The grotesque in contemporary British fiction

Manchester University Press

The grotesque in contemporary British fiction

Robert Duggan

Manchester University Press
Manchester and New York
distributed in the United States exclusively by Palgrave Macmillan

Copyright © Robert Duggan 2013

The right of Robert Duggan to be identified as the author of this work has been asserted by him in accordance with the Copyright, Designs and Patents Act 1988.

Published by Manchester University Press
Oxford Road, Manchester M13 9NR, UK
and Room 400, 175 Fifth Avenue, New York, NY 10010, USA
www.manchesteruniversitypress.co.uk

Distributed in the United States exclusively by
Palgrave Macmillan, 175 Fifth Avenue, New York,
NY 10010, USA

Distributed in Canada exclusively by
UBC Press, University of British Columbia, 2029 West Mall,
Vancouver, BC, Canada V6T 1Z2

British Library Cataloguing-in-Publication Data
A catalogue record for this book is available from the British Library

Library of Congress Cataloging-in-Publication Data applied for

ISBN   978 0 7190 7891 0 hardback

First published 2013

The publisher has no responsibility for the persistence or accuracy of URLs for any external or third-party internet websites referred to in this book, and does not guarantee that any content on such websites is, or will remain, accurate or appropriate.

Typeset
by JCS Publishing Services Ltd, www.jcs-publishing.co.uk
Printed in Great Britain
by TJ International Ltd, Padstow, Cornwall

Contents

Acknowledgements	*page* vii
Introduction	1
1 The contemporary British grotesque	11
2 Angela Carter: the play's the thing	53
3 Martin Amis: the limits of comedy	83
4 Ian McEwan: below the waves	117
5 Iain Banks: improbable possibilities	150
6 Will Self: under the influence	182
7 Toby Litt: haunted by the grotesque	216
Conclusion	248
Bibliography	254
Index	273

Acknowledgements

The early research for this book took place at the University of Kent, where I was fortunate to be part of a vibrant postgraduate community, with particular thanks going to Antony Barron, Brian Dillon, Felicity Dunworth and Páraic Finnerty. I am also indebted to the staff at Kent for their advice, especially the encouragement of Lyn Innes and Abdulrazak Gurnah and most importantly Thomas Docherty, whose guidance and support during and after my PhD are much appreciated.

My colleagues at the Department of English and Creative Writing at the University of Chichester have been admirable in helping me try to balance research and teaching, with special thanks to Benjamin Noys, Fiona Price and Mark Mason, and I am grateful to the university's Research Facilitation Fund for funding to help complete the writing of this book.

A special thank you must go to the many people in English and American Studies at the University of Manchester who have made me the lucky recipient of both their warm welcomes and critical insights.

I am grateful for the advice (and patience) of Matthew and Kim at Manchester University Press and would like to thank The Little Artists for the cover image.

Final thanks go to Anastasia, who invariably asks the right questions and whose support in all things continues to be invaluable.

Introduction

Contemporary British writing moves in a variety of directions, and the object of this study is the exploration of a particularly fertile path some recent British fiction has taken. 'The grotesque' as a term currently used in the media is a quality or set of qualities that seems to be ubiquitous and indispensable while at the same time being an extremely vague category or characteristic. One might speculate that the term's vagueness constitutes its usefulness for the commentators involved, whether it is used in connection with contemporary writers such as those examined here or with artists such as Jake and Dinos Chapman, whose recreations of Goya's *Disasters of War* have drawn praise and condemnation in almost equal measure. It is therefore a productive critical step to approach the grotesque in scholarly and historical terms and from this perspective to investigate its presence in and importance for contemporary British fiction. My exploration begins by examining the grotesque and developing a set of attributes associated with it that is then utilised in the individual chapters devoted to each writer's fiction.

Angela Carter, Martin Amis, Ian McEwan, Iain Banks, Will Self and Toby Litt have different approaches to writing fiction but as a group they share family resemblances, that is to say their fiction shows a set of different but related characteristics that can be termed grotesque. My discussion of texts by these authors will illuminate this family resemblance and, rather than pursuing a single quality of the grotesque through their works, will instead draw a web of links between the various contemporary novels and short stories. The writers selected for this study have been chosen in order to show how different but interrelated aspects of the grotesque are embodied in contemporary British fiction and how the family resemblances between the contemporary authors find a parent in the tradition of the grotesque. The writers are shown to be drawing on a shared set of discourses and influences that are part of the tradition of the grotesque in art and literature described in the first chapter of this book.

The writers in this group are frequently thought to be out to shock the reading public, and their sometimes disturbing subject matter is often contemporary in nature, including explorations of late capitalist consumer society, pornography, drug culture, destructive contemporary gender roles and dysfunctional families. This initial similarity, however, tends to obscure the significant differences in narrative method shown by these authors: Carter's political playfulness, Amis's hyperbole and exuberance, McEwan's 'clinical' and honed prose, Banks's combination of oddity and novelistic 'craft', Self's intertextual intoxication and Litt's subversive take on familiar genres. My purpose is to trace the way in which these quite different approaches to writing contemporary fiction have their roots in the tradition and discourse of the grotesque, and thus to use the grotesque to shed light on the tangled system of connection between these writers. There are a number of reasons why these specific authors were chosen, the most obvious being the closeness of the family resemblances between them. There is a network of influences, including Rabelais, Swift, Kafka and Thomas Mann, from the history of the grotesque that traverses the works of these writers. My examination of their novels and short stories taken together reveals a contemporary literary scene exploiting the principal features of the grotesque as a literary and artistic tradition as it has been historically articulated, including preoccupations with the human body, parodies, inversions, transgressions, intoxication, play and discourses of 'diseconomy'. In the course of this discussion I will also be addressing the most prominent and distinctive features of these authors' approaches to writing fiction, showing how the grotesque is central to an understanding of each writer's oeuvre.

While there are perhaps other contemporary writers who might be included in a study of this kind on the grotesque, it is Carter, Amis, McEwan, Banks, Self and Litt who offer the most diverse and simultaneously coherent set of relations to each other and to the grotesque. The diversity can be seen in the different ways these writers engage in a variety of fictional enterprises and their distinct styles, from the baroque and kinetic texts of Carter, Amis and Self to the more controlled prose of McEwan, Banks and Litt, enable a discussion of a very broad set of literary idioms, themes and subject matter. This book sets out to show how this diversity nevertheless displays a strong coherence when placed in the critical and aesthetic context of the grotesque, where these dissimilarities can be understood as distinct but related aspects of the grotesque and its symbolic inversions and reversals, play of form and scale and mixture of humour and horror. This selection of authors thus spans writers whose literary careers began in the 1970s to those who books first appeared in the 1990s, and all of whom (with the exception of Carter) continue to produce new work. This contemporary British grotesque therefore is a steadfast facet of current writing, not simply a moment, with its aptitude for challenging borders and hierarchies and recombining elements in novel ways a strong factor in its enduring appeal.

As I discuss in Chapter 1, criticism historically has often represented the grotesque in the work of an author as the product of the personal habits and idiosyncrasy of the writer (for example, Walter Scott on E.T.A. Hoffmann). An exploration of the works of these contemporary authors recasts the narrative deformations, reversals and 'shocks' of their writing not as evidence of the peculiarity of the author's psyche but as evidence of the contemporary articulation of the grotesque in British fiction. It is important at the outset to consider the difficulties in a critical approach that would search for the roots of the contemporary grotesque only in contemporary circumstances. Historical problems soon arise in trying to ascertain the social and cultural conditions that, for example, Rabelais, Swift, Kafka, Mann, Dickens and Martin Amis have in common that are catalysts for grotesque literature. Given the grotesque's distant historical roots and its presence in different epochs, how to determine the factors in a culture that are auspicious for the emergence of the grotesque becomes uncertain. Another issue with an approach that is narrowly historicist is the temptation to portray the grotesque as essentially a realist mode, where the grotesqueness of the contemporary situation is mirrored by contemporary writers' grotesque fiction. Such an argument, frequently used in relation to Dickens – as I discuss in Chapter 1 – is attractive in its unity and the neat correspondence between lived reality and artistic mode; however, it is likely that it has the effect of eroding the distinctiveness of the grotesque as an artistic mode, and of imposing a univocal (mimetic) orientation on literature and art generally. As such, the argument of mirroring tends to rescue the text from the 'ignominy' of the grotesque, and 'saves' the work by pointing to a supposedly quasi-ethical purpose embodied in the text ('representing the real') and simultaneously downplaying the significance of the (grotesque) aesthetic approach taken. Ruskin's recuperation of Dickens that I discuss in the first chapter is a key example of such a move.

I have therefore sought in this study to preserve the possibility of the grotesque outside this kind of interpretation, and to avoid the temptation of reading the contemporary grotesque as being essentially constituted only as a response to current social or historical circumstances. So, while I am not suggesting that the writers discussed are not interested in contemporary culture and society, I am proposing that the aesthetic roots of, and the discourses which pervade, their fiction lie in the tradition of the grotesque. This study intends to move from an approach where the grotesque is registered as an abstract, ahistorical, loosely descriptive term, to one where the grotesque is understood as a literary tradition and an aesthetic discourse in European art and literature that permeates the tropes, narrative strategies, images and preoccupations of much contemporary British literature.

In terms of literary history the works of these writers do not fall easily into a specific category. Although there are some aspects of the fiction under discussion that might be considered postmodernist, many of the novels and stories do not appear to be notably 'avant-garde'. Rather, as this study will show, there is a clear pattern of a 'new voicing' in this contemporary reworking of the tradition of the grotesque, with its play of scale and perspective, reversals, parodies and mixing of forms. The grotesque in contemporary fiction is therefore not some master principle to which these six writers have subscribed, nor an aesthetic model simply demanded by the times in which we live. Instead we should consider the grotesque as being closer to the negation of a master principle and the deformation of received aesthetic models. Jean-François Lyotard begins his essay 'Answering the Question: What is Postmodernism?' (1984, first published in French 1982) by claiming that 'This is a period of slackening – I refer to the colour of the times' (71). While Lyotard is concerned with, and about, the trend against experimentation in contemporary art and literature, we can apply his description to the contemporary fiction explored here, where there is no accepted aesthetic master principle, no prominent regulating system of taboos and no strong imperative towards aesthetic economy. Rather, we are faced with the interlacing outline of the tradition of the grotesque.

What Lyotard's evocative use of 'slackening' suggests is a contemporary looseness in critical discourse on the arts, where a former tightness and clarity are being lost. This apparently retrograde step, while perhaps depressing from the point of view of those championing the avantgarde, may also inaugurate a looseness that entails an expansion and elaboration of artistic and literary practice into diverse modes. The consequence of this slackening is not simply a return to old verities, since the new looseness precludes such a close adherence to set patterns. In literary terms the turn away from the avantgarde therefore does not effect an unproblematic return to the old 'classical' forms of art, but rather the continued dissolution of the 'strong' normative aesthetic category of realism, without a new unified model superseding it. The proliferation of the grotesque in contemporary British literature arises from this cultural context where neither traditional forms of narrative realism nor oppositional modernist modes hold unchallenged sway over the literary imagination. Current British writing looks both to the 'Great Tradition' of nineteenth-century storytelling and the experiments of the 1920s and 1930s without pledging sole allegiance to either mode. It is within this gap that the grotesque's sustained engagement with the border between the serious and the playful, the beautiful and the ugly, the horrible and the funny comes into its own. This worrying of existing norms, as a dog might worry sheep, may well be worrying in the usual sense, often producing a mood of disquiet as readers wonder whether to wince, laugh or be moved by the grotesque narratives they read. As this book will show, reactions to these writers have frequently been polarised, which comes as a direct result of the authors' apparent impatience with conventional canons of 'good literature'.

With increasing numbers of writers having honed their skills on university creative writing courses, the hardening of resistance among some writers to what Toby Litt has called 'the novel of polite form'

(Marshall, 2003a) has sometimes been perceived to stem from a desire to distinguish oneself in a crowded literary marketplace. The desire of these writers to shock has sometime led to accusations of cynical publicity hunting, a reputation that can be difficult to shake off. As I discuss in Chapter 1, the visual arts have a long history of providing critics and writers with artistic parallels for discussing literature, and the grotesque as a discourse often issues from the intersection of pictorial art, literature and social practices, including carnival. Looking at the relationship between art and literature in contemporary Britain in terms of shock tactics, it would seem that the artists lead the way. A volatile mixture of provocation, controversy and commercial success has been seen as central to the careers of a number of Young British Artists or YBAs, as critiqued by Julian Stallabrass (1999) in *High Art Lite*, most notoriously in the *Sensation* exhibition at the Royal Academy in 1997, consisting of works from the Saatchi Collection by artists including Damien Hirst, the Chapman brothers and Tracey Emin. The work by The Little Artists on the cover of this book translates Jake and Dinos Chapman's *Great Deeds Against the Dead* (1994) into Lego, amplifying the focus on scale, play and seriousness apparent in the original sculpture that is itself an uncomfortably playful reworking of an etching featuring mutilated bodies from Goya's *Disasters of War*. The Little Artists' work, which could be described as 'the grotesque squared', thus stands both at the end of a chain of ambiguous reiteration and at the forefront of artistic reinvention.

Nicola Allen (2008) argues that recent *aesthetic* 'marginality' in contemporary fiction is closely tied to the increased prominence of the formerly *socially* marginal in literature; the precise relationship between the two remains unclear in her analysis, however. The coincidence or non-copresence of these two very different axes of marginality is not always predictable and perhaps sometimes coincidental in the conventional sense. To obtain a clearer view it may be more worthwhile to consider how contemporary culture is in two minds about the grotesque's play with convention, with plaudits and brickbats arriving in equal measure. So, rather than resorting to the evocation of a contemporary zeitgeist marked by alienation and anomie, as Wolfgang Kayser (1963) does in his classic work on the grotesque, I aim to trace how the contemporary British grotesque has thrived in the *absence* of such a single dominating mood and in the absence of critical consensus over what constitutes desirable aesthetic norms in art and literature. As I will show in the subsequent chapters, the texts of these writers are invariably engaged in the contestation of normative standards across a range of domains including subject matter, genre and narrative economy as well obscenity, the human body, violence and the division of the playful and the serious. Such persistent interrogation and frequent confounding of aesthetic norms has been key to the emergence of this group of authors as inheritors of the mixed tradition of the grotesque.

Since the works of these writers are quite different in terms of language, subject, theme and tone, and because the works examined embody different aspects of the grotesque, a range of theoretical approaches has been used in each chapter devoted to an author's oeuvre. Theoretical perspectives derived from structuralism and poststructuralism, psychoanalytic criticism and gender theory are employed to explore these different authors' writings and the different aspects of the grotesque exhibited by them. In general, the orientation of this study is towards an aesthetic although not simply formal understanding of the grotesque since, as I will show, the grotesque as a literary and artistic tradition cuts across many categories and cannot be adequately considered only in formal or thematic terms, just as a purely historicist approach to its contemporary manifestations would itself be limited. Therefore a combination of approaches has been used to trace the presence of the grotesque in different areas of the works – whether in the handling of the narrative or the described images, or in the structure or the language used or the subject matter or the theme.

How to identify the grotesque is the task of the first chapter of this study, which examines the history of the grotesque in visual art and literature together with historical and more recent theoretical accounts of the grotesque. A theory of the grotesque centred around but not limited to the human body, perspective, reversal, 'diseconomy' and non-classical aesthetics is elaborated. I analyse the relationship between the novel and the grotesque through an exploration of the discourses of realism and the grotesque and their historical development and interrelation. The discourse of realism is considered as a literary articulation of broadly classical aesthetics and from this is developed a theory of what I term the 'economy of realism' as an artistic mode. Following this first chapter are the chapters devoted to the grotesque in the work of each of the contemporary writers: Angela Carter, Martin Amis, Ian McEwan, Iain Banks, Will Self and Toby Litt.

Chapter 2 is devoted to the late Angela Carter, who mixed fantasy and politics to spectacular effect in her fiction, which is shot through with the grotesque. Established Bakhtin-influenced readings of Carter novels such as *Nights at the Circus* (1985, first published 1984) and *Wise Children* (1992, first published 1991), so prevalent in scholarly criticism, are developed and extended to offer a more nuanced and comprehensive account of her place within the contemporary grotesque. The playful seriousness of Carter's explorations of the human body and her works' dynamic traversals of the material and the imagined are reframed to offer a new account of the author's aesthetic project that addresses Carter's interest in the theatrical. The interpretative framework provided here reveals how the tradition of the grotesque shapes the innovative postmodernist forms utilised by Carter and relates her unique sensibility to wider cultural formations of the grotesque in contemporary art and literature. The following chapter offers an account of Martin Amis's oeuvre that reveals the centrality of the grotesque in his fiction, from *The Rachel Papers* (1984a, first published 1973) to the literary landmarks of *Money* (1985a, first published 1984), *London Fields* (1989) and *Time's Arrow* (1991), and his fiction's scatological and eschatological preoccupations are related to his use of hyperbole and comedy. As perhaps the most admired stylist of his generation, and a controversial figure often in the limelight, Martin Amis has been and continues to be hugely influential, and his metafictional adventurousness and linguistic prowess combined with his interest in the grotesque body and black humour mark him out as a prominent exponent of the contemporary British grotesque.

The chapter on Ian McEwan charts his development from macabre explorer of dysfunction and psychosis in early works such as *The Cement Garden* (1980, first published 1978) and *The Comfort of Strangers* (1982, first published 1981) to celebrated public figure and Booker Prize winner. While the elements of taboo, horror and the abject have been identified in his early work, this section makes a new case for considering his trajectory as a writer as continuing his engagement with the grotesque, albeit in new ways. McEwan's continued importance in the British literary scene, as shown by his novel about post 9/11 anti-war protests *Saturday* (2005) is matched by the persistence of the grotesque in his investigations of the human psyche and biology. The evolution of McEwan's presentations of abnormal mental states and of 'human nature' has developed the writer's preoccupation with the grotesque and scientific theories of human development and social organisation. In contrast to the prolixity of Amis and Carter, McEwan's grotesque is 'dry' and Kafkaesque, intrigued by dark origins and the pre-linguistic.

Since his shocking debut *The Wasp Factory* (1990a, first published 1984) Iain Banks's fiction has often encompassed the taboo and excessive, and Chapter 5 investigates how his work's grotesque use of horror, black humour and games transforms his novels into mechanisms of fiendish intent and elaborate plotting. Banks's writing often embodies a duality characteristic of contemporary literature, a disjunctive fusion of violent force with carefully calibrated and organised literary form from which emerges a distinctive grotesque play with improbable possibilities and ingenious inversions and reversals, as found in *The Bridge* (1990b, first published 1986). The grotesque provides a theoretical model capable of investigating both the principal narrative energies and the controlled structures of Iain Banks's fiction, acknowledging his place within the Scottish literary tradition and its interest in the grotesque, from James Hogg to Alasdair Gray.

Chapter 6 considers the hallucinating characters, monstrous metamorphoses and disorientating play with perspective and scale that all point to the importance of the grotesque within Will Self's fiction. His short stories and novels bear the traces of Swiftian satire and Rabelaisian scatology in their vividly imagined fictional worlds and the transfigurations of *Cock & Bull* (1993, first published 1992), intensely violent *My Idea of Fun* (1994b, first published 1993) and Swiftian *Great Apes* (1998, first published 1997) are part of a literary project that has seen Self become a media celebrity and a satirist on a daunting scale. Like Amis a renowned stylist, Self has produced a large body of journalism and creative writing marked by a distinctively baroque style that, with its mixture of erudition, comic hyperbole and physical description, has become the hallmark of the contemporary British grotesque.

The final chapter looks at the growing prominence of Toby Litt as marking a new development in the contemporary British grotesque, with his fiction crossing different genres and exhibiting diverse stylistic approaches. His experimentation with the thriller, 'chick lit' and ghost stories are tinged with both desire and disgust while the disturbing *deadkidsongs* (2001) echoes the dysfunctional males of Ian McEwan and Iain Banks's fiction and *Ghost Story* (2004) figures the grotesque as just beyond the border of the real. A descent into violence and/or madness haunts many of his novels, and this chapter shows how the grotesque has become an ever-present threat to 'normality' in Litt's oeuvre.

Chapter 1

The contemporary British grotesque

The object of this chapter is to give a brief account of the historical tradition of the grotesque in literature and the visual arts and so to develop, rather than a singular *definition* of the grotesque, a set of core qualities and theoretical debates in which the grotesque partakes and with which we can examine the works of Angela Carter, Martin Amis, Ian McEwan, Iain Banks, Will Self and Toby Litt as well as the links between their texts. Through an examination of manifestations of the grotesque throughout history and in the light of more recent work on the subject by critics such as Mikhail Bakhtin, Arthur Clayborough and Geoffrey Galt Harpham, I will develop this set of core qualities while also engaging in the critical debates surrounding the use of the term 'grotesque'. It is out of this grotesque tradition that contemporary British fiction draws so many its preoccupations and narrative strategies.

Definitions and origins

Finding an accurate description of the grotesque has proved an insurmountable problem for the many critics who have explored the subject, yet it has remained an insistent impulse in their efforts. The profusion of examples of the grotesque from (just to take those which have generated a large amount of critical comment) the loggias of Raphael, the architecture of Venice, the engravings of Hogarth, the paintings of Bosch, to the writings of Swift and Pope, the plays of Shakespeare and the fiction of Dickens, Kafka and Poe has proved a seemingly open series with very few common qualities apart from the perceived presence of the grotesque. Arthur Clayborough's *The Grotesque in English Literature* (1965) moves from outlining what he sees as the principal features of the grotesque to listing the various strategies other critics have used in order to try and reach some definition of the subject (22), his taxonomy of the grotesque giving way to a meta-critical taxonomy of methodologies. As Margaret Miles (1997) points out, theorists of the grotesque 'frequently critique their predecessors on the basis of a few well chosen examples', although she cannot help but resign herself to a contribution to this 'time-honoured academic dynamic' (89). Frances Barasch in *The Grotesque: A Study in Meanings* (1971) argues that 'modern uses of "grotesque" differ remarkably from each other because the critics employing them have in mind separate historical traditions for the use of the word' (10), and so her book traces the history of the term from roughly 1500 to 1800 but even in this enterprise the term remains perpetually elusive among the proliferation of examples. Critics also differ in their assessment of the historical period of the grotesque: for Ewa Kuryluk in *Salome and Judas in the Cave of Sex: The Grotesque: Origins, Iconography, Techniques* (1987), the grotesque extends from the end of the Renaissance to the end of the nineteenth century (3), while Geoffrey Galt Harpham in *On the Grotesque* (1982) claims that the grotesque has existed from prehistory to today (48–76). The grotesque as a subject for critical inquiry has historically been used in relation to art and literature for a very wide range of places and eras, and it is my intention in this chapter to develop a set of thematic concerns, narrative techniques and aesthetic debates relevant to contemporary British fiction in general and to the writers discussed in this book in particular.[1]

The grotesque as an object of scholarship overlaps many areas of research, from literary criticism, visual studies and aesthetics to social history, philosophy, psychoanalysis and anthropology. Wilson Yates in 'An Introduction to the Grotesque: Theoretical and Theological Considerations' (1997) makes an attempt at a comprehensive description of the grotesque through a very broad synthesis of the major recent critical works on the subject, which is worth quoting at length:

> Grotesque imagery may point to the denial of our own mythic consciousness and the need to recognise the power and validity of mythic insight, about which Geoffrey Harpham writes; or the demonic in human experience that Wolfgang Kayser speaks of; or the oppression we have imposed on social groups as Ewa

Kuryluk insists; or the human body and its ideal relationship to nature and the larger communal body that Mikhail Bakhtin spells out; or the repression of psychic and emotional forces that Arthur Clayborough alludes to; or the denial of a classical world and its rational ordering of things as Vitruvius indicated at the time the first Roman grotesque forms were uncovered. (Yates, 1997, 40–1)

But even such an exhaustive attempt at accommodation and its consequently broad definition fails to include that strand in comment on the grotesque which hails the grotesque as precisely that quality which most approximates nature and real life, as seen for example in Victor Hugo's theory of the grotesque.[2]

The attempt to define the grotesque in relation to other terms is itself prone to a slide into an endless chain of signification as more related but heterodox concepts come into play: the ugly, the fantastic, the gothic, the sublime, the abject, the uncanny, the monstrous, the ignoble, the generically mixed, the insane, the immoral, the exaggerated and the macabre. Geoffrey Galt Harpham (1982) acknowledges the great difficulty in seeking a definition when he asks 'if the grotesque cannot be defined formally, thematically, affectively, or even by relation to other concepts, then what hope for clarity is left' (xx). What then is my own purpose in using the term in the present study? Suzanne Guerlac in her review of Harpham's book, suggests why we might need such an elusive term:

> Prof. Harpham's ambitious study makes painfully clear the kind of difficulties which a theoretical study of *the* grotesque faces. It would be tempting to advocate abandoning the generic, or nominal, terms 'the grotesque' and 'the sublime' altogether, were it not for the fact that there does seem to exist a rich and powerful textual field when it comes to the sublime. (Guerlac, 1985, 49)

I would argue that there exists an equally rich and powerful textual (and indeed visual) field for 'the grotesque' and so the term proves a necessary, if endlessly problematic, area of critical inquiry. My purpose at this stage is to create a web of meanings, in light of different critics' work, across a wide range of aspects of the grotesque and so to map this web of resemblance onto contemporary British fiction, reflecting both on the fiction's aesthetic qualities and the discourses employed in its critical reception.

Perhaps the only common point between the various critics of the grotesque is where they begin their analysis. Harpham, Barasch, Clayborough and Kayser agree in locating the first use of the word in connection with excavations during the late fifteenth century in Italy of Roman ruins and in particular with a certain sort of decorative art found on the walls of these uncovered rooms. The most important excavations were in the 1480s in Rome, where some of the ruins of Nero's Domus Aurea or Golden House built by the emperor between the great fire of 64 CE and his death in 68 CE still survived among the ruins of constructions ordered by later emperors, including Vespasian and Trajan.[3] As nearly all of the original Classical designs could only be viewed by crawling down tunnels beneath surface ruins, this style of artwork came to be known as *grottesche*, from *grotta* or cave. This style of decorative art had disappeared from view after the fall of Rome, and involved:

> graceful fantasies, symmetrical anatomical impossibilities, small beasts, human heads, and delicate, indeterminate vegetables, all presented as ornament with a faintly mythological character imparted by representations of fauns, nymphs, satyrs, and centaurs. (Harpham, 1982, 26)

Almost as soon as it emerged in Rome in the first century BCE this style of art had its notable detractors, the most famous of whom was Marcus Vitruvius Pollio, whose *De Architectura* (circa 27 BCE) criticised the use of monsters and hybrid human and vegetable shapes. He attacked the fantastic aspect of this style of painting for its deviation from nature in depicting things that cannot exist and for placing them in ludicrous configurations (Vitruvius, 1999, 91). Horace's injunction against the representation of fantastic creatures in *Ars Poetica* or 'On the Art of Poetry' (probably written between 12 and 8 BCE) derides such artwork and then goes on to warn against such strategies in literature:

> Supposing a painter chose to put a human head on a horse's neck, or to spread feathers of various colours over the limbs of several

different creatures, or to make what in the upper part is a beautiful woman tail off into a hideous fish, could you help laughing when he showed you his efforts? You may take it from me, my friends, that a book will have very much the same effect as these pictures if, like a sick man's dreams, the author's idle fancies assume such a shape that it is impossible to make head or tail of what he is driving at. (Horace, 1965, 79)

Horace, like Vitruvius, is criticising the fusion of incompatible elements in visual art and he makes the further suggestion that such incompatibility might inform literature (although this should be avoided); it is this aesthetic incompatibility that was to endure as a fundamental aspect of the grotesque. The discovery of the *grottesche* in the Renaissance, however, led to a new style of ornamental painting that proved to be popular among many eminent artists including Pinturricchio, Arcimboldo, Raphael and Giovanni da Udine.

The most famous critic of this Renaissance style, and perhaps of the grotesque as a whole, was John Ruskin, whose monumental three-volume work *The Stones of Venice* (Vols I to III 1908–12, first published 1851–3) examines the history and architecture of the Italian city. The third volume of the work includes a chapter on the 'Grotesque Renaissance' of Venice but also comments on the *grottesche* of the Vatican loggias created by Raphael and Giovanni da Udine:

> Those grotesques or arabesques of the Vatican, and other such work, which have become the patterns of ornamentation in modern times, are the fruit of great minds degraded to base objects ... If we can draw the human head perfectly, and are masters of its expression and its beauty, we have no business to cut it off, and hang it up by the hair at the end of a garland. If we can draw the human body in the perfection of its grace and movement, we have no business to take away its limbs, and terminate it with a bunch of leaves. (Ruskin, 1912, 142)

The *grottesche*, according to Ruskin, are a waste of great talents and the result of a perverse desire to mix heterogeneous elements including the human and the animal, the animal and the vegetable, and to indulge in the creation of fantasy. Raphael's arabesque design comes in for special criticism 'as mere elaborate idleness. It has neither meaning nor heart in it; it is an unnatural and monstrous abortion' (Ruskin, 1912, 143). In Ruskin's view, the growth of the grotesque as a prevalent artistic mode in Renaissance Italy marked the beginning of the end in cultural terms and presaged the gradual decline of cities such as Venice in terms of influence and power. His wonder at the peerless achievements of the artists of the time therefore is matched by his horror at their later debased tastes; a central preoccupation of his *The Stones of Venice* becomes how to identify the precise moment when the artistic life of the city lost its way.[4]

To further this attempt to find the watershed, Ruskin in the third volume of *The Stones of Venice* tries to subdivide the category of the grotesque into what he calls the 'noble' and 'ignoble', the true and false grotesques, to which end he introduces a comparison between two designs, each featuring a lion. His purpose in this is to create a dividing line between legitimate and illegitimate grotesque art; however, his attempts to divide the grotesque into two categories of 'terrible' and 'sportive' in order to recuperate the 'noble' grotesque are plagued by problems:

> First then it seems to me that the grotesque is, in almost all cases, composed of two elements, one ludicrous, the other fearful; that, as one or the other of these elements prevails, the grotesque falls into two branches, sportive grotesque and terrible grotesque; but that we cannot legitimately consider it under these two aspects, because there are hardly any examples which do not in some degree combine both elements: there are few grotesques so utterly playful as to be overcast with no shade of fearfulness, and few so fearful as absolutely to exclude all ideas of jest. (Ruskin, 1912, 124–5)

The inseparability of these categories in practical terms is down to the presence of play in both kinds of grotesque, which itself generates further critical attempts to gauge the degree rather than the kind of play involved, a strategy echoed by Bernard McElroy in *Fiction of the Modern Grotesque* (1989) when he suggests that when faced with the serious and comic 'the point to bear in mind is that the crucial factor separating these two apprehensions of the grotesque is the level of play involved in a particular work' (15). The grotesque is characterised by both fearfulness and the comic and as a quality resists critical subdivision, leading critics of many different epochs towards a more intense focus on the mind of the artist as they play with the fearful, a tendency that, as I will show, is alive and well in the reception of contemporary British writing.

In Volume III of *Modern Painters* (1906, first published 1856) Ruskin returned to the grotesque in order to distinguish between 'true' and 'false' grotesques, and, as in Volume III of *The Stones of Venice*, introduced a comparison between two representative designs – one 'true' and one 'false' – of a griffin. Again, it is the artist's state of mind that determines which grotesque is produced, but the state of mind is deduced by Ruskin from its choice of object:

> Such being the true and precious uses of the grotesque, it only remains for us to note carefully how it is to be distinguished from the false and vicious grotesque which results from idleness, instead of noble rest ... It is easy for the reader to conceive how different the fruits of two such different states of mind *must* be; and yet how like in many respects, and how apt to be mistaken, one for the other .... (Ruskin, 1906, 108)

Ruskin's definition of the grotesque itself becomes baroque and contorted, and we can see his frustration that the key to delineating clearly between positive and negative grotesques has become one of degree rather than of kind. This movement from a qualitative judgement to a quantitative one, and the consequent realignment of putative opposites along a single continuum is very significant and, as I will discuss in relation to caricature, the grotesque's violation of normative aesthetic economy becomes a key distinguishing characteristic.

The links between sickness (especially of the mind), dreaming and the grotesque have a venerable history: Horace (quoted above) likened fantastic designs to a sick man's dreams and, as Harpham points out, *grottesche* in Renaissance Italy were also known as '*sogni dei pittori*' (1982, xvii), the 'dreams of painters'. Walter Scott in his famous review of E.T.A. Hoffmann's stories described their fantastic elements as issuing from an imagination 'that was ill-regulated, and had an undue tendency to the horrible and the distressing' (1835, XVIII,

306). Edgar Allan Poe in his tale 'The Masque of the Red Death' (1986, first published 1842) links madness, dreams and the grotesque in his oft-quoted description of the masqueraders at the ball:[5]

> Be sure they were grotesque ... There were arabesque figures with unsuited limbs and appointments. *There were delirious fancies such as the madman fashions.* There was much of the beautiful, much of the wanton, much of the bizarre, something of the terrible, and not a little of that which might have excited disgust. To and fro in the seven chambers there stalked, in fact, a multitude of *dreams*. (Poe, 1986, 256–7, my italics)

Ruskin in the third volume of *The Stones of Venice* also saw dreams as a source of the grotesque, but claimed that this inferior sort of grotesque was a product of 'ungovernableness of imagination' (1912, 148). Dreams as unregulated products of the imagination are in this discourse associated with intoxication, and we find all the negative associations of the grotesque in Scott's characterisation of Hoffmann as a writer who used wine and tobacco to excess (Scott, 1835, XVIII, 294) and who was 'nearly on the verge of actual insanity' with an imagination 'so little under the dominion of sober reason' (306) and whose inspirations 'so often resemble the ideas produced by the immoderate use of opium, that we cannot help considering his case as one requiring the assistance of medicine rather than of criticism' (331). In the same vein Ruskin claims at the very beginning of the 'Grotesque Renaissance' chapter in Volume III of *The Stones of Venice* that the most 'degraded' grotesque architecture 'can sometimes hardly be otherwise defined as the perpetuation in stone of the ribaldries of drunkenness' (1912, 111) while the first illustration for the volume is entitled 'Temperance and Intemperance in Curvature'. So the grotesque as an excessive aesthetic mode is associated with psychological and bodily excesses and issues from the breakdown of the 'regulated' imagination in dreams and through intemperate drug and alcohol-fuelled intoxication.

Paulette Singley (1997), following Georges Didi-Huberman, has explored the importance of Ruskin's description of the grotesque mask of Venice's Church of Santa Maria Formosa for Jean-Martin Charcot's studies on hysteria:

While the head of Santa Maria Formosa, in Ruskin's analysis, reflects the mind of a suffering artist, it is Jean-Martin Charcot, writing in *Les Difformes et les malades dans l'art* of 1889, who directly links the head with the visage of a male hysteric and, in so doing, returns the grotesque from the fantasies of disturbed minds to the field of natural representation ... Charcot sees the signs of convulsion in works of art as representing actual physiological disturbances. (Singley, 1997, 117)

In Charcot's work, the grotesque becomes so identified with hysteria that it ceases to be a mode of exaggeration or distortion and becomes instead a vehicle of realistic representation. Scott's comments on Hoffmann come close to such a statement, implying that the author was representing, in some kind of realistic way, the phantasms of his diseased imagination. So the grotesque is seen to occupy, or more properly to issue from, a nexus of intoxication, delirium and fantasy with their concomitant qualities of immorality and deviancy. My subsequent analyses of the contemporary fiction selected for this study will show the persistence of this nexus of states of mind, play, imagination and intoxication in the critical reception of these works.

The grotesque body and carnival

Thus far I have been tracing the history of the grotesque in its form established by Renaissance ornamentation and discussing different critical strategies employed in attempts to analyse its elements. There is, however, another tradition of the grotesque that carries with it its own set of critical approaches and, rather than being primarily concerned with fantastic ornamentation, or with generic co-mingling or with the individual subject, this grotesque revolves around the grotesque human body, its artistic and literary representation and its cultural articulation in history. The major work concerning this 'other' grotesque is Mikhail Bakhtin's *Rabelais and his World* (1984a, first published in Russian 1965), and his thought continues to be a source of debate about the grotesque. One of the most intriguing features of the grotesque lies in the way its etymology does not quite fit a set of the word's common connotations. As I have already described, the term grotesque comes from the *grottesche*, which comes from the historical fact that the Domus Aurea ornamental designs were found in caves (*grotta*). However, as Harpham clarifies:

> Like Vitruvius' judgement, this naming is a mistake pregnant with truth, for although the designs were never intended to be underground, nor Nero's palace a grotto, the word is perfect ... *Grotesque*, then, gathers into itself suggestions of the underground, of burial, and of secrecy. (Harpham, 1982, 27)

This other tradition of the grotesque is not confined to *grottesche* and fantastic ornamentation but instead deals with the cave and its metaphors – the buried, the hidden, the dim and remote past, the inside and the cavernous body.[6] It is the grotesque as applied to the human body to which I will now turn.

While 'exaggeration, hyperbolism, excessiveness are generally considered fundamental attributes of the grotesque style' (Bakhtin, 1984a, 303), Bakhtin sees the human body as the basis of the grotesque in Rabelais, upon which everything is built:

> The material bodily element has here a positive character. And it is precisely the material bodily image that is exaggerated to disproportionate dimensions: the monastic phallus as tall as a belfry, the torrents of Gargantua's urine, and his immeasurably large, all-swallowing gullet. (Bakhtin, 1984a, 312)

Bakhtin claims that Rabelais's starting point is the concept of the body in medieval popular culture, and its potential as a means of accessing the 'unofficial' truth of life. His discussion links medieval festivals and *commedia dell'arte* and he describes comic inversion in terms of its focus on grotesque aspects of the body and through this the inversion of dominant power structures. A central idea is the 'uncrowning' of 'official' hierarchies and dogma through degradation and parody during the period of the medieval festival or carnival. The celestial, intellectual and spiritual aspects of people, all associated with the head or sky, are replaced by the terrestrial, anatomical and biological aspects of life, associated with defecation and dirt. The body as presented in carnival inaugurates what Bakhtin calls 'grotesque realism' – that is, a way of looking at the world which cuts through the dominant ideology and prevailing truth. The grotesque body of medieval popular culture, in its supreme manifestation as carnival, is regenerative, rebellious and democratic and for Bakhtin, writing in the totalitarian society of the USSR, the attractions of such qualities are clear.

Bakhtin's description of non-grotesque 'classical concepts of the body' (322) is of a body individualised and rendered static:

> That which protrudes, bulges, sprouts, or branches off (when a body transgresses its limits and a new one begins) is eliminated, hidden or moderated. All orifices of the body are closed. The basis of the image is the individual, strictly limited mass, the impenetrable facade. The opaque surface and the body's 'valleys' acquire an essential meaning as the border of a closed individuality that does not merge with other bodies and with the world. (Bakhtin, 1984a, 320)

If we think of a classical marble statue, static in temporal and physical terms, individual and sealed against the environment by its impenetrable surface, we are close to Bakhtin's idea of the classical concept of the closed body, which he sees as being the 'new bodily canon' replacing the body as represented in medieval popular culture. It should be noted that although Bakhtin refers to 'classical concepts of the body' he is referring to a modern canon of ideas about the body that is classical in structure and not to Classical, i.e. ancient Greek or Roman, conceptions of the body.[7] Whereas Bakhtin develops a theory of grotesque realism and the grotesque human body, Georges Bataille in 'The Big Toe' (1985, first published in French 1929) is intrigued by the role of certain parts of the body and, just as Bakhtin traces a movement upward in the grotesque body, with the bowels and genitals now taking precedence over the face as an expressive organ, so Bataille discusses the treatment of feet in different cultures. For Bataille, the foot in general and the big toe in particular come to represent the material nature of humanity:

> [W]ith their feet in mud but their heads more or less in light, men obstinately imagine a tide that will permanently elevate them,

never to return, into pure space. Human life entails, in fact, the rage of seeing oneself as a back and forth movement from refuse to the ideal, and from the ideal to refuse – a rage that is easily directed against an organ as *base* as the foot. (Bataille, 1985, 20–1)

Although Bataille sees that 'joy' may result from emphasis on the physical nature of people, he still claims that the toe is psychologically analogous to death,[8] whereas Bakhtin is far more positive in asserting the undying and collective nature of the grotesque body. For the latter, the grotesque is a carnivalised tradition because it partakes of this extra-official life of the people, and since the grotesque body is not individual but universal it cannot die.

Manifested in the excessive bodies of Gargantua and Pantagruel, the human body is multiple, extensive and interacts with the world:

> The grotesque body, as we have often stressed, is a body in the act of becoming. It is never finished, never completed; it is continually built, created, and builds and creates another body ... This is why the essential role belongs to those parts of the grotesque body in which it outgrows its own self, transgressing its own body, in which it conceives a new, second body: the bowels and the phallus. (Bakhtin, 1984a, 317)

The genitals and the anus are now the key elements in human interrelations and existence, and this formulation goes against classical ideas of the body that convey 'a merely individual meaning of the life of one single, limited body' (321). The grotesque body, on the other hand, is collective and universal in character and its images dominate 'the extra-official life of the people' (319). This collective, universal aspect of the grotesque body is, for Bakhtin, the guarantee of its eternal nature and so it is forever dying and being born. Both Swift in *Gulliver's Travels* (1973, first published 1726) and Rabelais in *Gargantua and Pantagruel* (1955, first published in French 1532–47) play with scale and perspective when representing the human body, and the works of both are frequently cited as examples of the grotesque. Gargantua and Gulliver (while in Lilliput) tower over the local inhabitants and their bodily processes are therefore magnified: Parisians drowning in urine in Rabelais and Gulliver putting out a fire in the royal palace in Lilliput by urinating on it. The body here has expanded beyond normal limits and the respective authors celebrate the biological aspects of this hyperbolic grotesque body. The narrative alters the reader's perspective of the human body and Swift of course provides a mirror image of this when Gulliver arrives in Brobdingnag where the bodies of the local inhabitants are outsized and consequently grotesque to the diminutive Gulliver.

Both in his work on Rabelais and in *Problems of Dostoevsky's Poetics* (1984b, first published in Russian 1963) Bakhtin seeks to situate his object of study within a wider historical context:

> Carnival itself (we repeat: in the sense of a sum total of all diverse festivities of the carnival type) is not, of course, a literary phenomenon. It is *syncretic pageantry* of a ritualistic sort ... We are calling this transposition of carnival into the language of literature the carnivalisation of literature. (Bakhtin, 1984b, 122)

The 'Grotesque realism' he finds in Rabelais is part of this carnivalisation of literature that is accomplished through the integration into literature of the spirit of medieval festivities, parodies, comic inversions and regenerative laughter which embodies the extra-official life of the people. The logic of carnival is also the logic of the grotesque:

> We find here a characteristic logic, the peculiar logic of the 'inside out' (*à l'envers*), of the 'turnabout', of a continual shifting from top to bottom, from front to rear, of numerous parodies and travesties, humiliations, profanations, comic crownings and uncrownings. (Bakthin, 1984a, 11)

In carnival hierarchies are suspended or temporarily overturned, the powerful are mocked and the solemn becomes travestied and the grotesque as part of the carnivalisation of literature follows this comic logic of inversion, reversal, the triumph of the low or base and the scandalous fusion of incompatibles.

Since folk culture lies at the heart of carnival and, for Bakhtin, the grotesque, he takes issue with later theorists of the grotesque who, he argues, view the grotesque through the prism of contemporary aesthetics. Thus the artists of the Romantic grotesque (*Sturm und Drang* drama, Hoffmann) and its theorists (Jean Paul, Fredrick Schlegel) form a kind of grotesque which lacks the laughter and the universal aspect of folk culture carnival (Bakthin, 1984a, 37–8). In the same way modernism's practitioners of the grotesque (Thomas Mann, Bertolt Brecht) are characterised by Wolfgang Kayser in *The Grotesque in Art and Literature* (1963, first published in German 1957) as constituting a grotesque preoccupied with fear, alienation and hostility that obliterates the laughter of carnival and its own past.[9] For Bakhtin, these developments in the literary tradition of the grotesque mark the triumph of bourgeois ideology, of the new bodily canon and the rejection of carnival. The grotesque realism of Rabelais, Bakhtin argues, gave way to the 'degenerate, petty realism' of later literary modes:

> The fact is that the new concept of realism has a different way of drawing the boundaries between bodies and objects. It cuts the double body in two and separates the objects of grotesque and folklore realism that were merged within the body. (Bakhtin, 1984a, 53)

We can also find traces of the grotesque in another of Bakhtin's carnivalised genres, the Menippean satire, or the wider genre termed 'menippea' in *Problems of Dostoevsky's Poetics*. The menippea as a tradition in literature includes writers who are also oft-cited examples of the grotesque: Lucian, Apuleius, Rabelais, Swift, Voltaire and later Dostoevsky. Northrop Frye in his *Anatomy of Criticism* (1957) had grouped the same set of authors under Menippean satire, or his preferred term 'anatomy', a form of writing which he distinguishes from the three other major 'strands' of writing: the novel, the romance and the confession (312).[10] As both grotesque realism and the menippea are carnivalised genres in Bakhtin's work, there is an explicable degree of overlap in their qualities, including use of the fantastic, slum realism, parody, dreams, insanity, scandals and eccentric behaviour (Bakhtin, 1984b, 114–18). In particular, the changes in scale and perspective that are so typical of the grotesque also form a feature of Bakhtin's menippea:

In the menippea a special type of *experimental fantasticality* makes its appearance, completely foreign to ancient epic and tragedy: observation from some unusual point of view, from on high, for example, which results in a radical change in scale of the observed phenomena of life ... This line of experimental fantasticality continues, under the defining influence of the menippea, into the subsequent epochs as well, in Rabelais, Swift, Voltaire (*Micromégas*) and others. (Bakhtin, 1984b, 116)

As I will go on to show in relation to the contemporary authors explored, this line of experimental fantasticality is a vibrant tradition within current British writing.

The link between the category of the grotesque and the female body has been discussed by a number of critics, including Mary Russo in her book *The Female Grotesque: Risk, Excess, Modernity* (1995, first published 1994) and Margaret Miles, who in 'Carnal Abominations: The Female Body as Grotesque' (1997) claims that 'twentieth-century analysts of the grotesque – Kayser, Bakhtin, Harpham – fail to notice the gender assumptions imbedded in grotesque art and literature, with the effect that they ignore a structural feature of this genre' (96). Miles sees the female body as central to the grotesque and argues that the dominant representations of women present the female body as grotesque in comparison to the male anatomical norm and therefore that 'gender constructions play a crucial role in constructing the category of the grotesque and therefore must be a part of any analysis of what constitutes grotesqueness' (112). Her identification of the female with the grotesque tends to be one-dimensional at times, however:

as grotesque, male bodies take on precisely the characteristics regularly attributed to female bodies; they lose form and integrity, become penetrable, suffer the addition of alien body parts, and become alternately huge and tiny. (Miles, 1997, 91)

This definition would seem too univocal in its gross literalisation of the female body; as Bakhtin points out, the grotesque body has both fertile depths, suggestive of female anatomy, and the 'procreative convexities' (Bakhtin, 1984a, 339) suggestive of male anatomy: the huge phalli, tongues and noses found so frequently in Rabelais. Female bodies may become alternately 'huge and tiny' in pregnancy but all bodies change in size and shape over time, particularly as people grow up. It is also difficult to justify modelling all changes in scale and perspective (found for example in Swift and Rabelais, but also in Kafka) on physical changes during female pregnancy.

Miles's assertion of a transhistorical essence to the grotesque which is identified with the female body, making it 'an essential – not an accidental – aspect of the grotesque' (1997, 90), exhibits a certain circularity in reproducing at the level of its own critical discourse the set of gross binary oppositions (male/female, mind/body, spirit/matter) it is supposed to be interrogating. Miles's essay also emphasises the genital aspects of Bakhtin's concept of the grotesque body without dealing with the other two aspects he discusses, the mouth and the anus, so while critics such as Mary Russo and Peter Stallybrass (1986) have a case in questioning Bakhtin's neglect of the issue of gender, Miles overstates the identification of the female body with the grotesque. Mary Russo's introduction explicitly warns against such a slippage between female and grotesque:

> It might follow that the expression 'female grotesque' threatens to become a tautology, since the female is always defined against the male norm. Indeed, in many instances, these terms seem to collapse into one another in very powerful representations of the female body as grotesque. The frequency, intensity and salience of the association of these terms suggests a mutually constituted genealogy, but this is not to posit an exclusive or essential relationship between the terms. (Russo, 1995, 12)

In her analysis of the female grotesque Russo argues that her examples of 'male grotesques' (including the twins in David Cronenberg's film *Dead Ringers* (1990)) are grotesque 'through an association with the feminine as the body marked by difference' and are 'set apart as heterogeneous *particular* men rather than the generic or normal men who stand in for mankind' (1995, 13). This critically established equivalence, although this time articulated via Russo's weakened 'association', between any term (female, grotesque, particular) defined by difference to the norm (Russo's undefined 'generic men') does, however, risk collapsing the terms into one another and losing purchase on what precisely is being mapped where.

Indeed, in her analysis of George Du Maurier's *Trilby* (2003, first published 1894) in a chapter subtitled 'Trilby's Left Foot, Nationalism and the Grotesque' Russo fails to pick up one of the story's dynamics of nationalism in her unquestioned acceptance of *Trilby*'s male characters' 'Englishness' (Russo, 1995, 133 and 148–9) and their supposed consequent homogeneity. As the names of the main characters signal, there may be more at stake in terms of Britishness than Russo's homogenising account acknowledges: Trilby O'Ferral (the 'feral' or 'wild' Irish); Taffy (from Yorkshire in Du Maurier's story, although 'Taffy' is slang for Welsh); the Laird (Scottish); Little Billee (Catholic, with 'just a faint suggestion of some possible very remote Jewish ancestor' (Du Maurier, 2003, 6)). More generally, while the 'female grotesque' has many powerful representations in Western art and literature, and in the work of contemporary writers like Angela Carter, Kathy Acker, Jeanette Winterson and Charlotte Roche, there also exists a venerable tradition of idealised and resolutely non-grotesque images of femininity as objects of contemplation and desire rather than disgust. In the light of all of these points we should avoid the temptation to make gender the principal preoccupation of studies of the grotesque.

More recently Bakhtin's theory of carnival has come under attack, particularly over the issue of political potential, and critics of his position point out that carnival is *licensed* festivity, and cannot be supposed to be oppositional in a political sense. Umberto Eco makes this argument in the course of his critique of 'the Bakhtinian metaphysic or meta-anthropology of carnivalisation' in his essay 'The Comic and the Rule' (1987, first published in Italian 1980):

> Carnival comic, the moment of transgression, can exist only if a background of unquestioned observance exists. Otherwise the comic would not be liberating at all. Because, in order to display itself as liberation, it would require (before and after its appearance) the triumph of observance. (Eco, 1987, 275)

Carnival, then, does not have the political potential for social change but is in fact a kind of social safety valve, a 'holiday from the law'. These critiques of Bakhtin's theory of carnival from a political perspective mean that Bakhtin's grotesque, as part of carnival, does not have an obviously 'progressive' character that can be co-opted into a wider political or social context. Harpham's critique of Bakhtin takes the metaphysical aspect of his theory, rather than carnival's political or social ramifications, as its target:

> The apprehension of the grotesque stands like a flaming sword barring any return to Paradise; the late medieval world is on the point of requiring the concept – a need Rabelais himself recognised, and, according to Bakhtin filled ... Underestimating the force of alienation in the grotesque, Bakhtin lays himself open to the charge Derrida makes against Lévi-Strauss, of imposing on his subject a 'sad, *negative*, nostalgic, guilty Rousseau-ist' sense of loss deriving from an unspoken 'ethic of presence ... of nostalgia for origins'. (Harpham, 1982, 72–3, second ellipsis in original)

For Harpham, Bakhtin is indulging in a metaphysics of nostalgia in his descriptions of a medieval, 'cosmic' understanding of the grotesque. Bakhtin's prelapsarian depiction of folk culture as a united collective at ease with issues involving death, and the human body is thus part of a metaphysical (in the Derridean sense) rather than an historical argument. Taking Harpham's points with Eco's critique, we can see that carnival represents neither a lost social reality nor a political alternative to the law. One way beyond this impasse in understanding the changing relationship between the grotesque and the novel, and which avoids both political oversimplification and metaphysical nostalgia, is offered by Peter Stallybrass and Allon White in their book *The Politics and Poetics of Transgression* (1986).

Building on the account of 'symbolic inversion' provided by Barbara Babcock's *The Reversible World: Symbolic Inversion in Art and Society* (1978), Stallybrass and White give a wide-ranging account of the concept of transgression that signifies a movement away from cultural norms, and a contradiction of cultural codes, shedding light on the relationship between decorum (both social and artistic) and the grotesque. In their investigation into the institution of the theatre in the seventeenth and eighteenth centuries Stallybrass and White show how changes over time in the way the plays were received in the theatres were focused on a regulation of the bodies of the spectators. From playhouses where the audience was standing and talking during the performance, leaving and returning, the theatre became a place where the audience was seated and was expected to attend politely to the performance. Stallybrass and White point to what they call 'transcoding', that is, the mapping of high/low distinctions between physical, social, cultural and geographical/topographical spaces, and they argue that the gradual regulation of the body of the spectator in the theatre was part of a more widely acting and socially articulated regulation of the body of the citizen, with the parts and functions of the lower body being unfit for polite conversation or public expression and in need of strict control.

What Stallybrass and White proceed to trace is the gradual accretion of an ideology of control that operated in the construction of the difference between 'high' and 'low'. Thus the passage of the eighteenth and particularly the nineteenth centuries saw a hardening of these categories in their aspects as separate, different and mutually exclusive, and a more strict enforcement of a policy of separation, whether it be the separation of different social classes or of human waste from the cities (1986, 125–48). For the authors the growth of this system of separation underpinned the gradual establishment of a bourgeois culture constituted by its rejection and denial of popular culture. They describe Dryden's Prologue to *Cleomenes* as:

> part of an overall strategy of exclusion which clears a space for polite, cosmopolitan discourse by constructing popular culture as the 'low-Other', the dirty and crude outside to the emergent public sphere. Dryden is doing more than policing a fundamental opposition between high and popular culture, he is also constructing it in this prologue, making sure that his audience knows they must choose one or the other – that to belong comfortably to both realms is a monstrosity. (Stallybrass and White, 1986, 87)

Thus bourgeois culture is created by its exclusion and to some extent demonisation of popular culture where the exclusion of the 'low-other' is the guarantee of the bourgeois culture's self-identity that 'produces and reproduces itself through the process of denial and defiance' (89). This labour of suppression and exclusion worked in different areas through the abolition of most of the great fairs, the social segregation of the city into prosperous neighbourhoods and slums, the fear of contamination from the lower orders, all of which reinforced the self-identification of the bourgeoisie through negation. Using models drawn from psychoanalysis, Stallybrass and White describe how the denial and exclusion of what is 'low', and its expulsion from bourgeois self-identity, creates a category that is a resource both of disgust and of desire. The establishment of a vertical hierarchy produces a situation where, as well as stigmatising it, the 'top *includes* that low symbolically, as a primary eroticised constituent of its own fantasy life' (5). The disavowal of the 'low-other' is therefore matched by its surreptitious movement towards forbidden and scandalous object of desire.

The realist novel and the grotesque

Debates about the relationship between the realist novel and the grotesque have often crystallised around the figure of Charles Dickens and, while much of the criticism on his novels tends to emphasise his role as a realist and his works' impulse towards social reform, as for example in Barbara Hardy's *The Moral Art of Dickens* (1970), there has also been interest in the part the grotesque plays in his narratives. Henry James in his essay 'The Limitations of Dickens' (1961, first published 1865) spoke for a number of critics when he dismissed Dickens's work because of the grotesque nature of his characters:

> In former days there reigned in Mr Dickens's extravagances a comparative consistency; they were exaggerated statements of types that really existed ... But among the grotesque creatures who occupy the pages before us, there is not one whom we can refer to as an existing type. (James, 1961, 49–50)

Where once Dickens had exercised sufficient control over his imagination, James saw his later work as having become careless and grotesque. The presence of the grotesque in Dickens's writing made it something of a conundrum for Ruskin, the arch-critic of the grotesque in its noble and ignoble forms, whose footnote in 'Unto this Last' (1907, first published 1862) makes it clear that Dickens's fiction is ultimately of a noble character:

> The essential value and truth of Dickens's writings have been unwisely lost sight of by many thoughtful persons, merely because he presents his truth with some colour of caricature. Unwisely, because Dickens's caricature, though often gross, is never mistaken. Allowing for his manner of telling them, the things he tells us are always true ... But let us not lose the use of Dickens's wit and insight because he chooses to speak in a circle of stage fire. (Ruskin, 1906, 120–1)

Here the inclination towards grotesque caricature produces a kind of optical effect, colouring its object but not ultimately distorting it, and the penetrating reader will be able to appreciate the fundamental authenticity of the work. The grotesque is conceived of as a veneer that can be separated from the underlying truth behind the text.

The visual register employed in this judgement can also be detected in Dickens's 1868 preface to *Martin Chuzzlewit* (1965, book first published 1844):

> What is exaggeration to one class of minds and perceptions is plain truth to another ... I sometimes ask myself ... whether it is always the writer who colours highly, or whether it is now and then the reader whose eye for colour is a little dull. (Dickens, 1965, 9)

The accusation of exaggeration, revolving around the quantitative question of extent, is not only rendered a subjective one by Dickens but also assigned a degree of superficiality through its association with colour rather than with form. The substance of Dickens's art is presumed to remain solid; it is only the gloss given to it that has become a source of disagreement. Nancy Hill in *A Reformer's Art: Dickens' Picturesque and Grotesque Imagery* (1981) describes Dickens's use of the grotesque as a means of getting people to see the world as it was. The 'corrective' of the grotesque for Dickens is in fact a step towards reality rather than away from it, Hill maintains, and quotes from Dickens in support of her view:

Greater differences will exist between the common observer and the writer of genius. The former accuses the latter of intentional exaggeration, substitution, addition, and has never been able in society to see the startling phenomena which he condemns in the romance as melodramatic and unnatural. The reason is, that such an individual has never *developed the sense required for seeing such things.* (Dickens quoted in Hill, 1981, 96–7, my italics)

Hill's discussion of the aesthetic category of the picturesque, and of Ruskin's suspicion and Dickens's satire of it, suggest the background to Ruskin's somewhat qualified praise of Dickens's work quoted above. Although Dickens may have been occasionally gross, he did not indulge in the superficiality of the picturesque aesthetic and certainly Ruskin's comments on Coleridge, whose writings 'are those of a benevolent man in a fever' (Ruskin, 1928, 268), show how he regarded writers who 'coloured' without such a realist impulse.

Michael Hollington in *Dickens and the Grotesque* (1984) and an earlier article on the same subject (1980) comes to conclusions similar to Hill's: that Dickens uses the grotesque to bring the reader into closer contact with reality. Hollington asserts that 'for Dickens grotesques are very much within nature, and not phantasmagoria' and that 'Dickens's project as a novelist was to show how the grotesque had become domesticated in England' (93 and 98). Mark Spilka in *Dickens and Kafka: A Mutual Interpretation* (1969) takes the opposing view that in Dickens's grotesque 'outer realities are made to seem fantastic through projected feeling, but there is nothing unreal about the total scene' (107), although he shares with Hollington an assertion of the reality of the 'total scene'. According to this view the grotesque may escape aesthetic censure if it has the authority of truth behind it and is engaged in a fundamentally realist enterprise. For these commentators realism is less a formal or aesthetic category and more like a moral or ethical one, as can be seen in Ruskin contrasting Dickens's 'main drift and purpose' with the artistic methods he uses. The realism of Dickens may not look like other narratives but ultimately that does not affect the 'essential' truth of his observations, according to such defenders of the author.

The development of the novel's complicated relationship to truth had by Dickens's time become more formalised than it was for innovators in the genre writing in the mid-eighteenth century such as Henry Fielding; however, painting and the visual arts were to provide a helpful discourse through which such questions could be articulated, just as they later would for Ruskin and Dickens. Fielding's preface to *Joseph Andrews* (1987, first published 1742) marks an important point in the development of the novel, or to use Fielding's rather unwieldy term, 'a comic Epic-Poem in Prose' (4). In the preface Fielding sets out what amounts to a definition and a defence of the emergent genre of novel, its subject matter and its representative mode. Fielding claims his own work is comic, rather than 'burlesque', which is another word for the grotesque:

> Indeed no two species of writing can differ more widely than the Comic and the Burlesque: for as the latter is ever the Exhibition of what is monstrous and unnatural, and where our Delight, if we examine it, arises from the surprizing Absurdity, as in appropriating the Manners of the highest to the lowest, or *é converso*; so in the former, we should ever confine ourselves strictly to Nature from the just Imitation of which, will flow all the Pleasure we can this way convey to a sensible Reader. (Fielding, 1987, 4)

The comic in writing, then, is a specifically realistic mode of representation, distinguished from the unnatural burlesque or grotesque, and Fielding's remarks define his comic novel as an essentially imitative form of art that will expressly eschew the topsy-turvy strategies and monstrosity of the grotesque.

Fielding then turns to the work of his fellow Tory supporter, William Hogarth, in order to build on his distinction between his own abstemious art, that of the 'comic epic' writer, and the excesses of the grotesque and the extravagant. Hogarth, like Fielding, is here a comic artist, not a burlesque or grotesque one:

> Let us examine the Works of a Comic History-Painter, with those Performances which the *Italians* call *Caricatura*; where we shall find the true Excellence of the former, to consist in the exactest copying of Nature, insomuch, that a judicious Eye instantly rejects any thing *outré* ... Whereas in the *Caricatura* we allow all Licence. Its aim is to produce Monsters, not Men, and all distortions and

Exaggerations whatever are within its proper Province. Now what *Caricatura* is in Painting, Burlesque is in Writing; and in the same manner the Comic Writer and Painter correlate to each other. (Fielding, 1987, 5)

So Fielding places both himself and Hogarth within an aesthetic mode that resists distortion and caricature and instead adheres to 'Nature', thus producing works worthy of respect due to their 'judicious Eye'. As Ronald Paulson notes in *Hogarth: His Life, Art and Times* (1971):

> By calling Hogarth's productions 'comic history painting,' and his own 'comic epic in prose,' Fielding is trying, as Hogarth had done, to secure a place in the classical (and contemporary) hierarchy of genres higher than satire, the grotesque, or the comic would command. (Paulson, 1971, 470)

In 1743, the year after the publication of *Joseph Andrews*, Hogarth returned Fielding's favour, as it were, in his *Characters and Caricaturas*, which includes the line, 'For a farther Explanation of the Difference Betwixt Character and Caricatura See ye Preface to Jo^h Andrews'. As Deidre Lynch argues in 'Overloaded Portraits: The Excess of Character and Countenance' (1994) and *The Economy of Character: Novels, Market Culture and the Business of Inner Meaning* (1998), Hogarth's etching:

> aims to polarise the grotesque overstatement and what Fielding called 'the exactest copying of Nature'. Yet the engraving seems instead to be about the *fine line* differentiating the mimetic structure of character from the mimetic structure of caricature. Only a fine line separates the marks that individualise the countenance from the marks that exaggerate it. (Lynch, 1994, 131–2)

Lynch demonstrates that attempts like Fielding's and Hogarth's to polarise the grotesque (caricature) and the copying of nature (character) collapse because they end up being about quantity rather than quality. The grotesque cannot occupy a position diametrically opposed to 'realistic' painting or the 'realist' novel as the grotesque and caricature are only to be distinguished by excess, by a quantitative and economic difference: 'Caricature, far from being the antithesis of character, may be read as its extension' (136). Caricature, the etymological root of which lies in the Italian word for loaded, signals the violation through excess of a normative aesthetic economy of representation.

Hogarth revisited the difference between character and caricature in *The Bench* (begun 1758, left unfinished on Hogarth's death in 1764), subtitled 'Of the different meaning of the Words *Character, Caricatura* and *Outré* in Painting and Drawing'. His description of an *outré* as 'a Giant' or 'a Nose or a Leg, made bigger than it ought to be' is reminiscent of Swift's *Gulliver's Travels*, for which he had produced engravings, and is close to Freud's later definition of caricature in *Jokes and their Relation to the Unconscious* (1960, first published 1905).[11] As Lynch notes, Hogarth later included reduction as another facet of the *outré* with the addition of 'a Dwarf' and 'or less' to his description, and she reads this as a sign of Hogarth's concern over the dangers of caricature being seen as merely an increase in character. William Hazlitt later observed in 'On Hogarth's Marriage A-la-Mode' (1934, first published 1814) the same danger in Hogarth's work, but thought that the latter's characters never quite extended to caricature: 'For his faces go to the very verge of caricature, and yet never (we believe in an single instance) go beyond it' (Hazlitt, 1934, IV, 29). Writing at around the same time, Charles Lamb is careful to distinguish between Hogarth's work and the grotesque.[12] The recurrent attempts to define the grotesque in economic terms and as an artistic failure issuing from excess are perhaps, like Ruskin's warnings about 'Intemperance in Curvature', a testament to the ease with which a realistic character in art or literature can become a grotesque caricature through careless immoderation and surfeit.

There is a line of distinction, then, between the comic-epic and the grotesque but the line is notable precisely for its permeability. The acceptance of Hogarth and Fielding as belonging to a genre between the grotesque and the ideal, between low farce and high art, by critics such as Hazlitt is in some ways a vindication of the efforts by the writer and artist to carve a niche for themselves in the hierarchy of arts. We can see, however, that the grotesque proves a threat to such attempts and that the early novel must repeatedly assert its difference to caricature and the grotesque. The disavowal of the grotesque low-other that Stallybrass and White trace more generally in the eighteenth century can be perceived in the 'significant pattern of disavowal' Lynch finds in writers' and artists' commentaries on how their work is very different to the grotesque. As she notes, for Fielding and Hogarth:

> [T]he finishing touch, the increase in detail that enables the image to realise its claim to truth value, is reconceived as, past a certain limit, something else – a something that disrupts rather than extends. As 'comic history painting' realises its generic identity, character breeds a monster – a caricature – and then disavows this constituent part of itself. (Lynch, 1994, 136)

The danger for artists and writers attempting to assert rhetorically this truth claim is that the final detail or the artist's finishing stroke may become a proliferation of details, an increase that leads to a disruption, not an extension of the 'realist' economy of the work. Such increases, if not controlled, may lead to caricature and the grotesque.

Dickens's concept of 'colouring' discussed above and Hogarth's and Fielding's attempts to bolster each other's claim to truthfulness are significant in terms of the relationship between ideas of literary realism and the visual arts. Fielding, in a letter to Caleb D'Anvers, distinguished between realistic and extravagant representation in terms of a visual artist's talent:

> The *Outré*, or Extravagant, requires but a very little Portion of Genius to hit. Any Dauber, almost may make a shift to portray a *Saracen's Head*; but a Master, only, can express the delicate, dimpled softness of Infancy, the opening Bloom of Beauty, or the happy Negligence of Graceful Gentility. (Fielding quoted in Paulson, 1971, 472)

Hazlitt had praised Hogarth's avoidance of 'the insipid tameness' and 'laborious drudgery' of the Dutch School painters (Hazlitt, 1934, IV, 29), but for later authors the Dutch School was to become the artistic equivalent of the novelist's realist enterprise, evident in George Eliot's 'delight in many Dutch paintings, which lofty minded people despise' (Eliot, 1980, 223) and Thomas Hardy subtitling his novel

Under the Greenwood Tree (1872) 'A Rural Painting of the Dutch School'. While Hazlitt had seen Fielding and Hogarth occupying a position between Dutch School 'copyists' and idealised high art and tragedy, Eliot positions her own work closer to the Dutch School and distances it from Fielding in her novel *Middlemarch* (1994, first published 1871–2):

> But Fielding lived when days were longer (for time, like money, is measured by our needs) ... We belated historians must not linger after his example; and if we did so, it is probable that our chat would be thin and eager, as if delivered from a camp-stool in a parrot house. I at least have so much to do in unravelling certain human lots, and seeing how they were woven and interwoven, that all the light I can command must be concentrated on this particular web, and not dispersed over that tempting range of relevancies called the universe. (Eliot, 1994, 141)

Eliot here defends her work as a project which is more concentrated and focused than Fielding's, invoking a peculiar argument which, like so many ideas of narrative and representation explored in this chapter, is pervaded by ideas of economy. Time is more valuable now, she implies, and this compels the artist to focus on a particular web rather than waste talent trying to 'cover' thinly a universe of diversity and possibility. The novel has become more abstemious in its artistic brief and writers are trying to strengthen its credentials as the literary counterpart to Dutch School painting and that school's intensive and concentrated depiction of real life. The dignity of the novel form will also be enhanced, Eliot suggests since what novelist, after all, would want to deliver 'thin and eager' chat 'from a camp-stool in a parrot-house'? Eliot's remarks demonstrate that a call for curtailment of the novelist's range and a more circumscribed description of the novelist's task is itself productive of a stronger claim to truth. The economy of the novel is to be more closely regulated and it is through this narrowed economy that realism is to be achieved.

As Margaret Anne Doody observes in *The True Story of the Novel* (1997, first published in the USA 1996), Eliot's berating of Fielding for his 'copious marks and digressions' in the course of her own lengthy digression (Doody, 1997, 148) might appear to contemporary eyes as somewhat hypocritical. In the same way, Eliot's comments on the parallels between artistic and literary practice in her digression in *Adam Bede* (1980, first published 1859) remain closer to Fielding's than might be supposed:

> Falsehood is so easy, truth so difficult. The pencil is conscious of a delightful facility in drawing a griffin – the longer the claws, and the larger the wings, the better; but that marvellous facility which we mistook for genius, is apt to forsake us when we want to draw a real unexaggerated lion. (Eliot, 1980, 222–3)

Eliot here aligns the 'real' lion with truth, the griffin with falsehood, as well as claiming her own mode of representation as the more demanding one. Only a few years earlier Ruskin had sought to demonstrate the difference between the true and the false grotesque using two images of a griffin; however, Eliot's statement does not admit to such a distinction and focuses instead on a real lion. A key term for our discussion is proportion, for proportion is the adherence to an economic law by which the artistic representation of an 'unexaggerated lion' is deemed true art while an artistic activity where 'the *larger* the wings, the better' is relegated to a subordinate, because non-mimetic, status. Hazlitt's claim in connection with Hogarth that 'it is easy to paint a face without a nose, or with a wry one; the difficulty is to make it straight. Few persons can draw a circle; any one may draw a crooked line' (Hazlitt, 1934, XX, 273) anticipates such a disavowal of the grotesque, since the accurate depiction is more difficult than a stylised one, and so of more intrinsic worth artistically and more fitting to be exhibited than anything 'exaggerated'. Fielding had made the same point in his preface to *Joseph Andrews*:

> [F]or sure it is much easier, much less the Subject of Admiration, to paint a Man with a Nose, or any other Feature of a preposterous Size, or to expose him in some Absurd or monstrous Attitude, than to express the Affections of Men on Canvas. (Fielding, 1987, 5–6)

This aesthetic of realism, then, operates a kind of economy whereby those texts that are excessive are cast into the outer darkness of the fantastic, where the effects they create are of little value.

Jane Austen in *Northanger Abbey* (1985, first published 1818) uses Catherine Morland's (mistaken) suspicion that General Tilney is a murderer to reflect on the kind of people depicted in Catherine's beloved gothic fiction, the characters of 'which Mr Allen had been used to call *unnatural and overdrawn*' (185, my italics). Like an excessive caricature, gothic characters are 'overdrawn' and of little use in helping a person perceive the truth that General Tilney did not murder his wife but is, as Catherine later reflects, not 'perfectly amiable' (202). When Hazlitt remarks that 'Coleridge's mind was unearthly, unsubstantial, with gorgeous tints and ever-varying forms' (Hazlitt, 1970, 232), the lack of *weight* in Coleridge's mind is central to the perceived failure of his work and to its lack of aesthetic importance, being all surface with no substance. As seen above, Ruskin's defence of Dickens was in spite of Dickens's artistic method, rather than because of it, while James accused Dickens of 'gratuitous distortions' (James, 1968, 51). What I want to draw on here is the way these comments construct the aesthetic mode of realism as 'the truth', while works which participate in the grotesque are outside this area and, because they do not conform to the economy of realism, take their place among 'insubstantial' works. This is the gap Eliot is talking about when she compares the griffin to the lion; the lion, because it exists in nature, demands an appropriate aesthetic response and the concept of proportion governs the legitimate means of its artistic representation. The danger for the artist is that the drawing of griffins does not prepare her for the more demanding enterprise of accurately depicting the real.

If this lessening of its problematic relation to reality is key to the development of the novel as a genre, then the suspicion with which the grotesque is regarded increases accordingly. In Eliot's remarks we can see a reciprocal movement: on one side a move away from the grotesque and towards a more strict economy, and on the other a consequent strengthening of realism's claim to truth. It can be observed that in place of the early novel's authorial disavowal has come the assumption of a coalescence of the realist aesthetic and the novel form. The novelist need no longer wear the mask of the historian as long as she is perceived to present the world in the realist mode. Lennard Davis's book *Resisting Novels: Ideology and Fiction* (1987) explores many of the ways in which much of what we have become used to in terms of realist narrative is not 'realistic' at all. Davis focuses on dialogue in realist narrative, showing how actual dialogue is characterised by pauses, intonation, turn-taking in the conversation, gesture and facial expression, whereas realist dialogue forgoes all of the above in favour of unified sentence units which are usually used in conversations between two or three characters. On character Davis comments:

> Suppose Flaubert had her [Emma Bovary] develop an interest in neoclassical architecture, or suppose he made her more ambivalent about sexuality. These minor changes would begin to undefine her – she would begin to become less strongly etched. In essence, the feeling that we get that we are watching a complex character is largely an illusion created by the opposite – the relatively small number of character traits that make up a character. (Davis, 1987, 114)

I do not intend to go too deeply into Davis's arguments here but, as we can see, the supposed close relation between realism and 'real life' may have as much to do with a growing familiarity with realist conventions than with an *a priori* correspondence between realism and reality. The dominance of the realist mode in the novel form throughout the nineteenth and, arguably, the twentieth centuries reinforces our understanding of the realist narrative as the norm against which narratives of the grotesque are defined as deviant.

A crucial area in our consideration of the historical development of grotesque, whether as a narrative mode and/or a type of subject matter, is the way that realist writers construct the grotesque as a disavowed low-other, where the normality of realism's economy and its sobriety and truthfulness, its Dutch School lack of glamour, stand in opposition to the wildness and exaggeration of the grotesque. Realism has its version of representational morality: George Eliot's digression in *Adam Bede* is in a sense providing the moral background to her novel, as well as instructions to the reader on how to read the book in terms of its author's project, whereas the grotesque is felt to be excessive and in James's words 'gratuitous', a freely given element beyond what is required by the economy of the narrative and an offensive addition to the work.

If we take realism to be fundamentally constituted from and structured by concepts of economy, we can see that the grotesque in literature disrupts this economy in a number of areas. Primarily this economy of realism is articulated through the desire for the abstemious depiction of real life where characters are not to be 'overdrawn' and levels of detail need to be controlled both in literature and in the visual arts. Within realism there is also an important economy of expression: the realist novel, like Dutch School painting, is 'merely' to mirror life, not to add to it. Hyperbole and excess must be avoided and proportion adhered to if the realist novel is to preserve and indeed strengthen its truth claim. Disavowal of the grotesque, of the excessive, is integral to this rhetorical assertion of realism's economy, an economy that also applies to issues concerning the imagination. If the novel is not to be fantastic, it must eschew Ruskin's griffins in favour of Eliot's lions since to depict the real is to have an automatic *raison d'être*, and so avoids charges of purveying fantasy and lies. Playfulness, which was subdivided into different categories of varying artistic worth by Ruskin in order to validate play in some form, is to be avoided by the realist novel that will instead value control. Ruskin's warning in Volume III of *Modern Painters* that 'the imagination, when at play, is curiously like bad children, and likes to play with fire' (1906, 100–1) seems to have been taken to heart by realist novels. Henceforth, the morality of truthfully representing life is to be pre-eminent and is, like an archetypal Victorian father, to take the bad child of the imagination 'in hand'. Within Ruskin's analogy we can also detect the inference that modern European artists, as mature individuals, should cast aside the toys of childhood and of previous generations. This result is that the grotesque understood as *sogni dei pittori*, involving dreams and the imagination, is increasingly suspect as an artistic mode.

The artist or writer who produces the grotesque is frequently seen to be violating non-aesthetic economies as well as aesthetic ones. Walter Scott, as discussed above, saw Hoffmann's grotesque as issuing from the writer's unbalanced mind, being the product of an ill-regulated imagination, in contrast to 'the virtuous, manly, and well-regulated disposition' of Wordsworth (Scott, 1835, XVIII, 305). Scott's suggestion that Hoffmann overindulged in alcohol, tobacco and perhaps even narcotics is part of the earlier discourse found in

Horace and Ruskin which blamed intemperance of the artist's body for excesses in his (and it was predominately his) art. The realism of nineteenth-century writers as an economy values sobriety of expression and attitude and is disturbed by excesses of body and mind, so that the grotesque, just as it disrupts aesthetic economies, is presumed to be a sign of disrupted physical or psychological economies and sometimes may be taken as a symptom rather than an aesthetic choice. To these economies of realism we might add the economy of reading that is sometimes employed when dealing with novels that are deemed grotesque or fantastic. This economy of reading views the reader as someone who places an investment in the text from which they must recoup a suitable return, as Scott's view of Mary Shelley's *Frankenstein* attests:

> In such cases the admission of the marvellous expressly resembles a sort of extra-money paid at the door of a lecture-room, – it is a concession which must be made to the author, and for which the reader is to receive value in modern instruction. But the *fantastic* of which we are now treating encumbers itself with no such conditions, and claims no farther object than to surprise the public by the wonder itself. (Scott, 1835, XVIII, 292)

Scott argues that if the encumbrance of instruction, which is the only valid excuse for a departure from realism, is cast off, then only lower quality work will result. This peculiar economy of reading is reiterated by E.M. Forster in his influential *Aspects of the Novel* (1976, first published 1927) that in its discussion of the fantastic uses an identical analogy (although there is no reference to Scott):

> It [the fantastic] demands an additional adjustment because of the oddness of its method or subject-matter – like a side-show in an exhibition where you pay sixpence as well as the original entrance fee ... So fantasy asks us to pay something extra. (Forster, 1976, 104)

Forster, like Scott, naturalises the reader's desire for reimbursement on reading fantastic literature and remarks that one dissatisfied reader 'though a genuine lover of literature, could not pay the additional sixpence – or rather he was willing to pay it but hoped to get it back' (Forster, 1976, 104). This economic narrative of sensible investment and return is contrasted with 'gratuitous' flights of fantasy that will leave the unwise reader out of pocket.

Stallybrass and White make an important point in their conclusion concerning theoretical debates surrounding the grotesque that is worth quoting at some length:

> We have had cause throughout this book to reflect on an unnoticed slide between two quite distinct kinds of 'grotesque', the grotesque as the 'Other' of the defining group or self, and the grotesque as a boundary phenomenon of hybridisation or inmixing, in which self and other become enmeshed in an inclusive, heterogeneous, dangerously unstable zone ... If the two are confused, it becomes impossible to see that a fundamental mechanism of identity formation *produces* the second, hybrid grotesque at the level of the political unconscious *by the very struggle to exclude the first grotesque*. (Stallybrass and White, 1986, 193)

The novel that we call grotesque is thus participating in both these moments as the normative code of realism and its 'classical' aesthetic of economy and proportion is formed by a supposed exclusion from the narrative of material drawn from the excess of the grotesque. Any subsequent inclusion of this grotesque, the 'low-other' in Stallybrass and White's terms, would constitute a mixing of forms, a transgression of aesthetic codes and 'boundary phenomenon' that is itself another kind of grotesque. Viewed in this way the novel reveals itself as an active participant in this discourse of the grotesque. The value of Stallybrass and White's book is in its relentless interrogation of culture's relation(s) to the grotesque, and the way their analysis resists a type of reversal in critical praxis which characterises some contemporary approaches to the subject. When, for example, Mary Russo in *The Female Grotesque* (1994) says, 'I begin this study on the side of the freak and the uncanny' (12) she risks taking part in criticism's 'speaking to itself in the delirium of its repressed others' (Stallybrass and White, 1986, 200) and overestimating the ease with which the processes by which 'freaks' are socially and culturally constructed can be reversed.

The grotesque, postmodernism and the gothic

The relationship between the postmodern and discourses of the grotesque with its various thematic, formal and affective aspects that I am tracing here, is in one sense problematised by the grotesque's historical tradition(s). In what sense can the grotesque tradition, which stretches back to Hoffmann, Swift, Rabelais and perhaps further into the past, be considered as especially postmodern or even contemporary? One way of approaching this problem is to adopt Bakhtin's approach to Romantic and modernist examples of grotesque and their contemporary theorists outlined above, where he argues that the literary or artistic movements of the time will interpret and renew the tradition of the grotesque in their own way. Bakhtin uses this approach when discussing carnival in *Problems of Dostoevsky's Poetics*:

> The degree of carnivalisation in each of the above authors[Voltaire, Tieck, Balzac, Ponson du Terrail] is almost identical, but each is subordinated to its own special artistic tasks (connected with its literary movement) and therefore each 'sounds' differently (we are not speaking here of the individual characteristics of these writers). At the same time the presence of carnivalisation defines them as belonging to one and the same *generic* tradition and creates, from the point of view of a poetics, a very *fundamental common ground* between them (we repeat, even given all the differences in literary movement, individual personality and artistic merit). (Bakhtin, 1984b, 160)

While we may not wish to endorse the entirety of Bakhtin's theory of carnival or the emphatically structuralist nature of his poetics, we can say that while the grotesque is articulated differently in contemporary art and literature, it still preserves important links to the tradition of the grotesque as it has changed across the centuries.

If we compare Bakhtin's poetics of carnival and the grotesque to Linda Hutcheon's *A Poetics of Postmodernism: History, Theory, Fiction* (1988), there is some common ground, particularly in the area of parody, although Hutcheon gives parody something of a poststructuralist twist.[13] Hutcheon's discussion of novels such as Angela Carter's *Nights at the Circus* (1985, first published 1984), which – as I will show in the next chapter – exhibits many features the grotesque, is notable in its careful avoidance of the term 'carnival':

> The ex-centric, the off-centre: ineluctably identified with the centre it desires but is denied. This is the paradox of the postmodern and its images are often as deviant as this language might suggest: the freak is one common example ... The multi-ringed circus becomes the pluralised and paradoxical metaphor for a decentred world where there is only ex-centricity. (Hutcheon, 1988, 60–1)

Christopher Nash in *World Postmodern Fiction: A Guide* (1987) seems equally keen to draw distinctions between postmodern literary forms and their precursors:

> But we need to keep alert to the fact that both satire and parody may be seen by the Anti-Realist precisely as the easy and perhaps exhausted conventions of philosophically more optimistic and credulous times. And that, when they now arise, the devices of a Voltaire or a Swift cannot be taken as prima facie evidence that – as with Voltaire and Swift – reorientations in ethical or political attitudes, for example, are offered as solutions to the kinds of crises the writer has in mind. (Nash, 1987, 220)

While accepting Nash's argument that postmodern satire and parody may not have the same political or philosophical orientation as earlier historical examples of these modes, we might question the extent to which Voltaire or Swift can be considered 'credulous' and ask whether Nash is splitting a formal/political dyad which was never cemented on a transhistorical basis in the first place. Brian McHale in *Postmodernist Fiction* (1987) is more willing to accept Bakhtin's account of the carnival tradition and its presence in postmodernist literature, and actually goes further in arguing (citing numerous examples, including Alasdair Gray, Thomas Pynchon and Flann O'Brien) that grotesque and carnival elements are typical of the projected worlds (or *topoi*) of postmodernist writing:

> Clearly this repertoire of Menippean and carnivalesque *topoi* overlaps at certain points with the repertoires of the fantastic and

science fiction genres, and thus with postmodernist adaptations of fantastic literature and science fiction. But in fact the overlap is more general than that: these characteristic *topoi* of carnivalised literature are also characteristic *topoi* of postmodernist fiction ... Grotesque imagery of the human body, a direct inheritance from carnival practices, is also highly typical of postmodernist fiction. (McHale, 1987, 173)

McHale follows Bakhtin in attributing the growth of carnivalised literature to the decline of popular carnival, although why postmodernist fiction should be especially interested in carnival when the popular carnival tradition has been in decline since the Renaissance, according to Bakhtin, is not addressed. If, for Bakhtin, Rabelais's work is part of the carnivalisation of literature, then it becomes difficult in a historically coherent way to identify carnival as a postmodernist form.

The grotesque is also a feature of the postmodernist novels mentioned in Allan Lloyd Smith's essay 'Postmodernism/Gothicism' (1996), albeit as a subcategory of the gothic in Lloyd Smith's argument (14). More broadly, the grotesque as being neither tragedy nor comedy, neither inside nor outside (the body), neither human nor animal, but in some sense both (and a problematic 'both') of the opposed terms, has been seen as an important part of the postmodern. Mark Taylor in 'Nuclear Architecture ...' (1990) suggests that architecture must be grotesque if it is to avoid classicism and become postmodern, and claims that when Peter Eisenman argues for a postmodern architecture, it is the grotesque he is describing:

A true postmodern phenomenon would accept the lack of a centre, and not attempt to put hierarchy back together again. It would attempt to see things in relativistic, non-synthetic way: fragmentation, decomposition, not seeing the world as hierarchical. That to me is the cognitive structure of postmodernism. (Eisenman quoted in Taylor, 1990, 11)

This current of the grotesque in postmodern thought can also be seen in Andrew Gibson's *Towards a Postmodern Theory of Narrative* (1996), where his analysis of monstrosity is linked to postmodern problematics of epistemology and ontology. Adopting the approaches of theorists, including Gilles Deleuze and Michel Foucault, Gibson discusses Beckett's *Trilogy* in order to examine 'elements of monstrous deformation in narrative' (Gibson, 1996, 259), and uses what we can now call a grotesque conception of the human body in his analysis of the bodies of Moran and Malone:

> On the far side of the world of the acceptable or manageable body as determined by a given *techne tou biou*, however, there is necessarily also a realm of physical monstrosity to which belongs the inadmissibility, even the horror or disaster of the aberrant body. This zone is the bodily equivalent – even the bodily representation – of epistemic illegitimacy. (Gibson, 1996, 262)

The grotesque can thus be seen to form a part, if not always a critically welcome one, of the postmodern both on the level of artistic or literary practices and also on the level of the postmodernism's cognitive and philosophical structures.

My object here has been to trace the grotesque and its relationship to the novel and realism and show how the grotesque has been a constitutive element of the discourse of realism not only conceptually but also historically. As my discussion of the work of Hogarth and Fielding, of Davis's account of the novel and Stallybrass and White's elaboration of transgression has shown, realism established its economies and what we can call its rhetoric through the denial and disavowal of the possibilities of the grotesque. I have sought to reveal the discursive labour that has gone into our (historically received) ideas of realism, and how the grotesque has been regarded as a threat to successful practice of realism due to its non-classical, low-other, mixed-form aesthetic status. In the context of the European novel, then, the grotesque reveals itself all the way from the novel's inception up to its postmodernist 'death' (rumours of which have been greatly exaggerated).

The historical relationship between 'gothic' and 'grotesque' has been explored perhaps most fully by Frances Barasch in *The Grotesque: A Study in Meanings* (1971), and it falls to me to argue that grotesque is a more suitable term than gothic to describe the work of the six authors discussed in this study. Examples of these writers' works being termed 'gothic' abound, and works by a number of them have been included in anthologies of gothic writing. The grotesque is frequently seen as a subsidiary feature to the gothic genre: for example, the book which accompanied a 1997 exhibition in Boston entitled *Gothic* (Grunenberg, 1997) contains an essay by the American short-story writer Joyce Carol Oates entitled 'Reflections on the Grotesque', although the relationship between the two terms is never discussed. In similar fashion, Neil Cornwell describes the grotesque as 'an accompanying or subsidiary feature to such literary forms as the Gothic and the Fantastic' (in Mulvey-Roberts, 1998, 273). Works by writers such as William Faulkner and Flannery O'Connor belong to the 'Southern Gothic' genre in Fred Botting's *Gothic* (1996) while exhibiting the grotesque as a feature (160). In their characterisation of the grotesque as an element (among others) within the gothic genre, these critics echo Ruskin in his use of the grotesque as an element within the gothic in the second volume of *The Stones of Venice* (1911) although the grotesque is rarely defined in these later instances.

The application of the term 'gothic' to the writers selected usefully emphasises some aspects of their work but in my view is too narrow. Something that most critics mentioned earlier have in common is terming the gothic a genre, and the grotesque a feature or element, which may stem from the gothic's greater coherence as a genre. This would mean that gothic rather than grotesque would be the term used to describe these examples of contemporary fiction generically. As I have discussed above, defining the grotesque formally (as well as affectively, thematically or in terms of subject matter) as a genre is extremely difficult, which may well account for the popularity of gothic as a description of the contemporary literature explored in this book. However, the use of the word 'gothic' in relation to these contemporary authors tends to obscure a number of qualities, influences and issues that 'grotesque' can accommodate and, as I will show throughout the course of this study, there is a long-established tradition of the grotesque that still animates contemporary British fiction and its reception.

Probably the most important element which the description 'grotesque' adds to the study of the contemporary novels and short stories examined in the subsequent chapters is the lack of emphasis on the supernatural and on the eighteenth-century gothic novels of writers such as Horace Walpole and Ann Radcliffe. This study will return again and again to influences that fall outside this historical genre of gothic but that are grotesque – Rabelais and Swift being the most important – and that represent a more important influence than gothic works of the 1790s on much of these contemporary writers' work. This study as a whole will demonstrate that grotesque is a more productive description for these contemporary works than gothic, not only in terms of the grotesque's greater historical, thematic or affective *breadth* of reference, but also in terms of the way the grotesque as a discourse brings together a number of issues to do with culture and form which run through much contemporary fiction. Elements which run through the works of Carter, Amis, McEwan, Banks, Self and Litt that are not generally regarded as being gothic include humour, the grotesque body and techniques of exaggeration, distortion and hyperbole. Many theorists of the grotesque have attempted to analyse the place of humour or the comic in the grotesque, often with a view to separating out the comic as the less worthy strand. Their difficulty in doing this attests to the closeness of the grotesque and the comic in literature and strengthens the argument for considering these examples of contemporary writing as grotesque rather than a gothic 'literature of terror'.

A productive way of rethinking the relationship between the gothic and the grotesque is provided by art historian E.H. Gombrich in his essay 'Norm and Form: The Stylistic categories of Art History and their Origins in Renaissance Ideals' (1966), which is discussed briefly by Harpham. Gombrich argues that the term gothic underwent a temporal reorientation in the eighteenth century:

> [T]he eighteenth century sometimes used the terms Gothic and Baroque interchangeably as descriptions for such bad or bizarre taste. Gradually the two terms for the non-classical divided their functions, Gothic being increasingly used as a label for the not-yet classical, the barbaric, and *barocco* for the no-longer-classical, the degenerate. (Gombrich, 1966, 84)

His point is that the gothic has historically become associated with the not-yet-classical, a type of formal arrangement that predates and as a consequence does not conform to classical conventions. We can see in the grotesque, however, characteristics of both the pre-classical and the post-classical, the unformed and the degenerate. This study will demonstrate repeatedly that this twin temporal orientation of the grotesque is prevalent in much contemporary fiction that is frequently regarded as being at once unformed and immature and at the same time decadent and debased. While Gombrich is interested in the baroque and the gothic as post- and pre-classical categories in mainly formal terms, we can see similar trends in the critical reception of the subject matter and themes of these contemporary works of fiction. Carter, Amis, McEwan, Banks, Self and Litt and their fiction are at once childish and decadent, immature and depraved, adolescent and degenerate. The grotesque, then, as non-classical, can be seen as both gothic and baroque in that its very lack of narrow definition makes it an umbrella term for that which transgresses conventional categories. The field of meanings opened up by the grotesque, and the relevance of the discourse of the grotesque to contemporary writing in general, makes it a far more productive category through which we may examine the works of the writers selected for this study. In this chapter I have elaborated a set of qualities of the grotesque from a wide variety of sources that include excess, hyperbole, exaggeration, degradation, changes in scale and perspective and the grotesque human body. As the subsequent chapters will show, the grotesque continues to play a key role in shaping both how contemporary works of fiction are written and the terms and expectations within which they are read.

Notes

1 Among these works on the grotesque are studies of the Renaissance grotesque or *grottesche* (Dacos, 1969), the American literary grotesque (Paula M Uruburu's *The Gruesome Doorway: An Analysis of the American Grotesque* (1986) and James Goodwin's *Modern American Grotesque: Literature and Photography* (2009)), the Augustan literary grotesque (C. Lawlor's *The Classical and the Grotesque in the Work of Alexander Pope and Jonathan Swift* (1993)), the Shakespearean grotesque (G. Wilson Knight's '*King*

Lear and the Comedy of the Grotesque' (1949)), the grotesque in postcolonial literature (Rod Edmond's '"Kiss My Arse!" Epeli Hau'ofa and the Politics of Laughter' (1990)) and in the work of artists such as Aubrey Beardsley (Kuryluk (1987)), Hieronymus Bosch (Wolfgang Stechow's 'Hieronymous Bosch: the Grotesque and We' (1997)), and Francis Bacon (Robert Newman's '(Re) Imaging the Grotesque: Francis Bacon's Crucifixion Triptychs' (1997)).

2 See the preface to Hugo's *Cromwell* (1968, first published 1827).

3 See Dacos (1969) for an account of the construction of the Domus Aurea frescos.

4 See Tony Tanner's *Venice Desired* (1992) for an exploration (for the most part textual) of Ruskin's approaches to the Venetian grotesque.

5 As Harpham notes, Poe had probably read Scott's review of Hoffmann's stories (see my earlier quote): 'The common inference is that Poe – overheated, sickly, tempted, tortured, and guilty – may have found Scott's article both precedent and program, modelling his art on Hoffmann's' (Harpham, 1982, 110).

6 As Paulette Singley observes: 'naming, the compulsion to repeat the root meaning, the etymological trap of grotto-esque, renders a chthonic descent into a myth of eternal return: every time we invoke the grotesque we must return to the cave' (Singley, 1997, 111).

7 'This boundless ocean of grotesque bodily imagery within time and space extends to all languages, all literatures, and the entire system of gesticulation; in the midst of it the bodily canon of art, belles lettres, and polite conversation of modern times is a tiny island. This limited canon never prevailed in antique literature. In the official literature of European peoples it has existed only for the last four hundred years.' (Bakhtin, 1984a, 319)

8 'Since by its physical attitude the human race distances itself *as much as it can* from terrestrial mud – whereas a spasmodic laugh carries joy to its summit each time its purest flight lands man's own arrogance spread-eagle in the mud – one can imagine that a toe, always more or less damaged and humiliating, is psychologically analogous to the brutal fall of man – in other words, to death.' (Bataille, 1985, 22)

9 'The modernist grotesque that inspires his [Kayser's] concept has almost entirely lost its past memories. It formalises the heritage of carnival themes and symbols.' (Bakhtin, 1984a, 47)

10 'The intellectual pattern built up from the [Menippean] story makes for violent dislocations in the customary logic of narrative, though the appearance of carelessness that results reflects only the carelessness of the reader or his tendency to judge by a novel-centred conception of fiction.' (Frye, 1957, 310)

11 '*Caricature*, as it is well known, brings about the degradation by emphasising in the general impression given by the exalted object a single trait which is comic in itself but was bound to be overlooked so long as it was only perceivable in the general picture. By isolating this, a comic effect can be attained.' (Freud, 1960, 201)

12 'It is easy to laugh at such incongruities as are met together in this picture [*The Harlot's Funeral*], – incongruous objects being the very essence of laughter, – but surely the laugh is far different in its kind from the thoughtless species to which we are moved by mere farce and grotesque' (Lamb, 1980, 318, first published 1811). Hazlitt disagreed with the extent of Lamb's praise for Hogarth's work, rather than its broad purpose, and for him both Fielding and Hogarth were above caricature but below high art: 'This attempt [Lamb's essay] to prove that Hogarth was something more than he was, shows that his bigoted admirers are not satisfied with what he actually was, and that there was something wanting' (Hazlitt, 1934, XX, 271).

13 'What I mean by 'parody' here – as elsewhere in this study – is *not* the ridiculing imitation of the standard theories and definitions that are rooted in eighteenth-century theories of wit. The collective weight of parodic *practice* suggests a redefinition of parody as repetition with critical distance that allows ironic signalling of difference at the very heart of similarity.' (Hutcheon, 1988, 26)

Chapter 2

Angela Carter: the play's the thing

> A universal cast of two-headed dogs, dwarfs, alligator men, bearded ladies and giants in leopard-skin loin cloths reveal their singularities in the sideshows and, wherever they come from, they share the sullen glamour of deformity, an internationality which acknowledges no geographic boundaries. Here, the grotesque is the order of the day. ('The Loves of Lady Purple' in *Burning Your Boats*, 1996, 42, first published in *Fireworks* 1974)

The invocation of the grotesque as the order of things is memorably marked in this short story by Angela Carter, 'The Loves of Lady Purple', a text that reminds the reader of the continued significance of puppets in her work, from her second novel *The Magic Toyshop* (1967) onwards. The marionette Lady Purple, who becomes the nemesis of her 'master', is part of a community of the marginal, of freaks who are objects of public curiosity and whose 'singularities' in appearance are, perhaps surprisingly, plural. As a group, these figures embody the grotesque in their collective deviance from supposed physical norms. The active construction of the grotesque as a paradoxical 'order of disorder' has been a hallmark of Carter's writing career, one sadly curtailed by the author's early death from lung cancer in 1992, and this chapter will explore the extent to which the grotesque forms an abiding core to her fiction that shaped not only her treatments of freakish bodies and sexual fantasy but also the evolution of her narrative modes and aesthetic vision. The presence of the grotesque in Carter's work, whether in the physical transformations of *The Passion of New Eve* (1977) and *The Bloody Chamber* (1996, collection first published 1979) or in the female performances of *Nights at the Circus* (1985) and *Wise Children* (1992, first published 1991), has been a hugely influential and at times controversial aspect of the work of this key post-war British writer. Carter's artistic legacy has inspired sometimes vexed critical debates over her fiction's engagement with sexual and cultural politics, not least in relation to Mikhail Bakhtin's work on carnival discussed in the previous chapter. It is the aim of this investigation of the grotesque in Carter's work to show how her writing's formal and thematic preoccupations constitute a particular contemporary form of the grotesque that is full of intertextual play and exuberant spectacles.

Carter's interest in the grotesque early on in her career can be seen in the choice of Leslie Fiedler's discussion of Herman Melville for one of the epigraphs for her 1969 novel *Heroes and Villains*: 'The gothic mode is essentially a form of parody, a way of assailing clichés by exaggerating them to the limit of grotesqueness' (Fiedler, 1997, 390, first published 1966). This quote brings together grotesque exaggeration with the interrogation of cliché, a potentially useful analogue for Carter's famous description of herself as being in the 'demythologising business' (Carter, 1997, 38). Her work seeks to challenge 'common sense' and through its drive to exaggerate, acts to explode clichéd and ingrained ways of thinking. Fiedler makes the gothic, a mode readily apparent in early work by Carter, part of a wider artistic strategy of satirical exaggeration that he aligns with the grotesque. In doing so he situates the gothic as a subset of the grotesque, something that this chapter will be bear out in its examination of Carter's fiction. Fiedler's 'limit of grotesqueness' is characterised as a liminal space in his quote, something stretched almost to breaking point, and he echoes this sense of an uncomfortable in-between space later in the book when he defines the grotesque as 'a perilous border-line between jest and horror' (1997, 486). The discordant combination of humour and horror within the grotesque discussed in the previous chapter is seen by Fiedler as leading to an uncomfortable reading experience. This discomfort has been readily apparent in the ways that Carter's own cultivation of the literary grotesque have led critics repeatedly to return to characterisations of her work dominated by dualisms of different kinds, which I examine below. The perilous borderline that is the domain of the grotesque therefore may be seen as part of the hinge around which Carter's work moves and that gives her work its cutting edge. When Marc O'Day writes that Carter's novel *Love* (1971) 'captures and grotesquely magnifies the waning of the sixties' (O'Day, 1994, 28) he attributes to the work a dual operation of representing reality in combination with distorting it, and it is the nature and possible risks of such distortion that this chapter will explore.

The perception that Carter's fiction is engaged in a 'perilous' act, to adopt Fiedler's term for a moment, is one that has infused much of the reception of her work, both negative and positive, with her admirers pointing to the daring success of her efforts where her detractors see unbalanced failure. Many of her texts focus on spectacular performances of different kinds, whether involving puppets (*The Magic Toyshop*), the cinema (*The Passion of New Eve* (1977)), the circus (*Nights at the Circus*) or the music hall and theatre (*Wise Children*) and, indeed, after the publication of *Nights at the Circus* and its evocation of high-wire and trapeze artists, it became almost de rigueur to present Carter as an author walking a tightrope between contradictions.[1] The projection of Carter as someone engaging in artistic modes that risked a fall had, however, long been a feature of critical responses to her books, as Peter Ackroyd's review of *The Passion of New Eve* shows:

> Now that the conventional novel has been embalmed with the sneer still on its face, certain 'modern' writers are veering wildly towards the grotesque, the fantastic and the merely silly ... That uneasy tone, perched somewhere between high seriousness and farce, unsettles the narrative as it leaps from one improbability to the next. (Ackroyd quoted in Gamble, 2001, 88)

Carter's novel is rendered as a literary performance involving jumping between precarious perches, an enterprise that seems almost doomed to disaster in Ackroyd's view, and the grotesque is presented as a limit point approached only at the author's peril. The wild, uncontrolled nature of the narrative and the difficulty in deciding whether the tone is serious or playful are all integral parts of the discourse of the grotesque as it has been elaborated through centuries of literature and visual art, and it is significant that Ackroyd sees this as part of a trend emerging after the apparent demise of the 'conventional' realist novel. The inference of decline and decay in artistic value is clear, with Carter's novel book being judged as mere play.

The impact on Carter of this kind of criticism of *The Passion of New Eve* is clear from interviews conducted many years after the book's publication, and she was clearly angered by the treatment of the novel 'as just another riotous extravaganza' (Haffenden, 1985, 86). The transformations of the protagonist Eve(lyn) and the revelation of the movie-star Tristessa's anatomy played out in a picaresque journey across a devastated and cult-ridden United States were, according to Carter, intended to be a 'deeply, deeply serious piece of fiction about gender identity, about our relation to the dream factory, our relation to Hollywood, our relation to imagery' (Evans, 1992). That the result of such a serious intention to reflect on the construction of gender through cultural images should be viewed as a silly bit of inconsequential play seems to be a result of the particular aesthetic mode that Carter cultivated, a mode notable for its generic mixtures and use of the fantastic. This mode brings together almost all of the features identified with the grotesque explored in the previous chapter, from grotesque bodies and metamorphoses to caricature, theatricality and the perceived lack of artistic control and sobriety. Such deviation from the realist tradition of English novel-writing, Ackroyd's 'conventional novel', has been aligned with the energy and vigor of Carter's writing, in contrast to the desired disciplined maturity of realist narrative. In such accounts of Carter's work, imagination and creativity are extolled, as one might expect in literary criticism; however, they are presented as lacking sufficient control from the author – as having run wild.

The grotesque as a literary and artistic mode has often been closely related to the issue of the authors' control of their material, as we have seen. The author is expected carefully to marshal ideas and images within a well-regulated and harmonious artistic system, and a fictional work that violates such norms has frequently been taken as a consequence of unbalanced authorial choice. John Haffenden in his interview with Carter hints at the enduring appeal of such an approach to aesthetics when he remarks:

> *Haffenden:* But I do think it's true that you do embrace opportunities for overwriting ...
> *AC:* Embrace them? I would say that I half-suffocate them with the enthusiasm with which I wrap my arms and legs around them. (Haffenden, 1985, 91)

What is remarkable here is how Carter, far from demurring from Haffenden's observation, instead confirms it and does so by employing a response that in its allusion to a sexually suggestive clinch itself embodies the overwritten and overplayed. Carter thus makes very clear that such supposedly un-realist, 'overwritten' fiction is a deliberate artistic strategy and not some error of 'craft' on her part, moving the conversation with Haffenden away from her work and towards wider arguments about normative literary standards. Her insistence that her writing can adequately address serious issues of substance despite its departure from conventional realist modes of narration can be read as a defence of the grotesque as valid artistic medium:

> I've absolutely nothing against realism ... the questions I ask myself I think are very much to do with reality. I would really like to have had the guts and the energy and so on to be able to write about, you know, people having battles with the DHSS [UK Social Services], but I haven't, I've done other things. I mean, I'm an arty person, OK, I write overblown, purple, self-indulgent prose – so fucking what. (Evans, 1992)

The overwritten and overblown qualities of Carter's fiction figure here not as evidence of artistic misadventure but as a calculated refusal to conform to a narrow set of social themes and narrative forms. The rejections of economy signified by the prefix 'over' place Carter's fiction within the excessive tradition of the literary grotesque and the profanity and pugnacity of her response balances her slightly self-mocking remarks, a stance simultaneously playful and deeply serious.

The struggle against her work not being taken seriously was, as the Evans interview shortly before her death quoted above shows, a persistent one for Carter and has arguably continued in a different form for scholars interested in her writing. In this latter case, Carter's writing has sometimes been adjudged unworthy of the critical interest shown in it, and this mood has been apparent in recent work, not least Dominic Head's influential and for the most part excellent *Cambridge Introduction to Modern British Fiction, 1950–2000* (2002). Head's broadside against Carter criticism encapsulates both a trenchant critique of theoretically inclined critical practice and dismissive comments on the quality of the fiction itself, using Carter as an example of negative trends operating within current literary criticism.

> Two of the problems I have been outlining here – the use of a theoretical perspective to determine rather than facilitate a reading, and the distorting claims that can be made for the flight from realism – are illustrated in the critical interest in Angela Carter. (Head, 2002, 3)

Head's linking of these two aspects, the use of theory in criticism and critical responses to 'non-realist' fiction through the work of Carter marks a degree of scepticism regarding the quality of Carter's work, with Head openly doubting whether her writing merits the widespread critical attention paid to it, arguing that Carter 'does not deserve the status of (by some margin) the most-written-about postwar British novelist' (3). No evidence is adduced to support this claim (nor indeed are any alternative candidates for the post suggested), and one might question the extent to which writers such as Ian McEwan, Kazuo Ishiguro and Salman Rushdie are less written about than Carter 'by some margin'. On a more substantive point, Head's argument proposes that the criticism on Carter must in large part issue from scholars with theoretical axes to grind, seizing on what Head regards as Carter's less-than-stellar fiction as a useful exemplar for their treatment of the latest theoretical fashion, leaving Head to wonder 'whether or not Carter is being used to illuminate the theory, rather than vice versa' (3).

Some of this may be down to academic fashion, with many scholars following similar lines of exploration at a particular time; how many academics look forward to another piece of student work, say, celebrating hybridity in Rushdie? The complex interplay of theory and fiction is also a site of anxiety for many scholars, particularly when faced with contemporary fiction that overtly displays connections to theoretical writings, as Carter's fiction so often does, risking becoming what the author called 'a kind of literary criticism' (Haffenden, 1985, 79). On a more serious note, however, Head's framing of Carter's fiction is quite damaging to her reputation as a writer and to the legitimacy of scholarship on her work, leaving it unclear why Homi Bhabha's theoretical work makes an approved 'obvious companion piece' (Head, 2002, 5) for a Rushdie novel but not Bakhtin for Carter. The singling out of Carter in this way and the sense that Carter criticism uniquely combines fiction of limited quality with crude theoretical heavy-handedness makes Carter carry the blame for a host of supposed faults in current scholarship. Head's claim that critical work on Carter invoking Bakhtin's theory of carnival is involved in 'a *de facto* cultural misrepresentation' (Head, 2002, 3) is especially peculiar given the fact that solemn warnings *against* the careless application of Bakhtinian theory to Carter's fiction are almost a commonplace of scholarly work on the author, found in work by Aidan Day (1998), Linden Peach (1998) and Paulina Palmer (1987), among many others. In fact, many commentators, such as Andrzej Gasiorek (1995), regard the limitations of carnival as a utopian project as a significant theme self-consciously explored and critiqued in her later books.

While Heather Johnson (2006) follows a positive (medieval, joyous) and negative (post-Romantic, threatening) historical division of the grotesque, we might more profitably focus on the contemporary British grotesque as vacillating between these two poles, being both funny and threatening. Indeed, as Johnson's footnote observes (134), her historical division between these two aspects of the grotesque is at the very least schematic, and as I have discussed in the previous chapter, contemporary accounts of the grotesque including Thomson and Harpham habitually seek to define the combined presence of the comic and the disturbing within the grotesque. We might instead think of Bakhtin as providing neither a blueprint nor a sourcebook for thematic readings of Carter but a set of identifications that complement Carter's intertextual allusions to grotesque writers: Bakhtin presents a narrative of a literary and cultural tradition, the grotesque, with which Carter's fiction engages and to the continued evolution of which it contributes. We might also remark on the important congruence between the carnivalesque and dialogic forms in Bakhtin's work, and how Bakhtin himself describes the English comic novel as a menippean tradition of a heteroglossic kind, full of different discourses and voices (Bakhtin, 1981, 301). From this perspective, Carter's work can be seen as not especially postmodern but instead a (re)turn to a particular strand of the history of the novel that has never really gone away despite nineteenth-century realism's disdain for its 'crude' forerunners. This is the longstanding tradition of the grotesque that Carter's fiction draws on and extends.

As to Head's argument about the 'flight from realism', Rushdie's prominence as an often-written-about post-war writer hardly marks a return to business as usual vis-à-vis literary 'realism' after Carter and, as Rushdie's interest in and praise for Carter might suggest (he wrote the introduction to her collected short stories), the 'flight from realism' is not just a Carter enterprise. Head's book's carefully qualified praise for Rushdie, with 'the Booker of Bookers' *Midnight's Children* (1981), a key British literary work of the post-war period, meriting only a mention in passing, may be of a piece with this distaste for the non-realist. Of course, a more charitable approach to Head's scepticism might claim that Carter, if not the most-written-about British post-war writer, may well be the most 'misread'. By 'misread' I mean the extent to which Carter herself was often shocked by readers' perceptions of her work, whether it was being asked to write about Stonehenge (Day, 1998, 4) or the presumption of an interest in fairies (Harron, 1984, 10). Between critics who regarded her writing as little more than 'high-falutin bluster' (Haffenden, 1985, 81) on the one side, and devotees whose apparent misinterpretations of her motives and viewpoint surprised her on the other, Carter's work has persistently formed a contested zone both in its immediate reception and later as a subject of scholarship. The recurrent possibility of readers not following carefully spun webs of intertextual reference was something that she reflected on, electing to follow a 'twin-track' approach that balanced complex cultural allusions with more straightforward literary entertainment: 'from *The Magic Toyshop* onwards I've tried to keep an entertaining surface to the novels, so that you don't have to read them as a system of signification if you don't want to' (Haffenden, 1985, 87). The coexistence of these different strata within the fiction indicates the complex nature of Carter's deployment and adaptation of a variety of narrative modes, creating an idiosyncratic contemporary oeuvre informed by the grotesque. If we are to do justice to such complexity rather than seeking to dismiss it as mere faddish gimmickry, then the grotesque forms the most effective avenue of inquiry to trace the development of Carter's aesthetic vision. Some attempts have been made in this regard; however, as I will show, they have been limited in scope and subject to contestation.

Carnival of carnivores: *The Bloody Chamber*

While some critical attention has been devoted to the grotesque in Angela Carter's work, it has tended broadly to follow two distinct paths that have sometimes seemed over-keen to distinguish themselves from one another. On the one hand are approaches in which theories of the body, carnival and gender play key roles, best exemplified by Mary Russo's *The Female Grotesque* (1994). On the other are analyses that seek instead to emphasise Carter's fiction's relationship to its sociohistorical context, and that are sceptical of the utility or even the legitimacy of some theoretically-inspired critical paradigms, such as Aidan Day's *Angela Carter: The Rational Glass* (1998). Analyses of the densely braided intertextual references to a particular author (e.g. Shakespeare, Swift) within Carter's prose have generally tended to particularise and so to weaken the potential correspondence between Carter's writing and a set of wide-ranging theoretical models. My purpose here is to offer a productive means of moving beyond the oft-repeated stand-off between theoretically inclined approaches to Carter's work and those which reject such perspectives in favour of what they propose as historically and contextually more coherent accounts. In order to acknowledge her grotesque's specific genealogies and its powerful cultural and theoretical resonance my exploration of her fiction will focus on the latter half of her career from *The Bloody Chamber* onward. My context-specific approach therefore seeks to avoid polarising debates and what Joseph Bristow and Trev Lynn Broughton call 'this after-the-fact "Butlerification" of Carter's writing' (1997, 19) in addition to what we may term 'after-the-fact Bakhtinification'. Carter's later work, in particular *Nights at the Circus*, *Wise Children* and the posthumous collection of stories *American Ghosts and Old World Wonders* (1996), reveals the evolution of her narrative modes in directions that deepen and complicate an engagement with the grotesque that has permeated almost everything she has written. Such a perspective acknowledges the strengths of the two poles of Carter criticism but resists seeing them as mutually exclusive, thus forming a bridge between two avenues of scholarship that has the capacity to reflect on and potentially critique the terms of the debate.

Carter's multifaceted adoption and development of the grotesque in her writing left her open to accusations of immaturity, silliness, pornography, sadism and fantastic irrelevance. Nowhere is this more evident than in the reactions to *The Bloody Chamber*, a collection which still inspires both adulation and suspicion in large measures. Having worked on a translation of the fairytales of Charles Perrault, Carter then decided 'to extract the latent content from the traditional stories and to use it as the beginnings of new stories' (Haffenden, 1985, 84). This *Interpretation of Dreams*-influenced approach to the fairytales, hinted at by her use of latent, was something she later described as an act that was 'illegitimate from the point of view of them being a certain kind of traditional narrative very much rooted in specific cultures, which is to analyse the imagery as if it was the imagery of the unconscious' (Appignanesi, 1987). Carter's point that her Freudian-inspired interpretations of and creative extrapolations from Perrault's stories make little concession to the specific historical and cultural context of the 'originals' can be seen as signalling not only an awareness of the very history/theory antithesis that has dogged so much of the scholarship on her fiction, but also a willingness to suspend anxieties around legitimacy in the cause of artistic autonomy. The fairytales are both the cultural product of a particular time and place and a reservoir of evocative images and scenarios loaded with sexual and gender import that are open to reiteration and re-signification in new and 'illegitimate' ways. As I will show, one of the most dominant features of Carter's oeuvre has been its enthusiasm for undeferential borrowing and illegitimate co-mingling. Indeed, illegitimacy may be regarded as a key preoccupation of Carter's fiction, from illicit collisions of high art and low culture to birth outside wedlock to the artistic gratuitousness and perversity identified by Ruskin as the hallmark of the grotesque.

The title story of *The Bloody Chamber* is based on the Bluebeard fairytale and tells the story of a girl from a modest Parisian background who marries a much older Marquis and moves into his castle, only to discover that he has tortured and murdered his previous wives. The heroine had been keen to leave behind her mother's house and enter the exciting and apparently liberated world of adulthood with a rich husband, but is shaken by her new status as a sexual prize to be inspected and enjoyed at leisure by the Marquis:

I saw him watching me in the gilded mirrors with the assessing eye of a connoisseur inspecting horseflesh, or even of a housewife in the market, inspecting cuts on the slab. I'd never seen, or else had never acknowledged, that regard of his before, the sheer carnal avarice of it; and it was strangely magnified by the monocle lodged in his left eye. (Carter, 1996, 115)

The emphasis on the voyeuristic pleasure enjoyed by the cyclopic Marquis in this description links his magnified and multiplied surveillance of the heroine with a desire that takes pleasure in the economic possession of the girl's body and longs to insert it into a fantasy tableau. In his eyes the heroine is reduced to a piece of meat that he has purchased, an equine prey to fall to his feline lust. Significantly, this transformation from flesh into meat for devouring is a process of which the heroine is aware. Carter suggests that she has seen this predatory look before but has not understood its malign instrumentality. Here the grotesque transmutation of the human body into meat is not a life-affirming humorous degradation of the kind one might find in traditional comedy but is one that is subordinated to a cruel system of sexual violence and patriarchal domination.

That it is the heroine's horse-riding and gun-toting mother, and not her brothers, who saves her from being killed is probably the most obvious deviation from Perrault's version of Bluebeard. However, on a deeper level the heroine's growing realisation of her predicament is the central engine of the story and adds a degree of sophistication to the revised fairytale plot. Her initial pleasure in the novelty of being the object of desire, and the promise of freedom and luxury it holds, give way to efforts first to understand and then to escape her deadly objectification in her husband's dungeon of horrors. The illustrated pornography he owns, the jewels he wraps her in, the ever-present mirrors and finally his fetishistic bloody chamber point to the dangers for a young woman of being commodified and of losing her way within the play of images generated in the service of masculine desire. 'The Bloody Chamber' stages the heroine's gradual awareness of her position within the castle and the murderous force ranged against her: an awareness that comes late but not too late to escape being consumed as a kind of sex-doll. In relation to the heroine's sense of herself as a piece of meat, Carter has described her experience of becoming politically aware in the 1960s in strikingly similar terms:

> There comes a moment when many of the things of which you have a theoretical knowledge actually start to apply to oneself. You could walk your calf past the butcher's shop for days, but it's only when he sees the abattoir that he realizes that there is a relation between himself and the butcher's shop – a relation which is mediated, shall we say, by the abattoir. (Haffenden, 1985, 78)

The political consciousness of one's place within controlling social structures is rendered here in shocking terms as the sudden consciousness of oneself as meat, liable to be consumed if one is not careful. It is this political understanding of how wider social forces affect the individual subject that *The Bloody Chamber* as a collection stages through its rewriting of traditional fairytales. The climax of the title story where 'the puppet master, open-mouthed, wide-eyed, impotent at the last, saw his dolls break free of their strings, abandon the rituals he had ordained for them since time began and start to live for themselves' (Carter, 1996, 142) conveys an iconic scene of liberation from patriarchal control that has echoes of the deaths of early Carter arch-manipulators such as Hoffman in *The Infernal Desiring Machines of Doctor Hoffman* (1972) and Uncle Philip in *The Magic Toyshop*. The serial repetition of submission has been overthrown by a violent revolution.

Meat-eating, as Linden Peach has observed, is a recurrent trope in Carter's work but finds its fullest expression in the lions, tigers, wolves and vampires that inhabit *The Bloody Chamber* and that follow differently gendered configurations of predator and prey. The stories present a series of variations on the themes of metamorphosis and of predation, with men and women becoming wild animals matched by beasts taking on human form in the different stories. At the opening of her story reinterpreting Little Red Riding Hood entitled 'The Company of Wolves' Carter plays on the wolf's role as 'carnivore incarnate' (Carter, 1996, 212 story first published 1977), that is, being a material manifestation of a human's disconcerting awareness of her own status as meat. While a wave of scholarship approaching fairytales in psychoanalytic terms, including Bruno Bettelheim's

The Uses of Enchantment: The Meaning and Importance of Fairy Tales (1976) and Jack Zipes's *Breaking the Magic Spell: Radical Theories of Folk and Fairy Tales* (1979), was emerging as *The Bloody Chamber* was published (and with which Carter's collection was in dialogue) the fairytale encounter between the girl and the wolf at the end of 'The Company of Wolves' is not coded as sexual in any simplistic way. Just as 'The Bloody Chamber' centred on the unnamed heroine's growing consciousness of her place within a gender-differentiated sexual order, so 'The Company of Wolves' focuses on the young girl's nascent interest in a sexual encounter, not in the role of passive object but as desiring agent: 'the girl burst out laughing; she knew she was nobody's meat' (Carter, 1996, 219). Entry into the sexual world of adults need not necessitate violent objectification and crude consumption.

Patricia Duncker's critique of *The Bloody Chamber* in general and 'The Company of Wolves' in particular warns of the dangers of using fairytale models in a modern context:

> But the infernal trap inherent in the fairy tale, which fits the form to its purpose, to be the carrier of ideology, proves too complex and pervasive to avoid. Carter is rewriting the tales within the straitjacket of their original structures ... Red Riding Hood sees that rape is inevitable – 'The Wolf is carnivore incarnate' – and decides to strip off, lie back and enjoy it. She wants it really. They all do. (Duncker, 1984, 6–7)

What Duncker sees as willed victimhood on the part of Carter's heroines, 'women voraciously, masochistically eager for the corruption of sexuality' (Duncker, 1984, 10), raises important questions about the degree to which Carter's newer stories could avoid reproducing the chauvinist aspects of earlier tales. The connections between meat-eating, carnal pleasure and economic commodification form a clear thread running through *The Bloody Chamber*, from the protagonist of 'The Tiger's Bride' who is bet and lost by her father in a card game to the happy girl in 'The Werewolf' who discovers her grandmother is a werewolf, raises the alarm and prospers in the inherited house after the old lady has been killed by the villagers. The young women who are the heroines of these stories seek to find a way to express their sexuality without being transformed into a deathly object to be consumed by men and without confusing their sense of self with their worth as a valuable commodity within patriarchal modes of exchange. In the same year that *The Bloody Chamber* came out Carter published *The Sadeian Woman*, her exploration of the place of women in De Sade's writings. The 'speculative finale' to the book is entitled 'The Function of Flesh' and notes the transformation of flesh to meat in de Sade's pornographic and 'inhuman' model of sexuality: 'The strong abuse, exploit and meatify the weak, says Sade. They must and will devour their natural prey' (Carter, 1979, 140). What Duncker regards as the 'reactionary' flaw in the collection issues from Carter's interest in de Sade, and certainly Carter's observation that some of de Sade's female characters when faced with male aggressors act 'as if a treacherous complicity finally unites them; as though, in some sense, the victim wills a victim's fate' (1979, 139) anticipates Duncker's unease with 'The Company of Wolves'. What de Sade's work holds out for Carter however, and that her stories hint at, is the possibility of free exchange, of a sexual politics stripped of its metaphysics and operating through mutuality, achieved through a radical social and political transformation. It is Carter's aversion to a new metaphysics (as opposed to a new politics) of sexuality based around female virtue and maternity that keeps de Sade and his radical pornography in the frame.

The Bloody Chamber's presentation of young women negotiating the often cruel world of patriarchal exchange and masculine sexual fantasy, fraught with the threat of 'beastliness' and the conversion of haptic flesh into comestible meat, can be read as part of a wider grotesque emphasis on human physicality in Carter's work. From the lavatorial comparison which fells a matriarch in her early short story 'A Very, Very Great Lady and Her Son at Home' (1996, story first published 1965) to the belching and farting of Fevvers in *Nights at the Circus*, the focus on the grotesque body in Carter's writing has fed into elaborate reflections on the construction of gender, sexuality and class. The material quality of the body marks an ambiguous site both of the 'infernal' conversion of women into things and of potential resistance to metaphysical and discursive framing. If, as Pauline Palmer has argued, Carter's early work has painted all too thoroughly the objectification and subordination of women within sexist social and fantasy structures, in a world where too often 'carnal knowledge is the infernal knowledge of flesh as meat' (Carter, 1979, 141), then her later work seeks to explore the possibility of achieving the opposite 'celestial' transformation, from traded things into people. This turn in Carter's work, where material apprehensions of the human featuring captivity are joined by utopian ones evoking flight and escape, plays an important role in acknowledging women's subjection to cruelty within forms of patriarchy but registering such social forms as historically produced and not hypostasising them as transhistorical structures. After Carter had written *The Bloody Chamber*, the next novel she would write was *Nights at the Circus*, which stages a dynamic fusion of the physical and material with the abstract and utopian, dreaming of what lies beyond the frequent sexual tyranny of the past.

The showgirl's revolution: *Nights at the Circus*

Nights at the Circus is a picaresque novel describing the many adventures of the 'Cockney Venus' Fevvers, an enigmatic and apparently winged star of the circus who travels around turn-of-the-century Europe with her dresser Lizzie, pursued by a curious male American journalist named Walser, who is determined to discover the secret of whether Fevvers can really fly. The book is divided into three sections based on the locations the characters visit – London, St Petersburg and Siberia – and the group's journeys chart the development of Walser and Fevvers's relationship in addition to hinting at Lizzie's clandestine role in the imminent revolution about to engulf Russia. The novel opens with Walser interviewing Fevvers about her past in her dressing room after one of her performances and details his intense scrutiny of her unique form, thus failing to observe the subversive nature of the newspapers Lizzie hastily hides from him. He struggles to reconcile Fevvers's image as a beautiful aerialiste with her vulgar behaviour and manners, and this binary opposition of heaven and earth affects everything he notices about her, from 'her voice of a celestial fishwife' (1985, 43) to his thought that there was 'not much of the divine about her unless there were gin palaces in heaven where she might preside behind the bar' (12). Having admired her feather-clad form gliding effortlessly through the air, he is surprised by her large size and matching appetite:

> [H]er mouth was too full for a ripost as she tucked into this earthiest, coarsest cabbies' fare with gargantuan enthusiasm. She gorged, she stuffed herself, she spilled gravy on herself, she sucked up peas from the knife; she had a gullet to match her size and table manners of the Elizabethan variety. (Carter, 1985, 22)

The conjunction of humble food, underdeveloped dining etiquette and the gross scale of her eating serves to reinforce Walser's sense of Fevvers's vulgarity and coarseness, qualities that are opposed to feminine beauty and refinement. The excessive physicality of this description, with its nod to Rabelais's Gargantua, thus complicates her role on- and off-stage as an object of desire for Walser and men more generally.

Walser finds something overwhelming about Fevvers's physicality, her face with 'its Brobdingnagian symmetry' (35), her powerful limbs and noisy flatulence posing a challenge to his sense of beauty. These allusions to Rabelais's Gargantua and Swift's Gulliver constitute a direct engagement with the literary tradition of the grotesque involving playing with scale, where the human body is rendered repellent and grotesque through detailed physical and often scatological descriptions of outsized bodies. As Anna Hunt (2006) has noted, the dressing room setting and revelations of a woman's private disrobing and digestive functions recall Swift's 'The Lady's Dressing Room' (1973, first published 1732) and 'Cassinus and Peter' (1973, first published 1734) poems and their juxtaposition of the conventions of love poetry with sordid biological detail. The hyperbolic qualities of Fevvers's anatomy lead Walser to question his aesthetic appreciation of her body, in particular the issue of how far size determines beauty. Following Rabelais and Swift's play with magnification, and recalling Edmund Burke's theories of what distinguishes the beautiful from the sublime, the sheer scale of Fevvers complicates any easy categorisation of her as something beautiful and precious. As Walser's interrogating gaze lingers on her, he is conscious of a vague imperfection that spoils her beauty:

The lightbulbs around Fevvers' mirror threw a naked and unkind light upon her face but could flush out no flaw in the classic cast of her features, unless their very size was a fault in itself, the flaw that made her vulgar. (Carter, 1985, 20)

Carter reveals how Fevvers's perceived vulgarity is located in her excessive size rather than in a particular feature. Instead of having a locatable defect, Fevvers by her size alone violates canons of moderation and decorum associated with female beauty in Western culture, creating a degree of aesthetic disorientation for Walser, whose head begins to swim in the heavy atmosphere of the dressing room. His metaphysical stupor is alleviated when he urinates behind a screen, where 'engaging in this most human of activities brought him down to earth again, for there is no element of the metaphysical about pissing, not, at least, in *our* culture' (52). Here Walser's own base physical needs restore his sense of himself, accompanied by a sly suggestion that the opposition between body and spirit regarded as fundamental to Western thought is a quaint provincialism not shared by all of humanity.

The grotesque physical body in this opening section of the novel can be read as a refinement of the fairytale metamorphoses between human and animal seen in *The Bloody Chamber*, where Fevvers occupies an ambivalent position as a possible freak or fraud poised between the worlds of people and beasts. The multivalent body that was subject to different forces and instincts from menstruation to vampirism in the forests and castles of *The Bloody Chamber* has become a single but more inscrutable phenomenon in *Nights at the Circus*, seen but not, in the carnal terms of the earlier story collection, consumed. This inscrutability is not only in spite of but also perhaps because of Fevvers's body's extreme visibility both within the narrative and before the fictional audiences she entertains. Walser's and by implication the reader's curiosity as to her 'nature' is matched by an awareness that Fevvers is involved in a performance before an inquisitive observer, a performance that deflects attention at least as much as it reveals. The novel opens with Fevvers's account of her past, where she was 'hatched out a bloody great egg' (1), but Walser and the reader are left wondering how far they should believe her. Scepticism as to Fevvers's real origins is something that even the author herself shared, as she claimed in tongue-in-cheek fashion in interview: 'We are talking about fiction here and I have no idea whether that's true or not. That's just what she says, a story that's being constructed' (Katsavos, 1994, 13). Beneath this light-hearted disavowal as to the 'facts' of her protagonist's birth lies an insistence on the fictional nature of what is being offered and on the contingent nature of the tale being told to Walser. In place of the biological pressures of *The Bloody Chamber* comes a heightened focus on the social and discursive framing of the human body, and the diverse and often misleading aspects it presents to the viewer within different contexts.

This stress placed on the artificiality of the spectacle involving Fevvers not only takes in the mystery as to whether she can really fly and is cleverly disguising her preternatural ability as a mere carnival trick, but crucially encompasses her life as a woman in patriarchal Western society at the beginning of the twentieth century. On stage, the Cockney Venus is a figure that may or may not be revealing a natural ability, and the description of her face 'thickly coated with rouge and powder so that you can see how beautiful she is from the back row of the gallery' (Carter, 1985, 18) points to the artifice of the spectacle she displays, where supposedly inherent beauty is a function of cosmetics. The sense of falseness persists when Walser reflects that her face even without its makeup 'might have been hacked from wood and brightly painted up by those artists who build carnival ladies for fairgrounds or figureheads for sailing ships' (35). The repeated emphasis on the theatrical illusion involved in this female performance points to the wider significance of the artificiality underlying gender construction, as Carter has made clear in interview: 'show-business, being a show-girl is a very simple metaphor for being a woman, for being aware of your femininity, for being aware of yourself as a woman and having to use it to negotiate with the world' (Evans, 1992). The artifice of theatrical presentation is offered not as an illusion disguising a hidden truth but rather as a fundamental and perhaps inescapable aspect of human interaction in the world. As a woman Fevvers presents an image to the world both on- and off-stage that the male characters in *Nights at the Circus* fixate upon in different ways, and try to incorporate into their own schemes of understanding and desire, with Walser no exception. What marks Walser out as different to the others is his experience of following the peripatetic Fevvers, a journey that leads him on a path of humiliation and rebirth. His name may be read as a nod to Swiss writer Robert Walser, a nomadic modernist known for his surreal 'anti-tales' as well as his descriptions of life as a clerk. Walser's role as a human chicken in Captain Kearney's circus closely follows the transformation of Professor Rath from a respectable schoolmaster to an object of amusement and derision as a clown as he pursues the performer Lola Lola (played by Marlene Dietrich) in Josef von Sternberg's film *The Blue Angel* (1930). First spotting Lola Lola as a feather-clad advertising image, Rath attends her cabaret performance and is smitten, but their subsequent marriage and his later role as a stage 'human chicken' splashed with eggs ends unhappily for him. While Walser undergoes a very similar bewildering experience of becoming a figure of fun and 'human chicken' his social disorientation ultimately ends on a positive note with his reunion with Fevvers, a New Man that is 'fitting mate for the New Woman' (Carter, 1985, 281) to begin the new century.

If many of the stories in *The Bloody Chamber* explore the infernal conversion of people, especially women, within capitalist patriarchy into objects to be consumed and so destroyed, then *Nights at the Circus* presents the reader with a potential reversal of this deathly process. The dangers of objectification still exist in *Nights at the Circus* and Fevvers must escape from her role as a tableau vivant in Ma Nelson's brothel and in Madame Schreck's museum as well as fleeing from the clutches of the Russian Grand Duke who wants to turn her into a miniature figurine. Her flight from these static roles, themselves reminiscent of the frequent paralysis of fairytale heroines, is aided by her apparent ability to defy gravity and take to the air. This means of breaking away from earthly bondage is a powerful emblem of liberation. However, as we can see from her physical makeup, this line of progress exists in a dialectic, balancing the ponderous ingesting and excreting material body and the feathery body of flight. Her relationship with the politicised Lizzie mirrors this disjunction between the possibilities for leaving the imprisoning mental structures of the past behind and the difficulty of achieving real social change, shown by Lizzie's response to Fevvers's description of a utopian future where

'The dolls' house doors will open, the brothels spill forth their prisoners, the cages, gilded or otherwise, all over the world, in every land, will let forth their inmates singing together the dawn chorus of the new, the transformed—'
'It's going to be more complicated than that,' interpolated Lizzie. 'This old witch sees storms ahead, my girl. When I look to the future, I see through a glass, darkly. You improve your analysis, girl, and *then* we'll discuss it.' (Carter, 1985, 285–6)

Nights at the Circus pairs the specifics of historical materialism that inform Lizzie's worldview with the utopian aspirations of Fevers and her hopes for the New Woman and the New Man. The storms Lizzie anticipates are the violent revolutions and wars that will convulse Europe in the first half of the twentieth century, and the radical political projects that despite their utopian rhetoric will lead to misery and genocide. The atmosphere of excitement and liberation Fevvers both feels and embodies notwithstanding, the future will be far more turbulent and difficult than she imagines.

This excitement and disorder can also be found in Walser's experiences with the circus clowns employed by Colonel Kearney, whose name is homonymic slang for carnival, and that involves slapstick violence of the kind described by Bakhtin in *Rabelais and his World*. The clowns are symbolically destroyed and reborn in their circus act, condemned to be ritually humiliated and reduced to objects over and over again but returned to life through the comedy of the grotesque body. Carter portrays the pleasure of the spectacle of these transgressions but is careful to note that such licensed reversals and inversions do not lead to political change. The clowns are 'licensed to commit licence and yet forbidden to act ... so that nothing would really change' (Carter, 1985, 151) and so they cannot effect real social transformation. Instead, their performance acts as a social safety valve, presenting disruptive energies that take over for a moment but that give way in a return to normality. The effect on an audience member is exciting but limited in scope: 'So then you'd know, you'd seen the proof, that things would always be as they had always been; that nothing came of catastrophe; that chaos evoked stasis' (151–2). Of course, what Lizzie with her secret plotting is trying to accomplish is precisely to make a revolution that will change things forever, a project that in the context of early twentieth-century St Petersburg is rife with dangerous possibilities. It is this historical dimension that Aidan Day is anxious to stress:

> The most important thing about the fantasy dimension of *Nights at the Circus* is that, for all its flamboyant craziness, it makes sense *specifically in relation to* the historical context that is sketched in by Carter. It is not gratuitous or surrealist fantasy, but fantasy whose symbolic meaning can be recovered in rational historical terms. (Day, 1998, 175)

While admitting the importance of Carter's evocation of a particular historical moment pregnant with dreams of transformation and a different future, we might also question what is at stake in Day's use of 'recovered' and whether such an approach risks jettisoning what are significant elements of Carter's novel, including its comedy and sense of narrative possibility. The recovery of rationality from 'flamboyant craziness' seems to continue the longstanding critical tradition of establishing a profound dualism within Carter's work and then privileging one side to the detriment of the other. The persistence of such dualism, although presumably intended to highlight the political 'relevance' of Carter's writing, also carries the risk of consigning many of its unique qualities to the critical dustbin.

The usefulness of Bakhtin's model of carnival and the grotesque body in relation to this novel has also been a site of critical anxiety, with scholars looking to reject possible Bakhtinian influence. Linden Peach is at pains to point out that 'the source of the carnivalesque element in *Nights at the Circus* and *Wise Children* was undoubtedly Shakespeare rather than Bakhtin' (Peach, 1998, 145), and similarly Anna Hunt argues that Swift rather than Bakhtin is the source of the grotesque in *Nights at the Circus* (Hunt, 2006, 147). Like Day's comments above, these identifications emphasise specific historical connections to canonical writers and shy away from the application of Bakhtin's theories to Carter. One can acknowledge the value of these intertextual claims, yet they seem perhaps too keen to sideline the extent to which Bakhtin's theory might draw together important aspects of Carter's work while also providing a possible genealogy for some of her most significant intertextual sources. If we view the carnivalesque and the grotesque as a part of a pre-existing cultural tradition that includes Swift, and to a degree Shakespeare and eighteenth-century novelists such as Fielding, then Bakhtin may be seen as *describing* rather *prescribing* a tradition. Such a perspective on Bakhtin may provide a means of understanding Carter and Bakhtin as together exploring and learning from common sources of the grotesque, sometimes engaging with common themes in similar ways, sometimes reaching quite different conclusions. The many qualifications placed on the application of Bakhtinian theory to Carter's novel may perform the important function of discouraging allegations of direct influence of the Russian theorist on the writer, since Carter claimed not to have read his work until later in her career. However, his work should not therefore simply be dismissed as a distraction or red herring in relation to Carter. Instead we might regard Bakhtin's work on novelists including Dickens as a way of theorising Carter's links to a tradition of the comic novel in which the grotesque is a prominent feature, as I have described elsewhere (Duggan, 2006). The Russian critic's careful exploration of the importance of heteroglossia within eighteenth- and nineteenth-century English fiction, and the applicability of such work to a contemporary author such as Carter shows the limitations of Head's categorical dismissal of Bakhtin's relevance.

The picaresque structure of *Nights at the Circus* and the generic status it may imply are another aspect of the book that has come in for comment, with Day arguing that:

> This eighteenth-century fictional device is invoked, it seems to me, in something other than a postmodern spirit. It is not invoked to be parodied or to be relativised as a narrative device. It is invoked straight, as it were, because Carter is using the device to explore issues and to say something about those issues in a way that she herself believes in. (Day, 1998, 169)

Given the exuberance of Carter's account of Fevvers's adventures, it may be that Day is being too straight with his account of the picaresque in the novel, and his model of authorial intention producing its clear fictional expression seems limited in comparison to the author's stated desire, quoted above, for her work to be read simultaneously on many different levels. Given that this picaresque and carnivalesque novel was written in 1984, its capacity to reproduce 'straight' eighteenth-century literary models must be attenuated and we might also question the extent to which the picaresque is opposed to the carnivalesque in *Nights at the Circus*. If we place this novel and Carter's later work in the tradition of the English comic novel and its enduring interest in the grotesque of the kind exemplified by Fielding and Dickens, we can regard the picaresque strategies as part of Carter's persistent and longstanding elaboration of the grotesque, even as the more prominent aspects of the gothic within early works such as *The Magic Toyshop* and *The Infernal Desiring Machines of Doctor Hoffman* begin to fade. The gothic strain within Carter's early novels that was, it must be admitted, more interested in freaks than ghosts – to borrow Leslie Fiedler's distinction in *Freaks: Myths and Images of the Secret Self* (1978) – gradually gives way to the carnivalesque of the final books but her grotesque can be seen as a central thread within her oeuvre, encompassing and shaping her use of these two modes. Her (re)turn to the 'unrefined' novelistic forms and grotesque narratives of the past is in order to find a means of accommodating both her earthy materialism and her flights of fancy.

Wise Children and the end of carnival

The doublings and dualisms I have been highlighting in Carter's fiction and in criticism on it come to a kind of humorous apotheosis in her last novel *Wise Children* and its protagonists Dora and Nora Chance, twin sisters looking back on their music hall careers and their family history, including their uncertain genealogy. The Chances are the illegitimate counterparts of the famous Hazard theatrical family, creating a proliferation of oppositions between high and low running through the novel. The strong connections between the two sides of the family, not all of which are openly acknowledged, suggest the symbolic but veiled dependence of the legitimate and prestigious on the low-class and vulgar. The all-singing and all-dancing Chances are the poor relations of Melchior Hazard, the foremost Shakespearian actor of the day, and his enigmatic twin brother Peregrine, who mysteriously vanishes and reappears at regular intervals. As Dora narrates, the twin girls struggle to gain recognition and acceptance from Melchior, whom they initially think is their father. However, they end up suspecting that perhaps Peregrine is their biological father and Grandma Chance their mother. Their search for acceptance and for their 'natural' parents sees them ultimately accept the absence of certainty in this regard, and the novel ends with the reunion of the two sides of the family and Nora and Dora taking on a new role as carers for baby twins who are apparently the offspring of their half-brother Gareth (himself a twin).

Wise Children's allusions to *King Lear* and its themes of paternity and ageing are only the most obvious signs of the concentrated network of intertextual references to the works of Shakespeare contained in Carter's novel. The web of allusions in *Wise Children* takes in many of his plays and its motifs of twins, multiple weddings, a feared drowning and an attempted poisoning point to a wide range of Shakespearean influences. The mood of the novel has been likened to the late romances rather than having a principally comic or tragic focus, and the happy atmosphere of reconciliation that permeates the latter part of the narrative evokes the plot resolutions of *The Tempest* and *Twelfth Night*. What Carter retains from *Nights at the Circus* is a picaresque plot and a heavily dramatised sense of narration, with Dora remarking at one point 'There I go again! Can't keep a story going in a straight line, can I? Drunk in charge of a narrative' (1992, 158). This loquacious and digressive narrator, whose idiom is reminiscent of Fevvers and Lizzie's working-class London style of speech, tangles up the chronology of the story and frames many of the twins' adventures as a process of experimentation and gradually gained self-knowledge. Born on 23 April, living on Bard Road and using bank notes showing his image, the women are never far from the multifarious cultural and commercial exploitation of the Bard of the kind that Michael Bristol describes in *Big-time Shakespeare* (1996), and the novel presents both high-quality artistic and crassly commercial appropriations of Shakespeare's plays. By marrying American film star Daisy Duck, Melchior Hazard 'thought he was marrying, not into Hollywood but Hollywood itself, taking over the entire factory, thus acquiring control of the major public dreaming facility in the whole world' (Carter, 1992, 148), continuing Carter's treatment of the American film industry as a colossal dream-machine in *The Passion of New Eve*.

One important episode of *Wise Children* involves Melchior's attempts to make a film of *A Midsummer Night's Dream* in which Nora and Dora play fairies and through which he plans to conquer the USA in the name of Shakespeare, a quest his father Ranulph had begun. The link between Shakespeare and cultural conquest is a subtle but pervasive thread in *Wise Children* as Nora and Dora's lifespan follows a general movement of decline in British military and cultural power abroad, charted through the expanding and shrinking of Gorgeous George's tattoos that map out the British Empire and his eventual decent into homelessness. This movement from British to American political supremacy is matched by film replacing theatre as the site of cultural hegemony, and the novel presents the reader with a shift of the centre of power across the Atlantic. Despite Dora's love of music halls and the theatre, when she imagines what the Hazards' departure to America would have looked like she thinks in cinematic terms: 'I see it in my mind's eye as if it were a movie – the ocean liner slipping her moorings, gliding away from the quay, the siren blaring, the crowd throwing flowers' (17). It is film's ability to colonise the mind's eye that enables it to turn the artifice of theatrical narrative and performance into something more potent, though still artificial.

The penetration of artifice into supposedly the most solid of domains is repeated again and again in *Wise Children*, with theatricality the order of the day, whether it is the 'real' identity of the twins' mother and father or even the reality of Grandma Chance's home in which they grew up as girls: 'the whole place never looked *plausible*. It looked like the stage set of a theatrical boarding house, as if Grandma had done it up to suit a role she'd chosen on purpose' (25). Their exchange of roles both on- and off-stage in *Wise Children* and the sometimes deceptive behaviour of their relatives and friends lead the twins to reflect on the nature of their search for their true father. The artificial and self-generated quality of their relationship with Melchior is signalled by his resemblance to an effigy in London's Notting Hill Carnival:

> 'And tonight, he had an imitation look, even when he was crying, especially when he was crying, like one of those great, big, papier-maché heads they have in the Notting Hill parade, larger than life, but not lifelike.'

Nora sunk in thought for a hundred yards.

'D'you know, I sometimes wonder if we haven't been making him up all along,' she said. 'If he isn't just a collection of our hopes and dreams and wishful thinking in the afternoons. Something to set our lives by, like the old clock in the hall, which is real enough, in itself, but which we've got to wind up to make it go.' (Carter, 1992, 230)

Following the path of Walser's pursuit of the truth of Fevvers's nature in *Nights at the Circus*, the twins' search for the truth of their family in *Wise Children* becomes a deeper process of self-reflection and an acknowledgement of the active role of their desires in constructing an object of perception out of a person. Dora and Nora's awareness of this lack of reality does not, however, engender a more direct access to truth, as Jacqueline Pearson has observed in relation to earlier works by Carter:

It is not that an 'apparent' world of phenomenon masks a 'real' world that we could see if we stripped away its deceptive veneer. It is rather that the whole nature of reality is problematised; and radically different modes of discerning, which seem to have equal validity, are depicted. (Pearson, 1999, 249)

Instead of swapping a false version of reality for a true one, Nora and Dora are left with a sense that the very fabric of reality is a thin layer of artifice fraught with the potential for delusion. This movement in both late novels, from a quest for truth to a questioning of the nature of reality, clearly resembles Brian McHale's (1992) well-known characterisation of postmodern fiction as exchanging ontological preoccupations for modernism's epistemological ones. The conclusions of both Carter novels end not with a revelation of final truth but a radical interrogation of the ontological status of women, men, fathers and mothers.

As Carter's comments about show business quoted above indicate, the endemic quality of pretence and performance in both *Nights at the Circus* and *Wise Children* blurs the line between the real and the artificial, and between the stage and the real world, problematising any notion of underlying truth. Commenting on the party at the end of *Wise Children*, Carter has remarked in interview that when Nora and Dora:

> put on the faces they used to have ... because they're now batty old hags, they recreate themselves as grotesque parodies of the girls they were. But in a sense, they know perfectly well that even when they were girls, they were grotesque parodies of the girls they really were. (Evans, 1992)

The grotesque here, in its combination of the comic and disturbing, arises from the apparent disjunction between the old women and their supposedly anachronistic makeup. However, Carter argues that the grotesque parody of femininity evident in the elderly twins' preparations for the party has in fact been a constant throughout their lives. Even as young women their 'war-paint' was a theatrical presentation of their gender not based in reality, and the Chance girls understood at an early age that they were not as they appeared to others. As I discussed in relation to *The Bloody Chamber* above, such self-knowledge is essential to avoid deriving one's entire identity from how one is perceived by others and becoming a puppet or living doll. *Nights at the Circus* and *Wise Children* at their conclusions therefore eschew any straightforward epistemological payoff via a clear solution to questions of identity and genealogy, and instead offer this quite different form of enlightenment. While W.B. Yeats may have asked how we can know the dancer from the dance, for Carter it is imperative that the dancer is capable of supplying an answer to the question herself.

The film production of *A Midsummer Night's Dream* in *Wise Children* takes place against a chaotic background of sexual intrigue and plotting, and when a large party involving the cast takes place the venue goes up in flames amid scenes of feasting and sexual licence. The incestuous sex between Nora and her uncle (or perhaps father) Perry and the burning down of the house recall the ending of *The Magic Toyshop*, and the apparent celebration of scandalous sexual pleasure leading to the disruption of order and hierarchies can be read as a sign of the power of carnival. Although such scenes contribute to the novel's celebration of the pleasures of performance and the possibility of reconciliation, it is important to note that Carter balances such exuberance with comparatively brief but nonetheless significant caveats about the limits of carnival's regenerative force. Chapter 4 begins, '"Let other pens dwell on guilt and misery." A., for Austen, Jane. *Mansfield Park*. I do not wish to talk about the war. Suffice to say it was no carnival, not the hostilities. No carnival' (Carter, 1992, 163) and the wider world of politics and wars cannot be wished away. The perhaps unlikely ally of Jane Austen is invoked by Carter's narrator Dora, who does not go into detail about the deprivations brought by war but acknowledges real suffering that resists carnival's comic inversion. This warning note about the boundaries of carnival returns when Dora confronts Peregrine, the back-flipping magician who appears in the Chances' lives with a flourish but who never stays around for very long:

> 'Life's a carnival,' he said. He was an illusionist, remember.
> 'The carnival's got to stop, some time, Perry,' I said. 'You listen to the news, that'll take the smile off your face.'
> 'News? What news?' (Carter, 1992, 222)

The play on the word 'illusionist' suggests that Peregrine as a magician is someone who disguises reality with a more entertaining appearance, and the category of artifice that for so much of the book is a positive quality, here for a moment takes on some of its more negative connotations of pretence and deceit. The news, of war and tumult, is not part of Peregrine's carnival ride, and Dora remarks, 'There are limits to the power of laughter and though I may hint at them from time to time, I do not propose to step over them' (220). Following on from the *Mansfield Park* quotation, Carter makes it clear that her 'overblown, purple, self-indulgent prose' should not be stretched to accommodate all circumstances and hints that its delights are in an oblique way the fruits of a broad but still finite scope. Rather than Austen's limpid and controlled prose, the digressive, picaresque style of *Nights at the Circus* and *Wise Children* owes more to the grotesque rough-and-tumble of eighteenth-century novels by Fielding and Swift. It is the tradition of the grotesque and unruly novel of Rabelais, Sterne and Dickens that offered Carter a means of creative liberation.

In relation to the oft-debated carnival aspect of Carter's late writing, Linden Peach has argued that:

the carnivalesque in her novels is a theme and not necessarily a position from which she writes ... If there is a single position from which Carter writes in *Nights at the Circus* and *Wise Children*, it is not the carnivalesque *per se* but the theatre. (Peach, 1998, 144)

While his emphasis on the theatrical, as this chapter has developed in more detail, is valuable, it is perhaps less certain that the theatre itself is best understood as 'a single position'. As I have been discussing, theatricality is a constant presence in Carter's fiction, in terms of both direct treatments of different kinds of acting, performance and spectacle and the deeper metaphoric resonance for notions of artifice and the 'unnatural' that Carter so effectively pursues. Both *Nights at the Circus* and *Wise Children* rely on the discourse and mechanisms of carnival for much of their literary vigour but Carter takes care to situate their often-comic narratives within wider contexts of historical change and its attendant troubles. The sometimes disorientating pull towards interrogating the real that both books generate, and their parallel movement from epistemological concerns to more ontological questions is pursued with unremitting drive and energy but is ultimately not permitted totally to overwhelm a consciousness of history. The reader will enjoy the excitement of Carter's stories but will also be gently reminded of something that Fredric Jameson eloquently sets forth in *The Political Unconscious: Narrative as a Socially Symbolic Act*:

History is what hurts, it is what refuses desire and sets inexorable limits to individual as well as collective praxis, which its 'ruses' turn into grisly and ironic reversals of their overt intention ... History as ground and untranscendable horizon needs no particular theoretical justification: we may be sure that its alienating necessities will not forget us, however much we might prefer to ignore them. (Jameson, 1981, 102)

Carter will not quite let us forget these necessities and it is within the bounds of this untranscendable horizon that the late novels of Angela Carter assert their prodigious imaginative potency and revel in the grotesque.

The Unfinished Angela Carter

Wise Children was published the year before Carter died and it is tempting to read it as being, among other things, a testament to reconciliation in the face of mortality and a celebration of the pleasure of artistic creation. Such a reading, however, risks obscuring the extent to which Carter's writing career was in so many ways unfinished. There are indications that her interest in Lizzie Borden, the axe-wielding heroine of American nursery rhyme explored in some of her short stories, might have led to a novel-length exploration, and her publishers were also left with a plan for a novel based on the character of Adela, Rochester's young female ward in Charlotte Brönte's *Jane Eyre*. So, while Jean Rhys's *Wide Sargasso Sea* (1966) famously opened up Brönte's novel along one axis, Carter's proposed book would have followed another, indicating the unfinished quality of all narratives and the loose ends thrown up by stories. As with so much of her writing, these uncompleted projects illuminate how Carter's intertextual fiction produced texts, rather than works, in the sense in which Roland Barthes contrasts the terms in 'From Work to Text' (1986a, essay first published 1971). The borderline between history and literature and between individual literary works becomes blurred in the world of Carter's fiction, and as this chapter has endeavoured to show, *The Bloody Chamber*, *Nights at the Circus* and *Wise Children* collectively form a vivid contemporary grotesque that stays unfinished in its treatment of the excessive body, its puncturing of high by low, its flirtation with improbability and theatricality, its lack of neat conclusion or definite *telos* and its appetite for breaking the bottles, shattering the myths and prising apart imprisoning structures.

Notes

1 See, for example, Salman Rushdie's comment that 'Carter's high-wire act takes place over a swamp of preciousness' (Carter, 1996, xiv), 'I want to argue that Carter maintains her balance on the tightrope between fantasy and rationalism' (Gasiorek, 1995, 127) and 'surely it is Carter's new way with words, her tightrope-walking risktaking' (Pykett, 1998, 59).

Chapter 3

Martin Amis: the limits of comedy

[I]n Angela Carter and Martin Amis, one finds Dickens's impress, in particular the interest in the self as a public performer, an interest in grotesque portraiture and loud names, and in character as caricature, a vivid blot of essence. (Wood, 2002, 11)

This chapter of the present study will look at the work of Martin Amis in the light of my earlier discussion of the grotesque in literature. I will be examining, among other works, his novels *Money: A Suicide Note* (1985a, first published 1984) and *London Fields* (1989) and will begin with a discussion of the importance of the body, which will be central to an understanding of Amis's fiction, and which will be considered from a number of perspectives. The discussion of the body in its different aspects will then lead to an examination of narrative technique, and questions of form, investigating Amis's oeuvre's relation to previous fiction, and its generic status. I will also show the extent to which the grotesque is present not only in Amis's early novels but is a strand which runs through his all his work, and approaches its most controversial embodiment in the grotesque reversals of *Time's Arrow* (1991).

Martin Amis's first novel, *The Rachel Papers* (1984a, first published 1973), is full of references to literature, as its protagonist Charles Highway attempts to gain entry to Oxford University and to sleep with fellow student Rachel Noyes. The narrative is set on the eve of Charles's twentieth birthday and structured around a series of flashbacks as he organises the eponymous 'Rachel Papers', the chapters beginning at 7 o'clock and ending at midnight. The grotesque is an important part of Charles's reading, as can be seen from early on in the novel:

This, then, was the humdrum background to the fecundities of my nocturnal reading. For I had begun to explore the literary grotesque, in particular the writings of Charles Dickens and Franz Kafka, to find a world of the bizarre surfaces and sneaky tensions with which I was always trying to invest my own life. I did my real study at home, of course, mostly on Rachel, and on English Literature and Language, which, or so it seemed to me, I was really fucking good at. (Amis, 1984a, 63–4)

Charles's twin principal subjects for study, Rachel and English Literature (he even terms his first attempt to impress Rachel a 'viva' (66)) thus also share space with the literary tradition of the grotesque. Charles even attempts a Kafkaesque 'Letter to my Father' (68) and returns to the grotesque when musing on why he claimed to a friend that he wished to sleep with an older woman, when he habitually remarks on how horrible old women looked:

I wonder. Transferred disgust of my own body? No; too boring. Dislike of women? Hardly, because I think male oldsters look just as dreadful, if less divertingly so. Sound distrust of personal vanity plus literary relish of physical grotesqueries? Could be. Sheer rhetoric? Yes. (Amis, 1984a, 88)

We can see a reflexive turn in Amis's writing here, something that could be termed an attempt to anticipate and counter negative interpretations of his work's preoccupation with the grotesque body — the grotesque in his prose is presented not as the result of the biographical or chauvinistic impulses that Charles's reflections suggest, but instead is part of a specifically *literary* tradition.

The grotesque tradition in literature is also invoked in the tenth chapter of *The Rachel Papers*, which is entitled 'Twenty-past: "Celia Shits" (the Dean of St Patrick's)'. Jonathan Swift was the Dean of St Patrick's Cathedral in Dublin, and it is his poem 'The Lady's Dressing Room' which contains the phrase 'Celia shits' as the protagonist Strephon explores his beloved's dressing room and is horrified by what he finds (Swift, 1992, 150–4, poem first published 1732). This disgust at discovering the biological nature of the beloved's body is echoed by Amis when Charles finds a stain on Rachel's underwear and is confronted by the graphic evidence that Rachel too possesses a biological body. Although Charles accepts this, "'Fair's fair, for Christ's sake,' I said out loud. "They do it too'", he also imagines confronting Rachel: "'Come, come, there's no use denying it; the proof's before you. *You ... shit*'" (Amis 1984a, 177). So, despite being able to rationalise the fact that his beloved has the same biological needs as himself, Charles still experiences some disappointment or disgust at the undeniable evidence of this:

> With what a ridiculous sense of grief and loss did I drop them into the laundry basket, and with what morose reluctance did I meet her eye when she returned that afternoon. (Amis, 1984a, 178)

The narrative works to disrupt the idea of Rachel's beauty in Charles's mind by his discovery of her biological, excreting body and shows how these categories are culturally defined in contradistinction.

The title of Amis's next novel *Dead Babies* (1984b, first published 1975), as James Diedrick mentions in *Understanding Martin Amis* (1995, 37) also recalls Swift as the author of 'A Modest Proposal' (1973, first published 1729), a satirical essay arguing that the impoverished Irish could eat children and thus save themselves from malnutrition and reduce child poverty. The genre of Menippean satire, which, as I have discussed earlier, has historically frequently coincided with the grotesque, also enters the frame as Amis uses a quote from Menippus as the epigraph to the novel.[1] The hilarious sexual and narcotic excesses of the characters of *Dead Babies* have been labelled grotesque and Swiftian by a number of critics (see Tredell, 2000, 24–7), and these early novels are thus situated, by their own intertextual signals, their content and the comments of the critics, within the literary tradition of the grotesque. A key aspect of the grotesque that is prominent in Amis's work, as these examples show, is the perception of the human body as grotesque and it is to this area that I will now turn.

The grotesque body

In the work of Amis the human body, like other aspects of the author's narratives, including his characters' appetites and the level of descriptive detail, is subject to a marked excessiveness, and this excessiveness takes a variety of forms. If we think about Bakhtin's description of the 'classical' body discussed in Chapter 1, it becomes clear that Amis's conception of the body is distinctly unclassical. The classical body, according to Bakhtin, is marked by its elevation (like a statue on a pedestal) and its perfection, static and inviolable to the external environment. For Bakhtin, of course, Rabelais's presentation of Gargantua's grotesque body is the antithesis of this static isolation. I will return to this idea of the grotesque body's openness later but for now we can see more generally that, in terms of harmony and health, the body in Amis's fiction is frequently dysfunctional and decaying. Looking at a wide range of characters from Amis's work, the reader is shown unhealthy rather than healthy bodies, from Terry's 'nasty hair', 'polychromatic teeth' and 'appallingly malarial eyes' in *Success* (1979, 184, first published 1978) to Tod Friendly's 'epic blemishes' in *Time's Arrow, or The Nature of the Offence* (1991, 17). One prime example is Keith Whitehead from *Dead Babies*, a persona upon whom Amis heaps all kinds of biological and anatomical misfortune:

> 'I've got very little imagination, nothing makes me laugh, I'm fat, poor, bald, I've got a horrible spotty face, constipation, B.O., bad breath, no prick and I'm one inch tall. That's why I'm mad now.'
> (Amis, 1984b, 149)

The grotesque body, as the earlier discussion of Bakhtin shows, goes beyond the ugliness of the not-beautiful and into the realm of the biologically dysfunctional body, moving from a consideration of surface and anatomy, proper to the aesthetics of classical beauty in Bakhtin's model, to a consideration of biology, of the depth of the body and its viscera and internal parts.

The body in Amis is not simply excessive in terms of a specific quality – for example, fatness or ugliness – it also fulfils Bakhtin's description of the grotesque body being open to the world, unlike the sealed and static classical body. Defecation (Marmaduke in *London Fields*), farting (Keith in *Dead Babies*), spitting (Richard in *The Information* (1995)), ejaculation (the porn John Self sees in New York in *Money*), vomiting (again John Self), masturbation

(Keith Talent in *London Fields* and John Self in *Money*) – all are part and parcel of Amis's narratives and are each described in detail. Bodily activities that are aligned with Stallybrass and White's 'low-other' (1986, 4–5), which should not be mentioned in polite society or become subjects of cultural production, are integrated into the fabric of the novel. However, Amis's desire to portray excess in an excessive manner applies even to those areas which would normally not be considered part of a low-other, so that in *Money* even the health of holidaymakers boarding an aeroplane home becomes grotesque:

> Girls in topheavy T-shirts and sawn-off jeans or else in superfemale parody of indigenous flounce and frill, the matrons also burgeoning in tight angular cords and a flush of freckly renewal ... Reacquainted with their bodies, warmed, oiled, attended to, they all have the sex tan: it is called *rude health*. (Amis, 1985a, 241)

As I discussed earlier in relation to the novel and the grotesque, the grotesque is characterised by excess and the transgression of economy and not simply by the not-beautiful. This grotesque of bodily excess is produced by a descriptive excess that is itself characterised by the presentation of the body as made up of disparate elements. Such a narrative strategy fits the description of Deidre Lynch's 'overloading' that violates artistic economy discussed in Chapter 1.

The body as excessive and grotesque is frequently achieved in Amis's work through the description of the human body as an aggregate of disparate parts. By breaking the body down into smaller units and focusing on specific aspects of these units, Amis magnifies, in both a visual and thematic way, the body's inherent grotesquerie. John Self's description of his taxi-driver's head on the first page of *Money* is a good example:

> My cabbie was fortyish, lean, balding. Such hair as remained scurried long and damp down his neck and shoulders. To the passenger, that's all city cabbies are – mad necks, mad rugs. This mad neck was explosively pocked and mottled, with a flicker of adolescent virulence in the crimson underhang of the ears. (Amis, 1985a, 1)

The language of the description of this mad neck is appropriately violent: virulent, crimson, explosive. These elements work in concert to show the reader the ugliness of the object, in this case the stereotypical New York taxi-driver whose aesthetic ugliness is matched by the moral ugliness of his racist views. One could make the point that Amis is using the taxi-driver's ugly body in order to encourage the reader to identify the driver as personally repugnant but it is important to remember that there is no privileged position of the ideal, healthy body. As we saw in the discussion of the stereotyped American body, the healthy body can also become grotesque and excessive.

The grotesque combination of qualities is also used by Amis in descriptions of the body, as can be seen from Keith Whitehead's 'puffed skin, at once babyish and corpselike' (Amis, 1984b, 191) or Tod Friendly's body 'smelling of poultry and peppermint' (Amis, 1991, 17). As Mary Shelley's Victor Frankenstein discovers, assembling a body from disparate parts seems to lead inevitably to grotesque monstrosity. Amis's description of Fat Lol in the short story 'State of England' (1998, first published 1996) is grotesque both in its comparison of the human body to cooked fatty food (where both the body and the food are rendered repellent by the likeness) and in its echo of grotesque portraits such as those of Arcimboldo, particularly *The Cook* (circa 1570):

> Fat Lol was what he ate. More than this, Fat Lol was what he was eating. And he was eating, for his lunch, an English breakfast – Del's All Day Special at £3.25. His mouth was a strip of undercooked bacon, his eyes a mush of egg yolk and tinned tomatoes. His nose was like the end of a lightly grilled pork sausage – then the baked beans of his complexion, the furry mushrooms of his ears. (Amis, 1998, 62)

As I outlined earlier in the discussion of Henry Fielding and George Eliot, the primary drive of realism centres on its economy, especially in terms of the descriptive potential of language. Viewing Amis's prose from this perspective emphasises its hyperbolic nature, as can be seen from John Self's reflections on his fellow citizens:

And these people aren't just mixed-up berks and babbling bagladies: they are haunted tinnitic taxmen, bug-eyed barristers and smart-bombed bureaucrats. Before, ... before, these tribes of spacefaced conquered would brood about God, Hell, the Father of Lies, the fate of the spirit, with the soul imagined as an inner being, a moistly smiling angel in a pink nightie, or a grimacing goblin, all V-signs, bad rug and handjobs. (Amis, 1985a, 330)

The alliteration of the first sentence draws attention to the artifice of the description, in which the supposedly everyday professionals are transformed into something alien and unnatural. There is little sense of economy at work in such a description and the subsequent two aspects of the inner spirit are described in John Self's peculiar idiom: 'rug', 'handjobs'. This piling up of descriptive elements can be seen as a characteristic feature of Amis's prose (and, as we shall see later, of Will Self's writing too), together with the peculiar vocabulary he mobilises.

Deidre Lynch's analysis of Hogarth and Fielding examines the anxiety surrounding 'the masterstroke' or 'finishing touch' that marks the end of the process of both pictorial and literary representation. A shared aesthetic where proportion and economy are the ruling principles emerged in discourse on the novel and its practice and reception, an aesthetic that the grotesque transgresses. The profusion of specific instances and their respective adjectives so frequently present in Amis's prose challenge any idea of descriptive economy, as presented in the catalogue of sexual harassment experienced by Selina in *Money*:

> [A] musk-breathing, toffee-offering sicko on the common, the toolshed interrogations of sweat-soaked parkies, some lumbering retard in the alley or the lane, right up to the narcissist photographers and priapic prop-boys who used to cruise her at work, and now the scowling punks, soccer trogs and bus-stop boogies malevolently lining the streets. (Amis, 1985a, 14)

Amis's work contains many such examples of what we can call a proliferation of details and of description, combined with his much-noted preference for verbal triads, which are frequently alliterative. This kinetic and swift-moving style is hyperbolic in the same way that the body in Amis is so often hyperbolic, seeking to exceed any economy. One example of the kind of people who harass Selina is not sufficient; each group must be mentioned and briefly described in its specificity to achieve this hyperbolic verbal flow. This differentiation harks back to Lynch's discussion of how 'caricaturists *flaunt* the ways in which the identity of the person comes to hinge, in their chosen form, on the production of a surplus' (Lynch, 1994, 127). 'Pictorial abstemiousness' (128) that is the equivalent in the visual arts of what I earlier called the economy of realism, reveals how the question of quality or kind is underpinned by a concern with quantity. Amis's books delight in metaphor, and in stretching each one to ludicrous proportions:

> My head is a city, and various pains have now taken up residence in various parts of my face. A gum-and-bone ache has launched a cooperative on my upper west side. Across the park, neuralgia has rented a duplex in my fashionable east seventies. Downtown, my chin throbs with lofts of jaw-loss. As for my brain, my hundreds, it's Harlem up there, expanding in the summer fires. It boils and swells. One day soon it is going to burst. (Amis, 1985a, 26)

Instead of a metaphor being something to be controlled and suppressed if necessary, the comparison between John Self's head and the socially segregated neighbourhoods of New York City is positively embraced and developed. The reader's attention is once again drawn to the particular construction of the metaphor, thus highlighting the writing, rather than its object, which runs counter to realism's enterprise and exceeds the economical use of 'the jewels of a few precious metaphors', as Barthes describes them in his discussion of *Madame Bovary* in 'The Reality Effect' (1986b, 144).

If we consider Barthes's '*effet de réel*', the issue of realism's economy becomes slightly more complex. As Barthes points out in relation to one of Flaubert's narratives, realism contains details that are semantically redundant, i.e. superfluous in terms of the communication of the story. In Barthes's theory such elements create reality effects because they signify the real, rather than denoting it: 'Flaubert's barometer, Michelet's little door, say, in the last analysis, only this: we are the real' (Barthes, 1986b, 148). Amis's proliferation of instances and his piling up of descriptive elements work along another axis: they do not signify the real by their singularity or semantic isolation, thus creating reality effects, rather the abundance of the elements signify their ultimate failure to signify the real, where the multiple instances do not form a whole. The real eludes such enumeration precisely *because* the elements retain their status as fragments and aspects that denote several instances of, rather than the category of, the real. The grotesque catalogue of Amis's description, by its length, presupposes further additions and development, rather than Flaubert's isolated detail that signifies the category of the real by its isolation and rarity.

Amis's play with perspective has been linked to the so-called 'Martian School' of writing (Diedrick, 1995, 54), and his poem 'Point of View' (1979) gives an early indication of its importance to his work. His novel *Other People: A Mystery Story* (1982, first published 1981) is the work most closely identified with the poem that supposedly inaugurated the school, Craig Raine's 'A Martian Sends a Postcard Home' (1979). *Other People* concerns the heroine Mary Lamb, an apparent amnesiac who views the world as if for the first time, with consequent descriptive defamiliarisation in the narrative, and who discovers that she may have been Amy Hide, a young woman who was murdered. The novel's title recalls Jean-Paul Sartre's representation of hell as other people in *Huis Clos* (1982, first published 1947), and the idea that the young woman repeats in death the cycle of her previous life is the 'consistent but not realistic' explanation Amis gives for the story (Haffenden, 1985, 17). The Martian School is also invoked in another of Amis's works, his short story 'The Janitor on Mars' (1998, story first published 1997) in which the eponymous robot describes humanity's development over thousands of years from the point of view of a far more technologically advanced civilisation. Martians also make appearances in *Money*, along with 'Venusians, pterodactyls, men and women from an alternative timestream' (Amis, 1985a, 2) but while examples such as these share features such as defamiliarisation with Raine's poem, we can also situate them within the wider context of Amis's play of perspective.

The commodified body, pornography and the fetish: *Money* and *London Fields*

There seems ample evidence that *London Fields*'s Keith Talent indulges, at one point or another, in all of the 'seven deadly sins' outlined in *Other People*: 'venality, paranoia, insecurity, excess, carnality, contempt, boredom' (Amis, 1982, 181), and a large part of *London Fields* is devoted to descriptions of the various forms such vices take. The novel's narrator Samson Young reminds us that 'Keith is modern, modern, modern' (Amis, 1989, 10), just as John Self describes himself as 'addicted to the twentieth century' (91). Keith Talent's life as a modern Londoner, like Self's, seems to be defined by desire, but desire that has been debased and that shows up his ignorance, greed and the poverty of his imagination (appearing in a televised darts match is his ultimate aspiration). Talent's status as the consumerist product of a materialistic society is at its most obvious after he has had sex with his ill and exhausted wife, having woken her up for this specific purpose: 'Keith turned over and lay there furiously wanting services and goods' (167). In *Money* and *London Fields* the human body is not to be exempt from the transforming powers of modern consumer society, powers that are at their most visible in the popularity of pornography.

Pornography plays a prominent role in *Money* and *London Fields* (as well as appearing in other works such as *Dead Babies*) and thought of as a fixation on parts of women's bodies, pornography also partakes in the strategy of portraying the human body only in disparate fragments, as Amis makes clear in his descriptions of Keith Talent's interest in pornography:

> Keith's screenings were usually over quickly, but some items, he found, repaid days or even weeks of study. Anything about lady wrestlers. Or women's prisons. The female body got chopped up by Keith twenty times a night: what astronomies of breast and belly, of shank and haunch ... Now the great thumb moved From Fast Forward to Rewind to Play. (Amis, 1989, 165)

It is this pornographic interest in women's bodies that Amis likens to the slasher movies that are also a staple of Keith's cultural diet.

Keith is in control of the temporal aspects (through Fast-Forward and SloMo) and so breaks up the narratives he watches into brief interludes of anonymous female nudity. He trawls through six hours of televised material to construct his own pornographic collage but this reorganisation is predicated on a savage destruction and dismantling of the female body and of the contextual narratives. This echoes *Money*'s John Self's experiences while conducting auditions for the part of a stripper in the film he is trying to make, where 'the girls tended to mangle and dismember in my mind' (Amis, 1985a, 197), their individual identities violently undermined. In this sense the disjointed female body depicted by pornography can be called grotesque in its lack of unity, its preoccupation with specific parts of the body and their visibility and its separation from social context and insertion into a retail industry.

John Self's business is pornography: pornographic films are the source of his wealth and *Money* charts Self's attempts to make such a film (provisionally titled *Good Money* or *Bad Money*). It is to this close link between money and sex that Amis returns throughout the novel, in the form of porn actors, prostitutes, strippers and women who work in massage parlours. Self's girlfriend Selina Street ('my shop-soiled Selina, my High-Street Selina, once more going cheap in the sales' (70)) unites money and sex for him: her tastes have the promise of 'brothelly knowhow', her underwear is 'top-dollar' (14), and he calls her underwear box a 'treasure-chest' (63). Pornography here is the conjunction of money and sex, where people use sex for money and vice versa; John uses money for sex (with Selina, and anyone else he can find), and in his role as a film producer he uses money to stage sex acts in order to create more money. Sex is seen as something some people are good at (for example Selina and Butch Beausoleil), a marketable skill rather than a source of pleasure, and it is noticeable how in Amis's fiction the deployment of sex by women can often be allied to destructive ends, including Gina Tull's infidelity for money and perhaps revenge in *The Information*, and Nicola Six's machinations in *London Fields*. Often in Amis's books sex has a value and is part of an overall economy whether it be a monetary economy (*Money*) or an emotional one (*Success* and *London Fields*).

As a novel *Money* repeatedly returns to the issues surrounding money, in particular its status as a fetish in Marxist terms (Marx and Freud are among the authors Self reads). The fluid nature of money and its fungibility and intangibility are a continual source of fascination to Self, and his flat, its contents and his car are all owned through complex arrangements of credit, his financial ruin at the end of the book showing how precarious his high-spending lifestyle was. *Money* itself can be read as a meditation on the lack of substance of capital since money is how John lives, how he maintains a relationship with Selina, how he plans to clean up his body, but ultimately money does none of these things for him. It is money that fuels pornography, another fetish that conceals a lack of actual sexual contact, an image of presence that is predicated on a state of absence. Money and pornography are Self's consuming passions:

> I realise, when I can bear to think about it, that all my hobbies are pornographic in tendency. The element of lone gratification is bluntly stressed. Fast food, sex shows, space games, slot machines, video nasties, nude mags, drink, pubs, fighting, television, handjobs. I've got a hunch about these handjobs, or about their exhausting frequency. I need that human touch. There's no human here so I do it myself. (Amis, 1985a, 67)

The business of pornography in *Money* displays a system of circulation without an end point in that people who work in the sex industry exchange sex for money, either in terms of prostitution or pornography, but the converse of this is that the consumers of sex exchange money for sex, again in terms of hiring a prostitute or buying pornography. This economy is at the heart of the novel and John Self is, to use economic terms, both a producer and a consumer of both pornography/commercial sex and money. The mutual exchange between pornography and money for John becomes clear when a young woman accosts him while he is looking at a pornographic magazine:

> 'How can you *look* at these things?'
> 'I've no idea.'...
> 'Why then? Why? Without you they wouldn't exist. Look at it.'
> We looked down again. The lovedoll was turned almost inside out.
> 'What does that say to you?'
> 'I don't know. Money.' (Amis, 1985a, 159)

This interrelation of money and pornography is also clear to John when he searches for pornography in Martina Twain's home: 'I don't know how to define pornography – but money is in the picture somewhere' (315). John worries about a war in the Middle East only insofar as it may cause currency problems (242) and despite or rather precisely *because* money is his central occupation, it is the circulation of capital that ultimately causes his ruin as he repeatedly signs himself up for debt.

Jean Baudrillard's works, particularly *For a Critique of the Political Economy of the Sign* (1981, first published in French 1972) and *Symbolic Exchange and Death* (1993, first published in French 1976), provide useful theoretical models within which to examine *Money*. What Amis is presenting to the reader in *Money* is the commodification of the body, and sexuality and health become in *Money* commodities subject to the law of exchange in which they are interchangeable with the ultimate fetish, money:

> What is fascinating about money is neither its materiality, nor even that it might be the intercepted equivalent of a certain force (e.g. of labour) or of a certain potential power: it is its *systematic nature*, the potential enclosed in the material for total commutability of values, thanks to their definitive abstraction. It is the abstraction, the total artificiality of the sign that one 'adores' in money. What is fetishised is the closed perfection of a system, not the 'golden calf', or the treasure. (Baudrillard, 1981, 93)

Money's interchangeability with everything, including the body, is clearly the source of John Self's 'adoration', as can be seen in his view of his sexual relations with Selina: 'the thrilling proof, so rich in pornography, that she does all this not for passion, not for comfort, far less for love, the proof that she does all this for *money*' (Amis, 1985a, 37). Pornography, to which Amis returns in *The Information*, is 'sex as spectacle' (1995, 410), whose actresses have been 'passed through some kind of lab or clinic, which reinvented them for male desire' (411). The commodified body in *Money*, with pornography as a paradigm, is central to understanding Amis's oeuvre.

Pornography in *Money* and *London Fields* is a series of images that share important characteristics of Baudrillard's simulacrum, 'never again exchanging for what is real, but exchanging in itself, in an uninterrupted circuit without reference or circumference' (Baudrillard, 1988, 170). Pornography is a simulacrum in that it bears no relation to reality, it is an image with no referent, as John Self is aware:

> That's the thing about pornography, that's the thing about men – they're always giving you the wrong ideas about women. *No* girls are like the girls in the men's magazines, not even Selina, not even the girls in the men's magazines. (Amis, 1985a, 236)

Pornography results in the ultimate 'elevation' of the body's image to simulacrum, and its dispersal via the mass media of print, television and video. The monetary equivalent of Baudrillard's era of simulation, involving the ceaseless circulation of the hyperreal, is evident in the comic cycle of Keith's cheating in *London Fields*:

> The other morning Keith had bought five hundred vanity sachets of Outrage, his staple perfume. At lunchtime he discovered that they all contained water, a substance not much less expensive than Outrage, but harder to sell. Keith was relieved that he had already unloaded half the consignment on Damian Noble in the Portobello Road. Then he held Damian's tenners up to the light: they were crude forgeries. He passed on the notes without too much trouble, in return for twenty-four bottles of vodka which, it turned out, contained a misty, faintly scented liquid. Outrage! The incident struck Keith as a sign of the times. (Amis, 1989, 113)

As Brian Finney observes, 'Keith's attitude to women and sex is entirely conditioned by the media, especially the porn industry' (1995, 11), which is why Nicola seduces him by making pornographic videos of herself for his viewing. When Keith cannot achieve an erection in bed with Nicola, she reminds him that it may be due to 'a little difficulty switching from one medium to another. That's what this whole thing is really about' (Amis, 1989, 429). Keith now inhabits the hyperreal world of simulation, where reality is no longer enough and objects are perceived only as mass media images and simulacra, as Samson discovers when he hears Keith summarising a football match: 'When Keith goes to a football match, that misery of stringer's clichés *is actually what he sees*' (97–8).

The nostalgic body and resistance to Money

Both *Money* and *London Fields* repeatedly emphasise the specifically contemporary nature of the body's commodification, evident in the way John watches women 'through my pornographic sheen. And the girls submitted to it, to the pornography. Professional city-dwellers, they were experienced in the twentieth century' (Amis, 1985a, 198). Nicola Six recognises much the same in Keith's view of women in *London Fields*:

> A reliable taxonomy of Keith's mind, his soul, his retractile heart – it couldn't be done. None of it parsed, none of it scanned. His libido would be all tabloid and factoid. Such a *contemporary* condition was pretty well recognised, if imperfectly understood. (Amis, 1989. 202, my italics)

In these examples Amis is describing a commodity culture that is specifically modern and that is produced by the media, whether by the tabloid press or John Self's pornographic varieties. For John, money is that which controls everything else and which can be exchanged for everything: clothes, cars, art, sex. John reads them all as signifiers of money, so the problem then arises that money in itself is an empty fetish, a sign which cannot itself be the ultimate referent for everything else. For *Money*'s anti-hero, money cannot deliver what he expects and all his dreams of money's potential remain unfulfilled because money is the fetishised general equivalent within a semiotic economy, subject to endless circulation. Self thinks money will be a passport to something else:

> And I mean *look* at my private culture. Look at the state of it. It really isn't very nice in here. And that is why I long to burst out of the world of money and into —into what? Into the world of thought and fascination. How do I get there? Tell me, please. I'll never make it by myself. I just don't know the way. (Amis, 1985a, 123)

Amis's novel is a dissection of Self's personal habits of consumption, although, as we can see above, Self wishes to escape from this debased and phoney culture. A metafictional reading of the quote is also possible – 'And that is why I long to burst out of the world of *Money* and into – into what?' and Amis himself has alluded to such a reading: 'He[Self] does end up dead in a way – outside the novel, outside money and *Money*, in endless and ordinary life' (Haffenden, 1985, 24). The epilogue narrated by Self is also italicised, tending to separate it further from the body of the text and suggesting that Self may now be outside the control of the fictional 'Martin Amis' (see Duggan, 2009 for an exploration of the intrusive author in *Money*).

Self is conscious that money cannot give him what he calls the 'human touch' (Amis, 1985a, 67), although he would be willing to try:

> If you were here now, I'd probably slip you some cash, twenty, thirty, maybe more. How much do you want? What are you having? What would you give me, sister, brother? Would you put an arm round my shoulder and tell me I was your kind of guy? I'd pay. I'd give you good money for it. (Amis, 1985a, 46)

For Amis, the escape route from money can be seen as culture, and John Self is culturally impoverished because he has not, and cannot, read, and he ends up financially impoverished because he has not read the contracts he has been signing.[2] The antidote to money is culture, a longstanding idea that Amis has asserted in interview in relation to his novel: 'The only way John Self is going to get over money as an idea – since he has no culture and has never read anything – is to be divested of it' (Haffenden, 1985, 14). Culture, then, is a resource standing against commodification, but one that requires effort, an effort John Self and Keith Talent are unable or unwilling to make. Even near the beginning of the novel, John acknowledges that all of humanity could do with a change as regards 'the human touch':

> It's for the touch, for the touch. After all we are only human beings down here and we could do with a lot more praise and comfort than we actually get. Earthling reassurance – it's in permanent

short supply, don't you think? Be honest, brother. Lady, now tell the truth. When was the last time a fellow-Earther let you rest your head on their heart, caressed your cheek, and said things designed to make you feel deeply okay? It doesn't happen often enough does it. (Amis, 1985a, 97–8)

Again the play of perspective is invoked, this time not to evoke the grotesque but to evoke human, 'Earthling', vulnerability. The same technique of scale comes into play in Amis's presentation of the human mouth, with the Rabelaisian and grotesque catalogue of what goes into it:

On the other hand, look what the human mouth has to put up with. I'm trying to see it from your point of view. Unimaginable, Third World food-mountains are churned and swirled through that delicate processor – pampas of cattle, fathoms of living sea, horizons of spud and greens, as well as conveyor belts of Wallys and Blastburgers, vats of flavouring and colouring, plus fags, straws, thermometers, dentist's drills, doctor's shears, drugs, tongues, fingers, feeding tubes. Is that any way to treat the mouth, the poor mouth, the human mouth? (Amis, 1985a, 268)

The image of the hand or fingers and of the human touch is central to *Money*'s visions of 'authentic' human interaction and here the vulnerable body is ranged against the industrialised modern world of mass-produced food and unpleasant intervention. Hands and fingers in *Money* come to take on the role of the body of authentic human contact outside a determining system of exchange and commodification, figured nostalgically as an 'authentic' era prior to semiotic or political economy. John Self's memories of his mother centre on the image of her fingers:

I hardly remember her. I remember her fingers: on cold mornings I would stand waiting at her bedside, and she would extend her warm hand from beneath the blankets to fasten the cuff buttons of my shirt ... I only remember her fingers, her fingerprints, her blemished nails and the mark of the white button on the contours of the tip. (Amis, 1985a, 206)

This is an example of what Kiernan Ryan terms 'recollections of original innocence' (1999, 215), and Self also scrutinises Martina Twain's fingertips, evidence that she is 'only human in all kinds of ways'(Amis, 1985a, 302). Fingerprints are also the site of individuality and the somatic signal of a person's uniqueness, their resistance to the kind of commodified body and sexuality industrially produced by pornography. In *Money*, however, the fingers and hand are also mediated by capital, indicated by Self wondering if Selina would recognise his handwriting: 'Had I ever shown her *my* hand? Yes, she'd seen it, on bills, on credit slips, on cheques' (Amis, 1985a, 69). Despite his occasional longing for an alternative form of human touch, Self's hand is dedicated to the world of money and credit. When John witnesses a father helping his son put his glasses on, the reader is reminded of his mother's hands:

> The child's face had the gently suffering look you sometimes get among the pale, the small, the hard of seeing: he showed his milky teeth, the expression rapt, expectant, forming a rightful entreaty. The father made his brisk adjustments – not unkindly, no, not at all. *The child's pale hand was raised and with its fingertips lightly steadied the darker, busier hand* ... (Amis, 1985a, 271, my italics, ellipsis in original)

Again the fingers, the image of touch, signal an encounter based not around commodities but on parental love. The human body in this aspect is part of the world 'outside' money that John so wishes he could reach. Unfortunately, just as Self still harbours a hope that money could secure him some of that 'human touch', parental human contact becomes for him a grotesque parody of maternal closeness as Caduta Massi (one of the actors Self is hiring) nurses him at her breast (107), and he has sex with his supposed mother-in-law, the stripper Vron, in his mother's bed (370). In a key episode, Self recalls receiving a bill for his childhood expenses from the man he thinks is his father, Barry Self: 'He submitted a bill for all the money spent on my upbringing. That's right – he fucking invoiced me' (178).[3] From his very beginnings then, the relentless power of money to shape all Self's relationships is evident.

Children's bodies have a particular importance in Amis's fiction and the threat of child abuse is a recurrent feature of his novels, from the death of Terry's sister at the hands of his father in *Success* (1985b, first published 1978), the abuse inflicted on Keith Talent's daughter Kim in *London Fields* and the suffering of children in Auschwitz in *Time's Arrow* to the undescribed events during the abduction of Richard Tull's son Marco in *The Information* and the abuse Cora Susan suffers at the hands of her father in *Yellow Dog* (2003).[4] Steve Cousins notes in *The Information* that 'many of the actors and almost all of the actresses on the pornographic screen had been abused as children' (Amis, 1995, 410). As Amis puts it in *Experience*, using a quote from Milton's *Paradise Lost* (see Amis, 2000, 133–5):

> Paedophiles hate children. They hate children because they hate innocence, and children *are* innocence. Look at them. They come here naked – but not quite. To the fit pair of eyes they come here thoroughly armoured: with native honour clad. (Amis, 2000, 141)

The child's body is vulnerable, but is not defined by absence (of protection) but rather by the positive presence of innocence, and William Blake's *Songs of Innocence and Experience*, along with *Paradise Lost*, provide the terms within which Amis describes children. The nostalgic body finds its source in the bodies of children and in the way that innocence and nakedness are entwined in our consciousness: 'Innocence and nakedness, like Adam and Eve, used to go hand in hand' (Amis, 2000, 133).

Despite the innocent and literally touching qualities of hand-holding, the nostalgic body may present some problems in terms of cultural theory. The body as a way of getting beyond a semiotic economy, of 'thinking' the body 'outside' culture throws up the whole problematic of nostalgia that Stallybrass and White argue we should avoid:

> If Ben Jonson, for instance, attempts to transcend the 'grossly physical', the 'return of the body' of so much recent theory is but the mirror-image of this prior repudiation. Both processes partake of the same mystification. (Stallybrass and White, 1986, 192)

Baudrillard's *Symbolic Exchange and Death* explores in detail attempts to re-evaluate the body, and a footnote to the chapter entitled 'The Body' is worth quoting at length:

After the history of the body's negativity comes the history of its positivity. The ambiguity of the current 'revolution' derives entirely from the fact that centuries of repression have based the body on *value*. Repressed, the body is charged with a transgressive virtuality of all values. Similarly however, we must understand that a long lasting and inextricable confusion between the body and a series of 'materialist' values (health, well-being, sexuality, liberty) has been at work in the shadows of repression ... But this liberation has something of the ambiguity of every liberation in that it is here liberated as value ... subjectivity is only ever liberated as a phantasm and sign-value in the framework of a planned signification. (Baudrillard, 1993, 124)

The body, according to Baudrillard, is therefore not recuperated value-free but as a sign within the semiotic economy whose value has been determined by a prior repudiation of the kind outlined throughout Stallybrass and White's *The Politics and Poetics of Transgression*. To take the part of the body, as it were, is merely to valorise the values assigned it by previous repression, not to arrive at the body *qua* body or to rediscover an original innocence:

The body is not at all the surface of being, a virginal beach without tracks, nature. It has only taken on this 'original' value through repression: and so, *to liberate the body as such in accordance with naturalist illusions is to liberate as repressed*. (Baudrillard, 1993, 106)

How then are we to approach the nostalgic body of Amis's fiction? One important point is to recognise the self-conscious way the nostalgic body is reproduced *as nostalgic*. The image of John Self's mother's fingers is one that is consciously nostalgic, being a fragment of childhood memory, and the same can be said of John witnessing the interaction between the father and son since it is in the context of childhood that this human contact has a resonance. The afterword to *Time's Arrow* expresses a memory from Amis's own childhood along similar lines.[5] The nostalgic body is also not represented as a way out of a system of exchange *in itself*: it does not indulge in a fetishisation of the body's naturalness or of freedom from ideology. The nostalgic body is not a body championed as some bulwark against reification and commodification but instead points to a context for human relations that are not subject to the economy of signs. It thus provides the means by which the 'human touch' can take place and the medium by which human love and affection can be physically, not verbally communicated. The body can therefore represent a site for a form of communication not subject to a generalised economy. The nostalgic body in Amis's work involves individualised bodies in contrast to the abstract, commodified body of pornography and the 'logistical' (to borrow from the afterword of *Time's Arrow*) bodies the Nazis catalogued and murdered in their masses. If the nostalgic body in Amis seems a rather ineffective and utopian opponent to late twentieth-century commodification, Baudrillard may offer the explanation:

> The strange thing is that the body is nothing other than the models in which different systems have enclosed it, and at the same time every other thing: their radical alternative, the irreducible difference that denies them. We may still call the body this inverse virtuality. For this however – for the body as material of symbolic exchange – *there is no model*, no code, no ideal type, no controlling phantasm, *since there could not be a system* of the body as anti-object. (Baudrillard, 1993, 114)

In this sense the nostalgic body in Amis is just such an 'inverse virtuality'.

Irony and the problem of form

In terms of the distance between Amis's fiction and earlier authors, *Money* seems textually to position itself as subsequent to the realism of older literature. When John Self asks 'Martin Amis' whether he has problems using 'bad behaviour', Martin replies:

> 'No. It's not a problem. You get complaints, of course, but we're pretty much agreed that the twentieth century is an ironic age – downward-looking. Even realism, rockbottom realism, is considered a bit grand for the twentieth century.' (Amis, 1985a, 248)

This aesthetic which finds realism 'a bit grand' would seem to be a possible analogue of Amis's own grotesque style with its emphasis on the grotesque body, the agglomeration of fragmentary disjointed details, the variations in descriptive scale and the excessive language which goes beyond realism's economy. In *The Information* Richard Tull makes some important points about literature in his discussion with his literary agent of a prospective work entitled *The History of Increasing Humiliation*, which is worth quoting at length:

> 'It would be a book accounting for the decline in the status and virtue of literary protagonists. First gods, then demi-gods, then kings, then great warriors, great lovers, then burghers and merchants and vicars and doctors and lawyers. Then social realism: you. Then irony: me. Then maniacs and murderers, tramps, mobs, rabble, flotsam, vermin.'
> She was looking at him. 'And what would account for it?'
> He sighed. 'The history of astronomy. The history of astronomy is the history of increasing humiliation. First the geocentric universe, then the heliocentric universe. Then the eccentric universe – the one we're living in. Every century we get smaller. Kant figured it all out, sitting in his armchair. What's the phrase? The principle of terrestrial mediocrity.'
> '... Big book.'
> 'Big book.' And he added, 'Small world. Big universe.' (Amis, 1995, 129)

It is at the end of this process of humiliation that the contemporary writer enters the scene.

If we view Tull's theory of 'Increasing Humiliation' as a possible clue to where Amis positions his own fiction, then we soon come upon similarly reflexive comments throughout Amis's novels, often exhibiting the same central question of genre:

> If Whitehead had been in a cartoon (which is probably where he belonged), he would simply have imploded to a third of his mass and drifted up into the air. (Amis, 1984b, 204)

And what am I starring in? It feels like slapstick to me. Pornographic slapstick, custard pie, the comic relief with the landlady or bellhop before the real fucking resumes elsewhere. (Amis, 1985a, 257)

What genre did his life belong to? That was the question. It wasn't pastoral. It wasn't epic. In fact, it was comedy. Or anti-comedy, which is a certain kind of comedy, a more modern kind of comedy. Comedy used to be about young couples overcoming difficulties and then getting married. Comedy wasn't about that now. (Amis, 1995, 179)

What all these quotes have in common is a meditation on the question of what genre Amis is writing in. If we link these passages with Richard Tull's theory of the development of literature, then Amis is seen as constructing a particular context for his work and in a sense his comments on the novel and on comedy are the descendants of George Eliot's famous digressions in *Adam Bede* and *Middlemarch* that I discussed in the first chapter. They function as guidelines on how to read the texts, in the same way Eliot's references to Fielding, to the Dutch School of painting and to the differences between drawing a lion and a griffin are guidelines to reading her fiction. Both sets of comments work by engaging with readers' expectations and the comments inform the reader what to expect and present the rationale behind not only the particular text being read, but behind the genre as a whole, effecting 'the unmasking of dead *literary* conventions and the establishing of new *literary* codes' (Hutcheon, 1984, 38 first published 1980).

If both Eliot and Amis coincide in their use of such 'reader-orientation' episodes then there are also important differences between their pronouncements. An important one is the fact that Eliot contrasts two differing modes of representation in terms of subject matter while Amis is more interested in the mode of representation itself. Eliot's main thrust is to argue that the representation of 'the real' is its own justification (much as Barthes discusses in 'The Reality Effect'), and links the concept of plainness of subject matter (in terms of a person's physical appearance) with a plainness of style. Amis, on the other hand, is interested in genre and brings comedy and slapstick to bear on his account of the contemporary novel. An important example of Amis situating his work within the tradition of the grotesque occurs at the very beginning of Amis's career as an author in *The Rachel Papers*, where Charles Highway rewrites and reverses the maxim of Jim Dixon, the hero of Kingsley Amis's most well known novel *Lucky Jim* (1954). Instead of 'nice things being nicer than nasty ones', Charles suggests that 'surely, nice things are dull, and nasty things are funny. The nastier a thing is, the funnier it gets' (Amis, 1984a, 88). This kind of digression is important in signalling the kind of fiction Amis is writing – that is, fiction of the grotesque. As Diedrick notes in relation to this reversal of *Lucky Jim*:

> The fictions of Dickens and Kafka often combine cruelty and laughter. So do the satires of Jonathan Swift. What is emerging here is Martin Amis's own literary manifesto – one part exorcism of his father's precedent, one part declaration that his own province is the comedy of the grotesque. (Diedrick, 1995, 28)

While this reversal of *Lucky Jim* may not quite constitute a manifesto, Diedrick picks up on the clear orientation towards the grotesque and of course this direct and playful reversal of literary precedent is itself characteristic of the grotesque tradition.

The most important distinction between Eliot's and Amis's comments on representation lies in Amis's insistence on an historical background to changes in genre. His apologias for his aesthetic are firmly grounded in ideas of the twentieth century, as can be seen from the selections, particularly from *The Information*, quoted above. While Eliot justifies her aesthetic of realism in formal artistic terms, Amis is providing a historical rationale to why his texts are the way they are. He places his own works in a particular narrative of literature's development, and in a particular relationship to earlier novels: 'Then social realism: you. Then irony: me'. What both Eliot's and Amis's comments demonstrate is a desire to effect a transition from previous modes of narrative to the author's own, thus establishing the legitimacy of their own narrative modes. For Amis, the question of why his apologia is historical in emphasis is tied up with whether his particular aesthetic, revolving around irony and the grotesque, has any legitimacy. His reviews of the work of others (in this case Angus Wilson) also cast light on his own work:

The contexts, the great forms of the eighteenth- and nineteenth-century sagas, have been exhausted; realism and experimentation have come and gone without seeming to point a way ahead. The contemporary writer, therefore, must combine these veins, calling on the strengths of the Victorian novel together with the alienations of post-modernism. (Amis, 2001, 78–9)

The key concept emerging from Amis's comments on genre is irony, and he positions his own work in an ironic relation to past narratives and in so doing casts his texts not as refinements of earlier narrative modes but instead as ironic deformations of them.

One clue for gauging the relationship between *Money*, *London Fields* and earlier instances of the novel is to look to the frequency with which Amis works towards a grotesque debasement of canonical works or the characters of such works. These incidences of short-lived irony are scattered throughout Amis's oeuvre but emerge very clearly in *Money*, where Fielding is the name given to the con man who swindles John Self. In some ways the thrust of the metafictional aspects of the book is to do with the status of realism, as shown by John Self's conversations with his writer, 'Martin Amis'. Fielding reappears in the form of a character named after Henry Fielding's eponymous hero Joseph Andrews in Amis's *Yellow Dog*, which partly reprises the London criminal scene and themes of paternity and incest explored in *Money*. This running correspondence casts Fielding as a paternal influence, and Amis in interview has remarked that in terms of learning from the writing of his father, the novelist Kingsley Amis, 'the most obvious thing is the English tradition of writing about low events in a high style, which is the tradition of Henry Fielding' (Haffenden, 1985, 24). As I outlined in Chapter 1, such a combination of low subject matter and elevated exposition in Fielding's work made him especially concerned about the tangled relationship between the tradition of the grotesque and the emergent form of the realist novel. John Self is himself is a debaser of previous 'classic' narratives, for example his advertisement for a new snack called Hamlette in which he uses an actor dressed in black, and the fact that the Oedipal aspects of Shakespeare's work are played out, as it were, in both *Good/Bad Money*'s plot and John Self's own life. Other intertextual references include John's reading of Orwell's *Nineteen Eighty-Four* as well as *Animal Farm*.

It is important to note that the irony present in Amis's work is often an irony of form, depending on the alteration and frequently the reversal of received forms, literary or otherwise: a woman repeats the cycle of her own death (*Other People*); an elaborate confidence trick which has no declared motive (*Money*); a murder story where the victim must seek out her killer (*London Fields*); the story of a Nazi doctor told in reverse (*Time's Arrow*); a suicide that seems to have no motive, and which may not even be a suicide (*Night Train* (1997)). This type of irony and parody is closely related to the grotesque in that it takes classical forms (in the sense of being regulated by formal rules) and then deforms them, so that instead of the beauty promised by the classical form we get 'ugliness', instead of proportion, monstrosity, and instead of economy, excess. Against the classical form of the realist novel and its abstemious presentation of daily life, Amis creates a hyperbolic linguistic excess; instead of the consolations of plot there is a radical lack of motive and instead of beauty the reader is presented with ugly and grotesque images and characters. As Stallybrass and White argue, the formal distinction between each element in these oppositions of economy/excess, high/low and beauty/ugliness of necessity paves the way for the grotesque as a *mixed form*, and a hybrid and corrupt deformation of the privileged term. Amis's grotesque aesthetic, with its mixtures of comedy and pain, its humour and threat, its gleeful wallowing in the present and melancholic nostalgia, is profoundly mixed in this sense. Amis's work also involves the mixture of genres, with the novels using mystery stories to explore wider social or metaphysical concerns as can be seen in *Other People* (what is Mary Lamb's past?), *London Fields* (who is the murderer?), *Money* (who is John Self's mystery caller?), *Night Train* (how and why was Jennifer Rockwell killed?) and *Yellow Dog* (who has attacked Xan Meo and why).

Examining the textual positioning of Amis's fiction in this manner highlights the way the novel as a genre is rendered problematic in his work. *London Fields* motions obliquely towards this problem of form, for example in Nicola's washing-up (1989, 395) or Samson's musings:

> The form itself is my enemy. All this damned romance. In fiction (rightly so called), people become coherent and intelligible – and they aren't like that. We all know they aren't. We all know it from personal experience. We've been there. (Amis, 1989, 240)

Money also meditates on this problem of form and on a larger scale the plots of many of Amis's novels have what we might call deformations of plot, including *London Fields* and its murderee, reversed time in *Time's Arrow*, and *Money* as a suicide note. In interview Amis has described his work as 'the comedy of humiliation' (Fuller, 1995) but Richard Tull might call it 'anti-comedy'. The way Amis's work positions its grotesque self as historically appropriate is not so much due to the lack of a suitable aesthetic but rather the necessity of an aesthetic that actively engages in the problematic of representation. The grotesque serves as just such an aesthetic approach, a suitable response to 'the realism problem' that John Self worries about in *Money* (1985a, 361). Amis's pronouncements on the comedy of his work display a similar historical context:

> Among the many mysterious processes under way in this century is a breakdown of genre, so that comic novels can take on quite rugged stuff. It seems clear to me – now that I can look back on my work – that what I am is a comic writer, and that comedy is a much looser form than it once was. (Haffenden, 1985, 10)

Amis's fiction presents its irony as historically and therefore artistically fitting – in Hutcheon's terms 'establishing new literary codes'. Amis's grotesque does not just deform received literary forms but presents such deformation as a legitimate aesthetic in its own right due to its historical suitability, and in this impulse towards cultural legitimacy functions in remarkably similar ways to Eliot's digression. From this perspective Amis's work positions itself textually in relation to earlier 'classical' forms by legitimising narratives which are problematic in terms of form and discursively reflecting on these problematised relationships. The grotesque novels of Martin Amis, in terms of violating the economy of realism, do not offer themselves as manifesting an aesthetic solution to such problems of representation but on the contrary are meditations on these very problems. As such, they do not represent a departure to a new poetics but the emergence of an aesthetic approach to narrative that 'works through' the problems of representation. If Randall Stevenson is correct in arguing that 'postmodernism not only radicalises forms, but also satirises them, exposing their incapacities to connect with reality and the possibilities for distortion that result' (1991, 25), then Amis's grotesque partakes of this postmodern mode. When Harpham states that '[g]rotesqueries confront us as a corrupt or fragmented text in search of a master principle' (1982, 43) it is precisely this lack of a master principle of representation that arguably defines contemporary literature and is the ground from which Amis's grotesque fiction emerges.

Grotesque reversals and *Time's Arrow*

The trope that is probably most typical of Amis's fiction is ironic reversal or inversion and, as I explored in the first chapter, symbolic inversion or transgression is closely linked to the grotesque. The grotesque deforms through reversing or inverting a literary genre or cultural code, and many of the most well-known examples of the grotesque such as topsy-turvy 'inverted worlds' involve reversal and inversion is also a prime feature of Bakhtin's grotesque body and of carnivalised literature in general. My analysis of Amis's work so far has thrown up a number of examples of inversion, including *The Rachel Papers*'s reversal of Jim Dixon's 'nice things are nicer than nasty ones' and the reversal of the thriller plot in *London Fields*. A particularly good example of this is the theme of impotence, which fails once more to rear its ugly head in *The Information* when the precise action of Richard Tull's impotence with his wife is explained to the reader:

> He was impotent with her every other night and, at weekends, in the morning too – when those boys of his gave him half a chance! ... Sometimes, when the Tulls' schedules conspired, he would be lazily impotent with her in the afternoons. Nor did the bedroom mark the boundary of their erotic play. In the last month alone, he had been impotent with her on the stairs, on the sofa in the sitting-room and on the kitchen table. (Amis, 1995, 89–90)

Here the contexts are kept the same but the outcome is inverted and where we expect consummation there is only impotence, but an impotence that keeps to the form of the expected consummation so that the polarity of the reader's expectation is reversed.

Amis's short stories frequently follow this pattern and 'Career Move' (1998, first published 1992) describes a world in which poets are rich celebrities and science fiction film scriptwriters are doomed to futile attempts to get published. In 'Straight Fiction' (1998, first published 1995) it is homosexuals who are the social norm and heterosexuals who are a loathed and barely tolerated minority, while in 'The Time Disease' (1988) it is the old people who are frightened of becoming young as time moves backwards.

It is, however, Amis's novel *Time's Arrow or the Nature of the Offence* that demonstrates to the fullest extent the author's preference for this kind of grotesque reversal or inversion. The novel in Amis's account of it 'is narrated by the soul of one of Mengele's lesser assistants at Auschwitz-Birkenau' (Amis, 2000, 289) and this unnamed narrator is unaware that it is journeying backwards in time through the life of its 'host', Odilo Unverdorben (*'verdorben'* means 'corrupt' or 'rotten' in German, so Odilo's surname is 'uncorrupted'). The narrative thus moves from Unverdorben's American exile in old age (under the names of Todd Friendly and John Young) back to his prime during the Second World War, and later on towards his birth and childhood innocence. The narrating soul is aware that Unverdorben has a secret towards which they travelling: 'I will know the nature of the offence. Already I know this. I know that it has to do with trash and shit, and that it is wrong in time' (Amis, 1991, 73) and it transpires that Unverdorben worked as a doctor at Auschwitz helping 'Uncle Pepi' (Mengele's surrogate) murder and experiment on the prisoners. The narrator, however, is travelling backwards into the past,[6] and in this chronologically reversed perspective it is causality which is reversed: garages destroy cars and leave them at the side of the road, people receive their nourishment from refuse and, most importantly, doctors do not relieve people's suffering but on the contrary cause it. For the narrator it is writing and paintings 'which seem to hint a topsy-turvy world in which, so to speak, time's arrow moves the other way' (95). Thus when Unverdorben has regressed back to his time at Auschwitz, the narrator sees the Nazi doctors as servants of humanity, creating the Jews out of smoke and ashes: 'The world, after all, here in Auschwitz, has a new habit. It makes sense' (138).

There are a number of important sources for Amis's book that he mentions in the afterword: principally the work of Primo Levi (from which the phrase 'the nature of the offence' is taken) and Robert Jay Lifton's *Nazi Doctors* (1986). Lifton's book analyses the historical reversal which characterised the doctors working in Nazi death camps and it is this central reversal, which Richard Menke calls 'this grotesque paradox' (1998, 967), that lies at the heart of Amis's book: the grotesque transformation of doctors from saviours of humanity into torturers and murderers. Lifton's book provides the important concept of doubling, which is 'the psychological vehicle for the Nazi's doctor's Faustian bargain with the diabolical environment in exchange for his contribution to the killing' (1986, 418). Doubling recurs in Amis's work (Terry and Gregory in *Success*, Marmaduke and Kim in *London Fields*, Gwyn Barry and Richard Tull in *The Information*, the doubles of Amis such as Martina Twain and Mark Avery) but the split between Unverdorben's self and his 'soul' can be seen to lie within Lifton's model.

Kurt Vonnegut also provides an important source for *Time's Arrow* in terms of the temporal reversal used in *Slaughterhouse-Five or The Children's Crusade* (1972, first published 1969). The 'certain paragraph – a famous one' (Amis, 1991, 175) of temporal reversal to which Amis refers in the afterword to *Time's Arrow* occurs in *Slaughterhouse Five* when the protagonist Billy Pilgrim becomes 'slightly unstuck in time' and watches a war film in reverse (Vonnegut, 1972, 54–5), and earlier examples of temporal reversal in fiction occur in Lewis Carroll's *Sylvie and Bruno* (1889) and in Philip K. Dick's *Counter-Clock World* (1967). Amis had first used the trope of reversed temporality at the end of his story 'Bujak and the Strong Force *or* God's Dice' (1988). Vonnegut's *Mother Night* (1997, first published 1966) provides a textual parallel for Lifton's theory of doubling where its narrator Howard W. Campbell Jr. broadcasts pro-Nazi propaganda while including secret intelligence for the Americans in his very popular speeches, and his preface is a precursor to Lifton's theory of the Nazi Doctor's split self:

> I would prefer to dedicate it [the book] to one familiar person, male or female, widely known to have done evil while saying to himself, 'A very good me, the real me, a me made in heaven, is hidden deep inside.' (Vonnegut, 1997, xi)

Vonnegut goes on to have Campbell, who at first seems an atypical figure, position himself at the centre of the Nazi psyche: 'This book is rededicated to Howard W. Campbell, Jr., a man who served evil too openly and good too secretly, the crime of his times' (xi). Campbell's duality is thus raised to a general psychological condition under Nazism that enables genocide, and Unverdorben's split self in *Time's Arrow* is such a doubling taken to extremes.

The critical reception of *Time's Arrow* was mixed, with some reviewers admiring it while others baulked at the combination of the Holocaust subject matter and the reversed narrative employed by Amis (see Tredell, 2000, 127 for a summary of reviews). James Buchan in his review opined, 'I find it creepy to see Primo Levi rearranged for literary fun and profit', while the Irish journalist and author Joseph O'Connor (in a long diatribe against the collapsed state of British fiction) made space to register a similarly shocked reaction to the narrative reversal.[7] The tenor of the negative reviews is neatly summed up by *The Economist*'s reaction, particularly its allusion to Lewis Carroll:

> But, above all, this Looking Glass perspective is plain wrong. This means that Mr Amis's narrator has nothing of interest to say about the real Holocaust ... Bereft of relevance to anything real, Mr Amis's tale becomes no more than a nasty little game.[8]

For such reviewers Amis has gone too far in mixing a grotesque narrative mode with the serious subject of the Holocaust, and their resistance to the novel is on the grounds of its grotesque and immoral mixture of the important history of mass murder and narrative 'tricks'. The grotesque mixture of the machinery of comedy (reversal/inversion) with perhaps the most solemn material imaginable is cast as an unacceptable offence by the book's detractors. As I discussed in the first chapter of this study in relation to Ruskin, the grotesque here has become synonymous with a game, with childish and idle play, something that should on no account be combined with a serious subject. The reviewers' comments recall Ruskin's edict that if we are masters of the human form (or in this case realist narrative) then we have no business changing it.

Time's Arrow thus represents a prime example of a grotesque novel: the ironic narrative reversal is a central trope of the grotesque, and its scandalous mixture of serious subject matter and 'playful' narrative is intolerable for many readers. For some critics and researchers 'Auschwitz is a bad subject for any kind of art' and the Shoah is regarded as 'unfit for artistic representation',[9] and so Amis's grotesque narrative is even more unwelcome. However, as I have shown, Amis has always worked on the basis of the mixture of genres, in particular the broadening out of our concept of comedy and tragicomedy and the prevalence of irony; as he remarked on his decision to write a book which involved the Holocaust: 'But once you have got over that you have to say to yourself, very early on, that I bring what I bring to this subject. I can't become another kind of writer because of the subject' (Bigsby, 1992, 173). As Diedrick notes, apart from the narrative reversal (albeit that the reversal has profound and diverse effects), Amis sticks very closely to the historical account set out in Lifton's book (Diedrick, 1995, 173).

The first chapter of this study explored how the grotesque spans both comic and serious subjects and for many critics (Ruskin, despite his attempts at taxonomy, is one) it is the mixture of comic and serious elements that is the problematic essence of the grotesque. The grotesque can use the machinery of comedy, in this case inversions and reversals, and also doubling and repetitions, but by doing so produce a serious effect and not (or not only) a comic one. It is the use of inversions and reversals without a purely comic effect that is the mark of the grotesque, and the grotesque aspects of *Time's Arrow* are precisely the trope of inversion without a purely comic effect. David Lodge has observed that the effect is 'comically grotesque at first, and then increasingly disturbed and disturbing as the story approaches the horrors of the Holocaust' (Lodge, 1992, 78–9). I would contend that the later effect is grotesquely serious or tragic – it does not cease to be grotesque as it becomes serious. Instead of the 'Swiftian (and very Martin Amis-like) attention to the grotesque reversed thermodynamics of the body' (Menke, 1998, 972), the reader is propelled into the topsy-turvy world of Auschwitz where trained doctors help murder children. The reviewers and critics who see the novel as a obscene 'game', a 'gimmick' or childish 'play', are writing from a position that demands the rigorous separation of comic and serious artistic modes and that denies that anything serious or important can emerge from inversions or reversals.

The grotesque as a literary and artistic tradition had frustrated, and will continue to frustrate, such regulatory aesthetic systems and defy the desire for clear boundaries. So what non-comic effects might this grotesque temporal reversal in *Time's Arrow* achieve, given the especially grave nature of its subject matter? The reversal can be seen as a narrative analogue for the original and historically constituted grotesque reversal that Lifton's book explores; that is, the healing-killing reversal of the Nazi death camp doctors. In the light of doctors' roles in the camp, we can see that the historical Auschwitz death camp did in reality become a topsy-turvy, satanically inverted world. For the reader, the novel's effect is to make them re-recognise the historical narrative, and so the reversed temporality produces a systematic defamiliarisation of the acts committed in Auschwitz. As Sue Vice puts it, '*Time's Arrow*'s narrator tries to make us see the overdeterminedly meaningful site before it gained those meanings' (2000, 24). The reader must reorder events themselves, must themselves (re)construct the narrative of Unverdorben's actions. The historical events at Auschwitz become the reader's destination and because the events have already happened, the reader is in some sense compelled to follow the temporal stream back to its source, to once again encounter senseless mass murder. In *Time's Arrow* it is not the future that is inevitable; there is no Nazi 'destiny' and the 'biological soldiers' like Unverdorben were not simply 'obeying orders' deprived of any agency. It is only the past that is forever set in stone and therefore tragic in its inevitability and unchangeability. The disturbing events the narrator and the reader move towards are tragic in the dramatic sense because we know that they are inescapable. In *Time's Arrow* it is ironically the irreversible nature of time and of the past that is emphasised, and through the grotesque what has been a mechanism for comedy becomes a means of engendering deep pathos and horror.

Notes

1   See Diedrick (1995, 33–4) for a discussion of the parallels between *Dead Babies* and Denis Diderot's Menippean satire *Rameau's Nephew*.

2 'I don't know what it's like to write a poem. I don't know what it's like to read one either ... About me and reading (I don't really know why I tell you this – I mean, do you read that much?): I can't read because it hurts my eyes. I can't wear glasses because it hurts my nose. I can't wear contacts because it hurts my nerves. So you see, it all came down to a choice between pain and not reading. I chose not reading. Not reading – that's where I put my money.' (Amis, 1985a, 42, ellipsis in original)
3 In a bizarre echo of this, a couple attempted to sue their local health board after they conceived following the husband's vasectomy operation. The House of Lords later rejected their claim for £110,000 in expenses incurred in raising their daughter. (*The Independent* 21 July 1999, p. 5)
4 *The Information* is dedicated to Amis's two sons and to his cousin Lucy Partington, who was abducted and murdered by the rapist and serial killer Frederick West (see *Experience*).
5 'This book is dedicated to my sister Sally, who, when she was very young, rendered me two profound services. She awakened my protective instincts; and she provided, if not my earliest childhood memory, then certainly my most charged and radiant. She was perhaps half an hour old at the time. I was four.' (Amis, 1991, 175)
6 Amis's narrating soul in *Time's Arrow* travels backwards into the past and so may be seen as a reversed image of the Angel of History of Walter Benjamin's 'Theses on the Philosophy of History' in *Illuminations* (1969), which travels backwards into the future, unable to see the approaching events.
7 'Martin Amis wrote a skilfully executed but deeply shocking book called *Time's Arrow* about the holocaust, where time went backwards. The best writer of his generation reduced to gimmicks and gameshow trickery, in the face of the most appalling event of the twentieth century. It was a telling moment in the history of British culture.' (O'Connor, 1994, 142)
8 *The Economist* 321: 7727 10 May 1991 p. 101.
9 See Wheatcroft (2000). Wheatcroft quotes Philip Gourevitch's point that 'violence and the grotesque are central to the American aesthetic, and the Holocaust museum supplies both amply' (10).

Chapter 4

Ian McEwan: below the waves

> I will know the nature of the offence. Already I know this. I know that it has to do with trash and shit, and that it is wrong in time. (Amis, 1991, 73)

The presence of the grotesque, with its characteristic contradictory elements, in Ian McEwan's fiction is most easily visible in the author's use of grotesque images and scenarios. As my earlier discussions of the concept of the grotesque have shown, the admixture of contradictory elements, such as death and the comic, has traditionally been described as grotesque. A good example of such contradiction is the episode at Mother's deathbed in *The Cement Garden* (1980, first published 1978):

> Julie took hold of the sheet and tried to draw it over Mother's head. Because she was sitting up the sheet would not reach. Julie pulled harder, the sheet came loose and she was able to cover the head. Mother's feet appeared, they stuck out from underneath the blanket, bluish-white with a space between each toe. Sue and I giggled again. Julie pulled the blanket over the feet and Mother's head was revealed once more like an unveiled statue. Sue and I laughed uncontrollably. (McEwan, 1980, 50–1)

Here, any pathos associated with the death of the children's mother is undermined by the comic show of the blanket being too short for the woman's corpse. The scene does not therefore become simply comic, however; instead the comic and pathetic elements coexist in the scene, forming an inappropriate and thus grotesque combination. The children's laughter is therefore grotesque in its ambivalence, that is in the copresence of the comic and the threatening in the episode.

The uncontrollable aspect of the children's laughter forms part of a wider interest in instinct in McEwan's work, which will be discussed later in this chapter.

Jack Slay sees the grotesque as a strand running through McEwan's work:

> In his next works [after *The Cement Garden*] McEwan abandons the disturbing and angst-filled world of the adolescent in love and trouble, focusing instead on the world of the adult, discovering it to be as repulsive, as grotesque. (Slay, 1996, 50)

Kiernan Ryan, however, grapples with the notion of an 'early' McEwan and a 'late' McEwan although he is understandably cautious about dividing McEwan's work in this way:

> It casts the author as a kind of Prodigal Son, who gradually grows out of his nasty adolescent fantasies and into a responsible adult novelist. The story it tells looks suspiciously contrived and reassuring, but it is difficult to deny its plausibility as one reflects on the distance McEwan has undoubtedly travelled between the appearance of *First Love, Last Rites* and the publication of *Black Dogs*. (Ryan, 1994, 2)

Nonetheless, Ryan seems committed to some kind of distinction between these two periods:

> A failure to distinguish between early and later McEwan plays straight into the hands of those keen to label him solely as the sick delinquent confrère of Genet, Burroughs, and Céline or solely as the mature male feminist anxious to address the nation on matters of vital political importance. On the other hand, exaggerating the difference ... either boils his career down to a gratifying tale of political enlightenment or it opens him to the charge of sacrificing art to moralism, of swapping the risks of the imagination for the safety of progressive pieties. (Ryan, 1994, 4)

While Ryan is obviously aware of the risks in making a distinction between early and later works by McEwan, he is somewhat anxious to recover McEwan from the 'sick' trinity of Genet, Burroughs and Céline and arguably it is the effort to distinguish between early and later McEwan, and not (as Ryan contends) the failure to do so, which is fuelled by the tendency to label McEwan as either 'sick' or 'pious'. The desire to erect such a division risks serving to isolate and privilege specific aspects of McEwan's oeuvre and to avoid contamination from the 'other' McEwan, a process of differentiation that, as I discussed in relation to Stallybrass and White in Chapter 1, is characteristic of a frequent aesthetic response to the grotesque. The aim of this study in relation to McEwan is not to make a case for the 'sick' McEwan to the detriment of the 'pious' one, but rather to examine the ways in which the grotesque pervades the author's fiction. This chapter will use the grotesque in McEwan's fiction as a means to approach issues that go to the heart of the author's work, including the human body, sexual and temporal differentiation, subject formation, rationality and instinct, and I will return to the question of early versus late McEwan at the end of this chapter.

The Innocent (1990), McEwan's espionage novel set in post-war Berlin, includes a notorious description of the dismemberment of a body clearly showing a grotesque treatment of the human body. Leonard, a young Englishman installing spying devices in tunnels beneath the city, has begun an affair with Maria and the lovers accidentally kill her former boyfriend Otto and decide to hide the body. McEwan has become in recent years frustrated with the amount of journalistic and critical interest in this episode, wondering 'what would have happened to that novel if that scene had not been in it. It would have forced everybody to have discussed the rest of the book' (Hanks, 1998, 14). While such a reaction shows a discomfort with the level of detail employed in taking 'the reader by the hand through every last detail of cutting this body up and putting it in two suitcases' (in Katz, 2012), perhaps this can be read as a back-handed tribute to the literally visceral power of this grotesque scene, in preparation for which McEwan attended an autopsy and consulted a lecturer in pathology. The scene is also reminiscent of the dismemberment episode at the end of Louis-Ferdinand Céline's *Death on the Instalment Plan* discussed in Kristeva's *Powers of Horror* and described by her as 'grotesque' (Kristeva, 1982, 150). After Leonard has cut open the corpse's belly and the guts have disgorged onto the floor:

the room filled with the close stench of musty air, which itself was a medium for other smells: of sweet earth sulphurous crap, and Sauerkraut. The insult was, Leonard had time to think, as he stepped hurriedly round the up-ended halves of the torso that were still joined, that all this stuff was also in himself. (McEwan, 1990, 182)

This emergence of the body's hidden contents brings us back to Bakhtin's concept of the grotesque body as described in *Rabelais and his World*, the body open to the world and in biological interaction with it. The body reverts from anatomy and from surface to biology, to the body as both being and containing matter and substance and the placing of ingestion and excretion side by side (as well as crap and Sauerkraut, McEwan uses 'liverish reds' and 'boiled egg bluish white' in the description of the dismembered body), echoing Swift's poem 'The Lady's Dressing Room' (1992).

The impact of cutting up Otto brings home to Leonard his own biology and the links along his own digestive chain, much to his disgust and affront. Indeed, this information is in fact an 'insult', offensive to Leonard's sense of himself and undermining his attempt to regard Otto as an enemy, whose crimes render him liable for dismemberment, just as the devastated city of Berlin is being carved up by the victorious Allies. McEwan soon reinforces the point: 'Was he hungry? The thought of taking selected parts of the solid world and passing them through a hole in his head and squeezing them through his guts was an abomination' (185). The normal process of eating has now been cast in a very different light for Leonard so that the biological fact of ingestion appals him and the exposure of the grotesque body in the narrative produces an unwelcome apprehension of a common biology. Ryan, commenting on this episode in *The Innocent* states that:

> The dead, dissected body is the point where signifying halts and hermeneutics ends, where the final ground of meaning is unmasked and metaphysical delusions implode. Hence the simultaneous horror and liberating gusto with which *The Innocent* assaults and defiles the human form. (Ryan, 1994, 59)

He makes a persuasive case, but we might add that McEwan is equally interested in this physical, grotesque body not as the end point, but as the beginning. This is our common biological origin, which in McEwan's work precedes everything else and to which the author returns again and again. His fiction is not so much concerned with the grotesque body as the end, but rather as the starting point out of which everything else (metaphysics, gender and social relations, the self) develops. In this he allies himself with Swift's point at the end of 'The Lady's Dressing Room':

> He soon would learn to think like me,
> And bless his ravished eyes to see
> Such order from confusion sprung,
> Such gaudy *tulips* raised from *dung*.
> (Swift, 1992, 154, ll. 141–4)

For Swift, such beauty cannot forget its origins, and McEwan's fiction evinces a similar awareness of the grounds out of which beauty is established. Indeed, as the subsequent sections will demonstrate, the grotesque in McEwan's work frequently involves an exploration of the grounds from which the subject is established as a gendered and socialised individual and of the processes entailed in such development.

In the first chapter of this study I discussed the various ways in which the grotesque has been classified, and subsequently focused on the grotesque as non-classical (the approach used by Bakhtin, Stallybrass and White, and Harpham, among others). It is worth quoting again from E.H. Gombrich, who makes a broad distinction between classical and non-classical art: 'gothic being increasingly used as a label for the not-yet-classical, the barbaric, and *barocco* for the no-longer-classical, the degenerate' (Gombrich, 1966, 84). It is my contention that the grotesque, in its amalgam of disjunctive elements and in its excess, falls into both these categories – pre-classical and post-classical, gothic and baroque and so violates the rules and disrupts the economy of classicism. The work of Martin Amis explored in the previous chapter tends towards Gombrich's '*barocco*', 'the no-longer-classical, the degenerate'. Amis's work, with its hyperbolic prose, points to the body as subject to decay and as moving towards dysfunction (just as the planet in general is moving towards decay in works like *Money* (1985) and *London*

Fields (1989)), to the extent that traditional concepts such as motivation are described as 'pretty well shagged out by now' (Amis, 1985a, 359). Amis's work can thus be characterised (and in fact has been by hostile critics) as decadent and debased in its relation to the tradition of the realist novel. McEwan's fiction, on the other hand, is closer to the grotesque as 'the not-yet-classical, the barbaric' and his interest in adolescent characters, in the processes of growing up and in human instincts, is part of this pre-classical trend. Instead of Amis's hyperbole and linguistic excess, McEwan's prose is characterised by an intense and narrow focus, and rather than looking at end points his work interrogates the foundations on which metaphysics, ideology and subjectivity are built. The following section examines the ways in which *The Cement Garden*, through its adolescent narrator Jack, explores the path of the human subject as not-yet-classical (i.e. not yet fully elaborated) on its journey towards adulthood.

Subject formation and *The Cement Garden*

McEwan's first novel *The Cement Garden* offers a sustained engagement with issues of subject formation, indeed the title itself invokes some of the concepts with which the book will grapple in terms of this stifling of the natural by that most artificial of substances, cement. The garden, however, is anything other than Edenic, and after his mother's and father's deaths, the narrator Jack relates how what remains of the family slowly draws in on itself, 'like burrowing animals', as McEwan has described it in interview (Haffenden, 1985, 171). This description recalls Kafka's short story 'The Burrow' (1999, first published in German 1931), the narrator of which seeks to render his underground burrow secure against a mysterious intruder. That story will later supply one of the epigraphs to McEwan's novel *The Innocent*, which describes a love affair against the background of Operation Gold, the secret attempt by Allied forces to burrow into the Russian sector of Berlin to tap telephone conversations. *The Cement Garden* sets up decisive oppositions between Jack and his father, which are given a manifestly Oedipal context by the opening line: 'I did not kill my father, but I sometimes felt I had helped him on his way' (1980, 9). Jack's father, who suffers from constipation (suggestive of adult unease with the body), has planned to cover the garden with cement but collapses and dies while moving the cement bags, while Jack masturbates upstairs in the house. The mother's death soon after leaves the children alone in the house, where Jack and his sister Julie gradually drift towards incest.

In psychoanalytic terms, the father can be seen as the upholder of the Law and crucially of the incest taboo who 'sustains the structure of desire with the structure of the law' (Lacan, 1979, 34, first published in French 1973). The children's dead father in *The Cement Garden*, however, is the now missing guardian against pollution and contamination, as Max Duperray argues:

> Le père est constamment associé au monolithisme des surfaces sans faille. Il meurt sous le fardeau de cette insurmontable tâche de purification, lutte mythique contre les désordres polluants du désir. Déja l'environnement immédiat portait les stigmates discrets d'une certaine souillure. (Duperray, 1982, 423–4)

> The father is constantly associated with the monolithic quality of surfaces without cracks. He dies beneath the weight of this insurmountable task of purification, the mythic struggle against the polluting disorders of desire. Already the immediate environment carried the unobtrusive traces of a certain soiling. (my translation)

The father is characterised by this desire for order, for a restraining structure both in physical terms (keeping the house tidy, covering over the garden) and in psychoanalytic ones (incest taboo) where Duperray's '*surfaces sans faille*' remind us of Bakhtin's classical body, so when the children's mother and father have died the house quickly deteriorates into a lawless state. Julia Kristeva remarks in *Powers of Horror*, in terms which seem to match *The Cement Garden* very closely, that:

> [T]he subject will always be marked by the uncertainty of his borders and of his affective valency as well; these are all the more

determining as the paternal function was weak or even nonexistent, opening the door to perversion and psychosis. (Kristeva, 1982, 63)

This closed world without authority leads to a breakdown in laws: Jack decides not to bother about personal hygiene or kitchen chores (McEwan, 1980, 72, 67). The patriarchal law-of-the-father is only a weak reminder for Jack, and as authority in the house is ceded to Julie, it becomes apparent that Jack has not inherited the role of the law-making father.

McEwan's comments on William Golding's *Lord of the Flies* (1954) shed some light on his reasons for writing a novel centred on children:

> The novel brought realism to my fantasy life (the glowing, liberated world without grown-ups) and years later, when I came to write a novel myself, I could not resist the momentum of my childhood fantasies nor the power of Golding's model, for I found myself wanting to describe a closed world of children removed from the constraints of authority. I had no doubt that my children too would suffer from, rather than exult in, their freedom. (McEwan, 1986, 159)

The children's development in McEwan's novel, then, is not towards liberation but towards suffering. In Golding's book the relics of socialised behaviour gradually disappear as the children develop into the author's primeval, and to some extent, quasi-Christian, archetypes (*Lord of the Flies* makes a later anecdotal reappearance in *Enduring Love* (McEwan 1998a, 170–1, first published 1997)). In contrast, McEwan is more interested in the children's development in psychological terms rather than in moral or ethical ones, and *The Cement Garden* charts Tom's increasingly infantile behaviour, including wearing a nappy and sleeping in a cot, with Julie as his surrogate mother. This movement is characteristic of the children's gradual absorption into their own circle, and of their degeneration into earlier modes of thought and behaviour: in other words of their regression, a key theme of many of McEwan's books, including *Enduring Love* (1998a) and *Saturday* (2005), but that perhaps finds its fullest expression in *The Child in Time* (1988, first published 1987), explored below.

Remarks made by McEwan in an interview with Ian Hamilton (1978) show how the author was interested in exploring oedipal issues in *The Cement Garden*:

> I had an idea that in the nuclear family the kind of forces that are being suppressed – the oedipal, incestuous forces – are also paradoxically the very forces which keep the family together. So if you remove the controls, you have a ripe anarchy from which the oedipal and the incestuous are the definitive emotions. From Jack's point of view Julie becomes something he aspires to sexually, even though she is his sister and also, in the circumstances acting as mother to his younger brother and to some extent to Jack himself. I suppose I'm suggesting a situation in which the oedipal and incestuous are identical. (Hamilton, 1978, 21)

At the end of the novel Jack is discovered nursing at Julie's breast after having sex with her and since Julie is his sister, this is sibling incest, but as Julie is a mother substitute for both Jack and Tom, calling them 'two bare babies' when she finds them together in the cot (McEwan, 1980, 123), Jack is fulfilling a quasi-oedipal drive. In this situation, as McEwan describes above, the incestuous and oedipal drives unite in moving away from differentiation, in the same way as Tom's return to babyhood denies temporal differentiation. McEwan has himself provided potential biographical clues for his interest in oedipal drives:

> One of my earliest memories is of seeing this figure [McEwan's father] in the rain, pushing his bicycle past the prefab window; when I saw him, I'd run behind the settee and call to my mother to send him away. As far as I was concerned, he was an intruder into my rather intense, pleasant relationship with my mother. (Hamilton, 1978, 10)

For Judith Butler in *Gender Trouble* (1990) the incest taboo, along with the taboo against homosexuality, is one of 'the generative moments of gender identity' (135), and Jack and Julie's incest can thus be read as a sign of Jack's failure to achieve a stable adult identity and his collapse into a childish state characterised by the stifling of differentiation and a union that can only lead to decay.

The obscene excesses of *The Comfort of Strangers*

The city of Venice forms a readily recognisable, albeit anonymous site (in that the author does not name the city) for McEwan's second novel *The Comfort of Strangers* (1982, first published 1981), forging a powerful intertextual connection to two works about Venice that are also important works in the tradition of the grotesque: Ruskin's *The Stones of Venice* and Thomas Mann's *Death in Venice* (1955, first published in German 1912). As J.R. Banks notes in 'A Gondola Named Desire', the English literary canon, from Ben Jonson to Henry James, has depicted Venice as a place of 'perversion, decadence, crime and sudden death' (Banks, 1982, 27), and McEwan's narrative of friendly strangers Robert and Caroline turning out to be killers is a contemporary contribution to this tradition. Ruskin's work on Venice is directly alluded to in *The Comfort of Strangers* as the unmarried English couple Colin and Mary who will be the victims of a murder plot sit on a café terrace in the unnamed city next to 'one of the great tourist attractions of the world' (McEwan, 1982, 47), and notice a baby at a nearby table staring at:

> the roofline of the cathedral where, it had once been written, the crests of the arches, as if in ecstasy, broke into marble foam and tossed themselves far into the blue sky in flashes and wreaths of sculpted spray, as if breakers on a shore had been frost-bound before they fell. (McEwan, 1982, 49)

The cathedral is Venice's St Mark's Basilica and the anonymous writer of the extravagant description (probably the most famous passage in *The Stones of Venice*) is Ruskin:

> [U]ntil at last, as if in ecstasy, the crests of the arches break into a marble foam, and toss themselves far into the blue sky in flashes and wreaths of sculptured spray, as if the breakers on the Lido shore had been frost-bound before they fell, and the sea-nymphs had inlaid them with coral and amethyst. (Ruskin, 1911, 67–8)

The clashing sounds of Ruskin's St Mark's, with the Austrian bands' 'martial music jarring with the organ notes' of the cathedral, become the 'dissonances and cross-rhythms' (McEwan, 1982, 48) heard by Colin and Mary, who are seated 'roughly equidistant from two orchestras', the music of which is 'simultaneously martial and romantic' (47–8), suggestive of Mars and Venus. The rich and antique hues in the art-critic's description of the basilica (gold, amber, ivory, azure, deep-green) are replaced by the banal colours of the baby's clown-like clothes, including 'a white sun hat, a green-and-white striped matelot vest, bulging pants frilled with pink lace and white ribbon, yellow ankle-socks and scarlet leather shoes' (48). Much like the music, these bright colours clash both in terms of colour and of their gender connotations as McEwan draws attention to the sex of the baby (like that of the people selling maps from kiosks) remaining unknown.

The startling contrast between the baby's grotesquely discharging body, with its 'snail trail of drool' and 'fat, weak legs ... splayed round the massive, shameless burden of its nappy' (49) on the one hand and the basilica's 'triumphant accretion ... of many centuries of civilization' (47) on the other will later be played out in microcosm in Robert's childhood story of being forced by his sisters to defecate in his father's sacrosanct study. The focus on the baby, combined with Robert's account of his childhood and Mary's feelings for her absent children further develop this sense of children and their treatment lying at the core of the novel. Robert's infertility seems to have been a catalyst for his initial violence against his wife Caroline and the narrative describes how a quasi-family structure emerges between the four people, a feeling enhanced by their lack of distinguishing surnames. As David Malcolm describes, in this schema Colin and Mary are gradually transformed into the role of dependent and obedient children who are powerless to stop the violence directed against them by their controlling and abusive father-figure Robert and his bullied but complicit wife (Malcolm, 2002, 82–3).

Christopher Ricks in his review of the novel, claims that 'it is in pondering Venice that Ruskin is driven to seize and to elaborate that distinction between the true grotesque and the false which is where any fundamental disagreement about McEwan's work must lie' (1982, 14) and, while wholeheartedly agreeing with such emphasis, I would contend that the stated desire to distinguish true from false grotesque is thwarted by the mixture and contradiction that lie at the heart of the grotesque, as explored in the first chapter of this book. The title of Ricks's review, 'Playing with Terror', infers that McEwan is engaged in creating 'true' rather than second-hand Venetian horror, hence the decision not to name the city or Ruskin explicitly; however, McEwan is clearly drawing on a literary tradition so that for his tourist couple 'the city, and their relationship to it, was littered with notions of possible death' (Haffenden, 1985, 181). *The Comfort of Strangers* therefore displays a self-consciousness in its deployment of the grotesque, both in terms of the human body and aesthetic tradition, which is of a piece with McEwan's sophisticated handling of oppositions and clashes within his fiction. It is this playful but serious self-consciousness that is apparent throughout his oeuvre, particularly evident in *Atonement*'s (2001) celebrated handling of narrative, which has done so much to secure McEwan's reputation as a key post-war author.

Disorientation and death are of course central to Thomas Mann's *Death in Venice* (1955), which explores Gustave von Aschenbach's fatal obsession with the fourteen-year-old boy Tadzio. In McEwan's story, however, it is Colin, the object of the obsession, who is destroyed rather than its possessor the sadist Robert. McEwan would later return to the theme of obsession in the person of Jed Parry, the man who becomes emotionally obsessed with Joe Rose, the narrator of *Enduring Love*. The striped matelot vest of the baby in St Mark's Square described above brings to mind the striped uniforms of Venice's gondoliers and Tadzio's 'English sailor suit' (Mann, 1955, 31). As Aschenbach arrives in Venice by boat, he is shocked to see that one of a party of young men on the boat is in fact old, and is dressed and made up to look young. Aschenbach is repelled by this grotesque 'young-old man':

> Aschenbach's brow darkened as he looked, and there came over him once more a dazed sense, as though things about him were just slightly losing their ordinary perspective, beginning to show a distortion that might merge into the grotesque. (Mann, 1955, 24)

The grotesque seizes Aschenbach as he arrives in Venice and is with him as he eventually surrenders to his obsession and pursues Tadzio through the city:

[H]e would follow him through the streets where horrid death stalked too, and at such times it seemed to him as though the moral law were fallen in ruins and only the monstrous and perverse held out a hope. (Mann, 1955, 77)

Aschenbach's thoughts here seem to follow Ruskin's explanation of the decline of Venice, where the grotesque architecture of the late Renaissance stands as the aesthetic outcome of the moral torpor and luxurious lifestyles of the Venetians. The fate of Aschenbach in the plague-ridden city also recalls the grotesque head of Santa Maria Formosa discussed in Chapter 1. Aschenbach dreams of Dionysus ('the stranger god') and of participating in orgies in honour of the god: 'in his very soul he tasted the bestial degradation of his fall' (Mann, 1955, 76). For Ruskin, the Santa Maria Formosa head is the worst example of the grotesque

> A head, – huge, inhuman, and monstrous, – leering *in bestial degradation*, too foul to be either pictured or described ... for in that head is embodied the type of evil spirit to which Venice was abandoned in the fourth period of her decline; and it is well that we should see and feel the full horror of it on this spot, and know what *pestilence* it was that came and breathed on her beauty, until it melted away like the white cloud from the ancient field of Santa Maria Formosa. (Ruskin, 1912, 120, my emphasis)

Aschenbach, through submitting to his obsession and finally succumbing to the plague, falls victim to both the bestial degradation and the pestilence that Ruskin saw as the city's surrender to the grotesque.

Colin and Mary are tourists in a city of tourists, and the novel is haunted by the camera and by the gaze, evident in the old man attempting to photograph his wife (McEwan, 1982, 16–17), the 'single camera lens' in a shop window, the camera Robert carries when he meets the English couple, Robert's grandfather's opera glass and the glass factory Colin and Mary try to visit. The supposedly innocent activity of tourist photography becomes something more sinister in the story, as the reader learns that Robert has become obsessed with Colin and has been secretly photographing him.

Robert, who indulges in sadomasochistic sex with his wife Caroline, believes women enjoy being dominated:

> 'And even though they hate themselves for it, women long to be ruled by men. It's deep in their minds. They lie to themselves. They talk of freedom, and dream of captivity.' (McEwan, 1982, 72)

Robert is, in Judith Seaboyer's words, 'an ugly case of oedipal desire, paternal violence, sibling hatred, and revenge' (1999, 968), and his sexist views are integrated into his mythology of the past, of the times of his father and grandfather: 'My father and his father understood themselves clearly. They were men and proud of their sex' (McEwan, 1982, 72). It is through murdering Colin, a 'feminised' man, that Robert and Caroline live out their sadism.

Geoffrey Harpham's examination of the grotesque as it appears in *Death in Venice* looks at the way in which 'sympathetic contaminations' (1982, 140) work in the novel; the plague in the city is refigured as the ways in which Aschenbach 'begins to dilute, or to "identify" with the various characters he encounters' (134). A prominent example of this is the way Aschenbach, after visiting the hotel barber, resembles the grotesque young-old man he saw on the boat, wearing makeup and having his hair dyed and so in a sense contaminated by the repellent young-old man he had earlier spotted. Colin and Mary are similarly 'contaminated' by Robert and Caroline and, having met the sadomasochistic couple, they joke about handcuffing themselves together forever and whisper to each other sexually sadistic stories 'that came from nowhere, out of the dark ... stories that won from the spellbound listener consent to a lifetime of subjection and humiliation' (McEwan, 1982, 81). We see the same contamination in Colin's newly acquired 'distant, rough authority' that is 'quite untypical' (43).

Another important link to *Death in Venice* revolves around Robert's 'shrine' (105) to his father and grandfather, which Colin ironically calls 'a museum dedicated to the good old days' (73), earning a punch from Robert. Robert tells Colin and Mary how his fearsome father had a moustache (for the reader, Hitler-like in its narrowness) 'and when it turned to grey he used a little brush to make it black, such as ladies use for their eyes. Mascara' (32), echoing the ruses of *Death in Venice*'s young-old man whose 'turned-up moustaches and small imperial were dyed' (Mann, 1955, 22). Robert therefore inadvertently reveals the theatrical nature of his father's appearance, based as it is on mascara and perfume. This chauvinist version of maleness is, as Seaboyer puts it, 'a masquerade of masculinity' (1999, 980), and the reader is left in no doubt that Robert's performance of masculinity is as dependent on the theatrical as his father's was on mascara to preserve his youthful appearance. The sexist stereotypes are shown to be as theatrical as the shop display in Venice, where the mannequins, although identical, are placed in 'male' and 'female' positions on a bed, the headboard of which is itself divided into a 'male' side resembling 'the control panel of a power station, or perhaps a light aircraft' and a 'female' one 'dominated by an oval, rose-tinted mirror' and equipped with 'magazine rack and a nursery intercom' (McEwan, 1982, 22). The theatrical nature of selfhood comes to the fore, in the case of Robert and also of Colin and Mary, both of whom have been involved in the theatre and so Venice's status as the home of masquerade, as well as of what the policeman calls 'these obscene excesses' (McEwan, 1982, 123) is thus asserted. If in *The Cement Garden* the grotesque body stands in opposition to the clean, impenetrable surface of paternal life, Robert's story from his childhood of fouling his father's study is another such violation of adult, masculine order by the grotesque body. In the bathroom Robert's father 'made a terrible smell, but it was covered with the smell of the shaving soap and his perfume' (32), and again adulthood is that which covers up, or more precisely attempts to cover up, the evidence of the grotesque body.

Regression and *The Child in Time*

The epigraph for this chapter is taken from Martin Amis's novel *Time's Arrow* (1991), in which the narrator describes the nature of the offence as having to do with trash and shit and being wrong in time, and both these qualities parallel the twin strands of the grotesque in McEwan's work. On the one hand we have the grotesque bodies of *First Love, Last Rites*, *The Cement Garden* and *The Comfort of Strangers*, of the dismembered corpse in *The Innocent* – the trash and shit. On the other we have the grotesque that is 'wrong in time', the grotesque of inverted or perverted time that has been an enduring feature of McEwan's fiction. The episode in *The Cement Garden* where Jack climbs into the cot and Julie encourages him to suck his thumb (1980, 121–2) echoes an early short story in *First Love, Last Rites* (1991, first published 1975) called 'Conversation with a Cupboard Man', about a man whose widowed mother never lets him develop and grow up:

> She tried to stop me growing up and for a long time she succeeded. Do you know, I didn't learn to speak properly til I was eighteen … She didn't like it when I got too big for my cot so she went out and bought a crib bed from a hospital auction. (McEwan, 1991, 75)

The effect such treatment has on this 'cupboard man' is far reaching:

> I don't want to be free. That's why I envy these babies I see in the street being bundled and carried about by their mothers. I want to be one of them. Why can't it be me? … I want to climb in the pram. It's stupid, I'm six feet tall. (McEwan, 1991, 87)

This fantasy of regression to childhood, to womb-like plenitude, is rendered grotesque and ridiculous by the detail of the man's height, by the absurd mismatch between his size and the dimensions of a pram. The cupboard man is, to use Amis's phrase, 'wrong in time', producing a contradictory and dysfunctional individual characteristic of the grotesque.

Other stories in *First Love, Last Rites* also involve such a grotesque perversion of time, including the disturbing 'Homemade' narrated by a fourteen-year-old boy who has sex with his ten-year-old sister. The extremely precocious narrator, who smokes tobacco and cannabis and drinks alcohol, tricks his sister Connie into having sex with him by playing with time, winding the clock back to delay her bedtime and inviting her to play Mummies and Daddies. This infantilised sex finds its popular parallel in Elvis Presley's song 'Teddy Bear' which the narrator whistles (25). The narrator is a grotesque combination of a fourteen-year-old who is also, according to McEwan 'meant to be a sort of Henry Miller-ish age, a wizened sixty' (Hamilton, 1978, 18). The sexual exploits detailed by Henry Miller, Havelock Ellis (the work of whom the narrator has been reading), Norman Mailer (mentioned in the Hamilton interview) and D.H. Lawrence (Connie's name recalling Lady Chatterley) become the grotesque and temporally perverted parody of sex described in McEwan's story:

> ... I felt proud, proud to be fucking, even if it were only Connie, my ten-year-old sister, even if it had been a crippled mountain goat I would have been proud to be lying there in that manly position, proud in advance of being able to say 'I have fucked', of belonging intimately and irrevocably to that superior half of humanity who had known coitus, and fertilised the world with it. (McEwan, 1991, 39–40)

Here the grotesque is put to work rendering the cultural tradition of asserting the virile power of masculinity into hyperbolic and destructive nonsense.

McEwan is also interested in the temporal contraction involved in regression, and his fiction frequently evokes the 'timelessness' of childhood, or of a regression to a childlike state. *The Cement Garden* and *The Child in Time* are both concerned with this lack of temporal perspective and the sense of an eternal present, something that is seen to be the prerogative of a child:

> 'It's funny,' Julie said, 'I've lost all sense of time. It feels like it's always been like this. I can't remember how it used to be when Mum was alive and I can't really imagine anything changing. Everything seems still and fixed and makes me feel that I'm not frightened of anything.' (McEwan, 1980, 123)

What McEwan is describing is a state of presence, of childhood plenitude and security, free from adult pressures and worries. However, to return to the author's comments on *Lord of the Flies*, the absence of any law-giving adult in *The Cement Garden* does not result in endless happiness for the children but rather in suffering and entropy. Freedom does not emerge from this parent-free zone but rather stasis and stagnation, as McEwan describes in an interview with Christopher Ricks:

I was trying to set up a situation where suddenly there were no social controls. Suddenly, children find themselves in the house – there are no teachers, no parents, no figures of authority, they have total freedom – and yet they are completely paralysed. The narrator is at first almost catatonic with freedom – can't move at all. (Ricks, 1979, 526)

The conflict between a childhood state of innocence and the pressures of adult responsibility is at its most extreme in the figure of Charles Darke in *The Child in Time*, who works as a minister in the British government and resigns his position in order to pursue his private fantasy of being a child again. He was a vocal fan of the protagonist's book *Lemonade* and tells him:

> 'Stephen, listen. Stephen, talk to a ten-year old in mid-summer about Christmas. You could be talking to an adolescent about his retirement plans, his pension. For children, childhood is timeless. It's always the present. Everything is in the present tense.' (McEwan, 1988, 32–3)

Where Colin in *The Comfort of Strangers* experiences the desire to escape adult responsibility, 'to be released from the arduous states of play of psychological condition' (McEwan, 1982, 104), as a momentary temptation, for Charles it becomes a growing obsession, as his wife Thelma describes:

> 'He wanted the security of childhood, the powerlessness, the obedience, and also the freedom that goes with it, freedom from money, decisions, plans, demands. He used to say he wanted to escape from time, from appointments, schedules, deadlines. Childhood to him was timelessness, he talked about it as though it were a mystical state.' (McEwan, 1988, 200–1)

Freed from responsibility, Charles has become a forty-nine-year-old schoolboy in Richmal Crompton's *Just William* mode, drinking liquorice water and hanging around a ramshackle tree house in the woods. Charles is attempting to turn back time but, as in *The Cement Garden*, this timelessness is not freedom, nor an escape from male adulthood, but in fact marks the ascendance of stagnation and decay. As Berthold Schoene-Harwood puts it, Charles 'begins quite literally to freeze into place' (2000, 161) as discovery of his corpse reveals:

> A two-inch layer of unmelted snow sat on Charles's shoulders and in the folds of his shirt along the arms. It had drifted deep on his lap and sat wedge-shaped on his head. It was on the line of his nose and across his upper lip. *The effect was comic, nastily so.* (McEwan 1988, 197, my emphasis)

This 'nastily comic' episode (reminiscent of the closing shot of Stanley Kubrick's film *The Shining*) with its mixture of humour and horror falls squarely into the realm of the grotesque.

Stephen's earlier encounter with 'the forty-nine-year-old schoolboy' Charles recalls both the cupboard man and Thomas Mann's young-old man in Venice. Time has been perverted here but the pretence of childhood is unsuccessful, as Stephen sees when he examines the contents of Charles's pockets:

> It was as if his friend had combed libraries, diligently consulted the appropriate authorities to discover just what it was a certain kind of boy was likely to have in his pockets. It was too correct to be convincing, not quite sufficiently idiosyncratic, perhaps even fraudulent. Momentarily, embarrassment overcame vertigo. (McEwan, 1988, 113)

Like the six-foot cupboard man wanting to get into a pram, the forty-nine-year-old schoolboy is a grotesque mismatch, evidence of a psyche that has become distorted. Charles's childhood objects are shown to be just as inauthentic and theatrical as Robert's little 'shrine' in *The Comfort of Strangers*, the objects of which 'suggested a memory game played at children's parties' (McEwan, 1982, 71). The children Colin and Mary meet in the street learn memory games as they are heard 'chanting a religious formula or an arithmetical table' (43) and are also subject to adult time as the school bell calls them: 'squeals of glee and congratulation ran through the crowd. Then the chiming ceased, and the remaining children fell silent and began to run grimly' (43). The final adverb stands in stark contrast to the image of happy children playing and the subjection of children to adult time (itself reminiscent of 'The Nurse's Song' from Blake's *Songs of Experience*). McEwan returns to such subjection in *The Child in Time* in one of the quotes from the fictional *Authorised Childcare Handbook*, for the ultra-conservative and sexist tone of which the reader eventually learns Charles is responsible:

> Make it clear to him that the clock cannot be argued with and that when it is time to leave for school, for Daddy to go to work, for Mummy to attend to her duties, then these changes are as incontestable as the tides. (McEwan, 1988, 27)

Conformity to such strictures is not without its negative effects, however, as Charles's fate shows.

According to his widow Thelma, Charles's case is part of a more general problem in which there are negative social consequences to men's failure to integrate their childhood selves into their adult lives:

> 'He could never bring his qualities as a child – and really Stephen you should have seen him, so funny and direct and gentle – he couldn't bring any of this into his public life. Instead it was all frenetic compensation for what he took to be an excess of vulnerability ... And quite honestly, when I think of my colleagues at work and the scientific establishment and the men who run it, and I think of science itself, how it's been devised over the centuries, I have to say that Charles's case was just an extreme form of a general problem.' (McEwan, 1988, 204)

The Child in Time offers a vision of men unable to preserve their childhood or adolescent qualities into manhood, and where the adoption of masculine roles is represented as a disjunction in a man's development, necessitating a 'jettisoning' of the child and his values. Kiernan Ryan comes to much the same conclusion in his discussion of *First Love, Last Rites* when he claims that:

> [G]rowing into a man means suppressing everything habitually identified with the mother and the feminine, everything which threatens to expose the brittle artifice of male autonomy. This

includes the animal functions and processes of the human body itself, the levelling evidence of our shared biological being, of the physiological affinities that traverse and mock the distinctions of gender we impose. But the will to remain hard, clean, and contained is repeatedly undermined by the yearning to relapse into that abject ecstasy in which manhood evaporates and the whole system of differences on which patriarchy depends collapses in scandalous confusion. Hence the notorious itch of McEwan's fiction to revel in the disgusting, to dwell on the secretions and excretions of the human organism – the mucus and saliva and menstrual flux – which returns us to the visceral reality of the flesh. (Ryan, 1994, 12)

Ryan is convincing when he talks of the drive in McEwan's narratives to relapse into an undifferentiated state; yet he perhaps overestimates the significance of gender in this relapse. Identifying the feminine with the body only reproduces the mind/body duality that Mars-Jones (see below) accuses McEwan of perpetrating in *The Child in Time*. The pull of regression and the drive to escape adult responsibility is not necessarily gendered, and Ryan's analysis – although correctly identifying the presence of regression and the 'visceral reality of the flesh' which McEwan presents to the reader – risks reproducing rather than deconstructing a masculine/feminine mind/body analogy. Regarding McEwan's portrayal of gender relations, Adam Mars-Jones in his polemic *Venus Envy* (1990) has accused McEwan of creating, in *The Child in Time*: 'a temporary blurring of identities, under cover of which the male, all the while extolling the sanctity of her privileges, usurps the female' (33), and claimed in a review of *Amsterdam* that 'there began, above all in *The Child in Time*, the invoking of certain values, particularly the decommissioning of the male ego in favour of a new personality more in tune with women and children' (Mars-Jones, 1998, 16). My discussion of McEwan's work, however, shows that the author is profoundly interested in 'the flesh', in the human body and its biology, and does not privilege the mind over the body. In fact, as this chapter has shown, McEwan constantly plays off the mind against the body, not to prioritise the mind, logic or rationality, but to stage the potential conflict between these aspects of being. His work reveals the limitations of rationality by focusing on the significance of those aspects of humanity which are not part of and do not conform to rationality: the body and its secretions, instincts, sexuality, erotic fantasies and the life of the emotions.

Both Ryan in his book on McEwan and Berthold Schoene-Harwood in *Writing Men* (2000) approach *The Child in Time* in terms of a Kristevan dynamic between the masculine symbolic and the temptation offered by the feminine semiotic to retreat into a regressed state which undoes systems of meaning. However, it is also possible – and I would argue more productive – to examine the novel in terms of regression and of narcissism. This section has linked the case of Charles Darke to earlier examples of regression in McEwan's work and it is clear that such regression is not an escape but a collapse into psychosis, as Kristeva notes in *Powers of Horror*:

> The edenic image of primary narcissism is perhaps a defensive negation elaborated by the neurotic subject when he sets himself under the aegis of the father. (Kristeva, 1982, 63)

Kristeva here suggests that the subject in his neurosis imagines his prior phase as some kind of paradise. The case of Charles in *The Child in Time*, who identifies with his imagined *Just William* past, is one such attempted return to Eden, but as *The Cement Garden* showed, such attempts are always doomed. There is no Eden, only entropy and the tendency to perversion and psychosis. In keeping with *The Child in Time*'s central theme of time, Stephen's parents meet each other when his father returns a broken clock to the shop where his mother works; the regression that as both theme and figure runs throughout McEwan's fiction has perhaps its fullest expression in this novel. Through a paranormal time-shift Stephen experiences his own episode of regression to the time he existed as an unborn foetus, staring at his parents through a pub window as they decide what to do about his mother's pregnancy. Like Charles, Stephen may also be said to be 'living in the past' in that his daughter Kate's kidnapping has split him off both from his wife Julie and from his future. Stephen allows for changes in his daughter's age but he is none the less fixed in time since he cannot move beyond his daughter Kate's disappearance, trapped like the traffic-bound cars he passes on a London bridge at the beginning of the novel. His search for his missing child imprisons him in a neurotic past-present that will not allow him a future and he can only move forwards when he stops living out a representation of the past. Stephen stops identifying with a ghost (unlike Charles and indeed Robert) and begins living the past not as the present, but as the past. Schoene-Harwood compares Stephen's reaction to Kate's disappearance to that of his wife Julie:

> Stephen finds himself consistently on the wrong track, taking an unnecessarily long-winded and circuitous route to the site of semiotic revelation at the end of the novel, which is symptomatically identical with the site Julie arrived at via a short cut many months before him. (Schoene-Harwood, 2000, 158–9)

However, while the critic sees the different reactions as due to gender differences, such a reading needs to include the element of time and the significance of things being, in Amis's phrase, 'wrong in time'. It is Stephen's neurotic mindset, his inability to work through this change in his life that is associated in the novel with his gender, as can be seen from his reflections on Julie:

> Such faith in endless mutability, in re-making yourself as you came to understand more, or changed your version, he had come to see as an aspect of her femininity. Where once he had believed, or thought he ought to believe, that men and women were, beyond all the obvious physical differences, essentially the same, he now suspected that one of their many distinguishing features was precisely their attitudes to change. Past a certain age, men froze into place, they tended to believe that, even in adversity, they were somehow at one with their fates. (McEwan, 1988, 54–5)

It is in men and women's contrasting approaches to time that they differ, but while the novel may advocate the 'feminising' of institutions (such as science and politics), Stephen does not make progress by somehow 'feminising' himself but by reconciling himself to his own past. Written during Margaret Thatcher's term as prime minister, *The Child in Time* is suitably ironic in demonstrating that having a female leader is no guarantee of liberating policies. In the novel the prime minister's gender is left unspecified, although the fact that 'Stephen had heard that there was a convention in the higher reaches of the Civil Service never to reveal, by the use of personal pronouns or other means, any opinion as to the gender of the Prime Minister' (82) leads one to suppose that the leader of the oppressive government in the novel is a woman.

Against Mars-Jones's claim that McEwan indulges in a blurring of gendered identities we can suggest that the novel offers instead a blurring of *time*. Stephen's route to happiness takes in regressions to his own in utero beginnings, to a school classroom and finally to a journey in the cab of a train, something he has wanted to do since he was a child. Stephen manages to make it to Julie's house in time to help with the birth of their child because he succeeds in doing what he had never dared do as a boy – asking a train driver to let him ride in the cab. As Paul Edwards outlines:

> The journey thus becomes emblematic of the fortuitous (but how else can it occur?) integration of the boy within the man, and thus forms a contrast with Charles Darke's willed and artificial second childhood. (Edwards, 1995, 49)

It is thus through a negotiation of temporal change that seeks simultaneously to preserve the past without becoming its prisoner, and to evolve in order to progress to a hopeful future, that Stephen recovers his life.

As well as showing an interest in regression to childhood, McEwan's fiction also frequently portrays humanity as literally devolved in the sense of being ape-like. Kafka's 'A Report to an Academy' (1999, first published in German 1917) is an explicit inspiration, and thus a useful starting point for McEwan's short story 'Reflections of a Kept Ape' from *In Between the Sheets* (1979, first published 1978), and it provides an epigraph to Will Self's *Great Apes* (1998, first published 1997), which is discussed in Chapter 6. Kafka's story concerns an ape captured on the Gold Coast who gradually learns to speak and adopts the behaviour and lifestyle of humans, and eventually presents his experiences to 'the Academy'. McEwan's story deals with the relationship between Sally Klee, an author, and her pet ape with whom she has enjoyed sexual relations. McEwan's ape is familiar with the work of Balzac, Yeats and Sterne but he dreams of married life with Sally:

> Yes, I saw myself, expensive fountain pen in hand, signing hire purchase agreements for my pretty wife. I would teach myself to hold a pen. I would be man-about-the-house, scaling drainpipes with uxorious ease to investigate the roof gutters, suspending myself from light fittings to redecorate the ceiling. Down to the pub in the evening with my husband credentials to make new friends, invent a name for myself in order to bestow it on my wife (McEwan, 1979, 32)

The grotesque relations between Sally and the ape ('This and my "bloody gibbering on the bed" precipitated the end of the affair' (34)) are rendered even more absurd by the cliché-ridden and chauvinistic fantasy the ape has of domestic life. The interest in portraying the ape-like characteristics of the human body and of human behaviour is not confined to this short story, however, as the first time we meet Robert in *The Comfort of Strangers*, his ape-like characteristics are emphasised: 'He was shorter than Colin, but his arms were exceptionally long and muscular. His hands too were large, the backs covered with matted hair' (McEwan, 1982, 26). As we have seen, Robert's sexist and antiquated views on gender relations are also of a type with the kept ape's dream of male power and privilege. There is another example in *The Comfort of Strangers* of what we can call devolution that occurs as Colin watches a man insistently cajole a nervous 'spindly girl' (92) into playing volleyball:

> She [the spindly girl] was gazing into the face of a square, ape-like figure who seemed determined to entertain her ... Like a newborn calf, the girl took a few aimless steps which faltered in embarrassment ... The ape came at her again and this time slapped her bottom, a skilful passing stroke, which made a surprisingly loud noise. The others, including the shorter girl, all laughed, and the ape performed an exultant, flailing cartwheel. (McEwan, 1982, 92–3)

The animal-like effect is emphasised by the dumbshow of the scene in that the lack of speech has the effect of presenting the reader with the essence of the encounter, over which speech would be merely a veneer. The idea that social situations often disguise a deeper, less pleasant reality is one that recurs again and again in McEwan's work, from *The Comfort of Strangers* through to *The Child in Time* and *The Innocent* to *Enduring Love* and *Amsterdam*.

Ape comparisons can be viewed as aspects of devolution and so of temporal and social regression, forming an important aspect of McEwan's interest in origins; that is, in our biological and psychological beginnings and how they influence us as adolescent and adult human beings. In the same way that *The Child in Time* figures Stephen's 'regression' as something positive rather than negative (in contrast to Charles's regression), so the novel offers a representation of devolution that is also positive, in the figure of a speaker addressing the childcare committee:

> His jaws and upper lip were smudged with closely shaved stubble which gave him the saddened, honest appearance of a chimpanzee, an impression furthered by large brown eyes and the black tangle of chest pelt, as thick as pubic hair, visible through his thin white nylon shirt and sprouting irreverently between its buttons. It seemed to Stephen that he held his hands still while he spoke to avoid exposing the unnatural length of his arms, whose elbows occurred an inch or two before they should have. (McEwan, 1988, 75)

This particular ape is 'Prof. Brody from the Institute of Development', a fictional organisation that spans McEwan's interest in both child development and biological evolution. The chimp-like Brody argues for a holistic approach to education and for 'the profound and immediate apprehension, which is the hallmark of a whole person, of the dancing interpenetration of the physical and the psychic, their ultimate inseparability' (76). This 'interpenetration of the physical and the psychic' comes close to McEwan's elaboration of the ways in which people are composed of a combination of physical and psychic elements, and Brody is twice identified as 'honest' as he pleads for a recognition of the whole person in the face of the fact that 'we are divided, deeply divided from ourselves, from nature and its myriad processes, from our universe' (76), reflecting some of the claims put forward in David Bohm's *Wholeness and the Implicate Order* that McEwan credits in the novel's acknowledgements. Stephen's rehabilitation is achieved by overcoming such divisions, firstly a division from himself in terms of the integration of his childhood self, but also divisions from nature and from the universe, the last being the subject of Thelma's lectures on the New Physics and perhaps resolved through his strange regression to the womb. Schoene-Harwood's identification of Brody's voice as 'an originary, primal voice, the voice of humankind's preliterate, prehistoric child' (2000, 166) points the way towards understanding this regressed human not as a baleful evolutionary throwback posing a threat, but on the contrary a representative of that part of our own being that our adult, rational selves need to acknowledge and incorporate.

The author in time: early versus late McEwan

Composer Clive Linley's decision in *Amsterdam* (McEwan, 1998b) not to help the woman he suspects may be in danger is a strong attack on the artist who removes himself from social responsibility, and whose behaviour is entirely conditioned by his own artistic or vocational needs and not anyone else's. This questioning of the artist's role brings us back to Ryan's comments regarding a distinction between an 'early' and a 'late' McEwan quoted at the beginning of this chapter. As I have sought to demonstrate through an examination of the grotesque and issues related to it, McEwan's work exhibits elements that span his entire oeuvre, such as evolution and obsession. However, McEwan's treatment of time and development in his fiction, particularly in *The Child in Time*, suggests self-conscious reflection on his own development as a writer. In the novel Stephen asks himself, 'Wasn't that Nietzsche's idea of true maturity, to attain the seriousness of a child at play?' (1988, 105–6) and later on, while helping his daughter build a sandcastle, he reflects that 'if he could do everything with the intensity and abandonment with which he had once helped Kate build her castle, he would be a happy man of extraordinary powers' (106–7).

While the seriousness of a child at play may have been Nietzsche's definition of maturity, it also fits exactly Freud's outline of the artist's work in his essay 'Creative Writers and Day-Dreaming' (1985, first published in German 1908). Freud claims that: 'The creative writer does the same as the child at play. He creates a world of phantasy which he takes very seriously – that is, which he invests with large amounts of emotion – while separating it sharply from reality' (132). Freud's essay also provides a background to Stephen's reflections on his daughter's sandcastle building:

> As an adult he can look back on the intense seriousness with which he once carried on his games in childhood; and, by equating his ostensibly serious occupations of today with his childhood games, he can throw off the burden imposed on him by life and win the high yield of pleasure afforded by humour. (Freud, 1985, 3)

The Child in Time, through the character of Stephen, depicts an attempt to close the gap between the intense seriousness of childhood and the adult's burdens. Charles Darke, in his infantile condition and in his role as MP, has split these selves apart. Stephen's book *Lemonade* is for Charles his own adult self addressing his childhood self (McEwan, 1988, 201), and he sees the book's genesis in the same terms, as he tells Stephen:

> This book is not for children, it's for a child, and that child is you. *Lemonade* is a message from you to a previous self which will never cease to exist. And the message is bitter ... You've spoken directly to children. Whether you wanted to or not, you've communicated with them across the abyss that separates the child from the adult and you've given them a first, ghostly intimation of their mortality. (McEwan, 1988, 33)

As Edwards (1995) points out, Charles's description of *Lemonade* makes negative what is positive in Wordsworth's 'Immortality Ode', and produces something that in the terms of this study is a grotesque inversion of Wordsworth's poem.

Freud's essay, *The Child in Time* and Wordsworth's poem all come together in McEwan's series of stories *The Daydreamer* (1995, first published 1994) which, like the fictional *Lemonade*, is aimed at both adults and children. The epigraph from Ovid's *Metamorphoses* ('My purpose is to tell of bodies which have been transformed into shapes of a different kind') situates the book once more in the realm of the grotesque, although the protagonist Peter's childhood adventures, as befits a book partly aimed at children, are generally devoid of menace. Echoing Freud's essay, McEwan presents day-dreaming and storytelling as similar activities: as Peter grows up he writes his dreams down and becomes an author as an adult. The final chapter of *The Daydreamer* recalls Charles and Stephen's discussion of time in childhood and of *Lemonade*, as Peter regards the group of adults and the group of children:

> Standing there that August evening between the two groups, the sea lapping round his bare feet, Peter suddenly grasped something very obvious and terrible: one day he would leave the group that ran wild up and down the beach, and he would join the group that sat and talked ... One day he would be an entirely different person. It would happen so slowly he would not even notice, and when it had, his brilliant, playful, eleven-year-old self would be as far away, as peculiar and as difficult to understand, as all grown-ups seemed to him now. (McEwan, 1995, 134–5)

This is the temporal disjunction between adult and child explored in *The Child in Time*, and just as *Lemonade* for Charles provided children with a glimpse of their future, so *The Daydreamer* shows Peter peering into his own future. In Wordsworth's poem the place where 'the children sport upon the shore' has in McEwan's text become the place where the children 'ran wild up and down the beach', and the book closes with the Romantic poet's 'immortal sea' transformed into time, into Peter's future stretching out in front of him:

> He turned and faced the ocean. It was sparkling, right to the wide horizon. It stretched before him, vast and unknown. One after the other the endless waves came tumbling and tinkling against the shore, and they seemed to Peter like all the ideas and fantasies he would have in his life. (McEwan, 1995, 143)

This tension between the child and the man and between the private and social selves in McEwan's fiction has important parallels with his career as a writer. McEwan's relationship to his early short stories has changed over time and he has said that he could not write such stories now, with their themes of incest and child abuse. The disturbing early fiction is now the work of a past self, according to the author: '"Thank god", McEwan has said in latter years, "one can't stay 22 forever"' (Walter, 1997, 3), and he has also admitted to being slightly disinguous in his past claims of being shocked by the controversy caused by his early work.[1] Asked by Haffenden in 1985 about 'Butterflies', his story about a man who abuses and then kills a young girl, McEwan responded: 'Yes, "Butterflies" is appalling; it's a story written by someone who knew nothing about children. I couldn't possibly write that story now, it would frighten me too much' (Haffenden, 1985, 172–3). The use of the third person here is suggestive in that the younger McEwan who wrote the short stories and early novels is referred to as a different person. There is a movement in McEwan's career, noted by many commentators, including Dominic Head (2007) and Kiernan Ryan (1994), away from the adolescent, introspective narrators and enclosed settings of the early stories and novels to more socially and politically oriented works such as *The Innocent*, *Black Dogs*, *Atonement* and *Saturday*. However, just as Stephen in *The Child in Time* seeks to integrate his childhood qualities into his adult life, so McEwan has been anxious not to leave the intensity and vividness of his early fiction entirely behind him. The author, while his comments distance his later self from his own past, represents himself as a writer as having 'grown out' of his early macabre phase, as having developed as an artist beyond his earlier preoccupations.

In McEwan's later work the tension between the child and the man, between infantile regression and patriarchal power that I have outlined above, has become in more recent novels a tension between private life and social obligation as *Amsterdam*, *Saturday* and *Solar* (2010) demonstrate. The diachronic tension between childhood and adulthood of much of the early work has now become the synchronic tension between the demands of the self and of the other. It is to this ethical dynamic that McEwan has turned, but explorations of the self, of sexuality and of obsession still persist, as can be seen both in the relationship between Joe and Clarissa and in Jed's erotomania in *Enduring Love*, and in the issues surrounding the evidence of Julian

Garmony's cross-dressing in *Amsterdam*. It is also worth noting that *Atonement*'s narrative of separation and possible reunion, while clearly embodying a detailed and profound engagement with history, is set in motion by the conjunction of sexual desire and adolescent incomprehension that was the hallmark of McEwan's early work. In the light of this, *Atonement* represents perhaps less a wholesale departure from the more obviously grotesque preoccupations of the early short stories and novels and more an integration of them into wider explorations of self and society. In a similar vein, the aggressive thought-processes of *Saturday*'s threatening intruder Baxter may well be the product of a deteriorating neurological condition; however, that does not reduce (and may in fact amplify) the terror experienced by Henry Perowne and his captive family at the end of the book. To borrow the terms used in *The Child in Time* to describe Julie's (in contrast to Stephen's) growth and development (McEwan, 1988, 54), McEwan has not 'jettisoned' his past self but on the contrary integrated it within a literary career that has explored historical events and the social and political world in concert with the pressures of the opaque depths of the human psyche.

Amsterdam contains a passage that encapsulates many aspects of the grotesque in McEwan's work. As Clive examines the photos of Julian Garmony in drag he reflects on our capacity to understand ourselves and each other:

> We know so little about each other. We lie mostly submerged, like ice floes, with our visible social selves projecting only cool and white. Here was a rare sight below the waves, of a man's privacy and turmoil, of his dignity upended by the overpowering necessity of pure fantasy, pure thought, by the irreducible human element – mind. (McEwan, 1998b, 71)

This image of an iceberg embodies many of the aspects of McEwan's work I have explored, particularly the ways humanity is presented as not quite less than its pretensions but rather as exceeding a narrow conception of a person as an essentially rational being. The visible social self is only a fragment of the human whole and the coolness of that social self is more than matched by the darkness below the waves, the realm of fantasy and desire which is intractable and which is not responsive to or governed by rational thought. Where Dominic Head finds 'a literary self-consciousness that can be submerged by the shock impulse' (2007, 34) within the disturbing early fiction, and traces its development into the complex use of narrative voice in *Atonement*, I have attended instead to the inescapable forces which remain 'submerged' within the later novels, despite their greater social orientation and far more detailed historical settings. The perpetual vulnerability of 'normal' everyday existence to irruptions of these submerged forces of violence, perversion, fantasy and mania is a quintessential feature of McEwan's writing and while the shocks, to use Head's phrase, may not be as immediately visible in the later novels, they have certainly not disappeared. This vulnerability, however, may not automatically be a cause for despair but on the contrary be a source of fascination with how 'the irreducible element' of mind exceeds people's social selves and their ability to mould themselves according to any culturally acquired model. One might say that McEwan's very model of humanity is itself grotesque in that it is a disjunctive entity composed on the one hand of rationality and scientific powers and on the other of perverse desires and strange fantasies. The iceberg is in many ways the perfect surface/depth model for McEwan's depiction of humanity: beneath the rational superstructure lurks an intractable and only semi-visible core that resists integration into our reason. In darkness then, below the waves, lie our origins: our biological, psychological and genetic beginnings that both preoccupy and pre-occupy our rational selves. The frequent conflict in McEwan's fiction engendered by the emergence of our non-rational aspects creates the grotesque by breaking social convention, violating decorum and subverting our sense of self. The 'rare sight below the waves' is the depiction of such intrusions and lies at the heart of McEwan's fictional enterprise.

This chapter has focused on the grotesque body and change over time as the two main strands of the grotesque in McEwan's work. While seemingly dissimilar, these two aspects of the grotesque in this author's work can be understood as part of the same phenomenon. If Bakhtin's grotesque body 'is a body in the act of becoming. It is never finished, never completed; it is continually built, created, and builds and creates another body' (Bakhtin, 1984a, 317) then in McEwan's fiction the human subject is always 'becoming' in terms of Bakhtin's grotesque body but also in terms of Freudian theories of development and Darwin's theory of evolution. McEwan's oeuvre presents the reader with the human subject as never finished, as being continually built physiologically, socially, psychologically and biologically in terms of our evolution as a species. We are always therefore in between, unfinished and becoming and thus we are always grotesque. In fact McEwan, as this chapter has shown, depicts the necessity of change over time, of being in-process, since without change there is stagnation and psychosis. The grotesque, considered in its pre-classical aspect, expresses McEwan's interest in origins and pre-symbolic legacies that runs all the way through his work from 1975 to the present.

Note

1 'I did want to be very vivid. The *TLS* accused me of writing to shock, and that stuck – when people asked me if it were true, I said no, but I guess now I'd say perhaps yes. I did want them[the early short stories] to be different.' (Walter, 1997, 3)

Chapter 5

Iain Banks: improbable possibilities

One of the reasons I loved Kafka was his ability to describe, in very naturalistic, very controlled prose, a situation beyond belief. (Ian McEwan in Grimes, 1992)

Since his disturbing debut *The Wasp Factory* in 1984 Iain Banks's fiction has often encompassed the taboo and excessive. While simultaneously establishing himself as award-winning science fiction writer Iain M. Banks, Banks's 'mainstream' fiction, which provides the focus for this chapter, is notable for its grotesque use of horror, black humour and games, transforming his novels into mechanisms of fiendish intent and elaborate plotting. Banks's writing often embodies a duality characteristic of much contemporary literature, involving a disjunctive fusion of violent force with carefully calibrated and organised literary form. From this dissonance emerges the grotesque play with improbable possibilities and ingenious inversions and reversals. The grotesque provides a theoretical model capable of investigating *both* the principal narrative energies *and* the controlled structures of Iain Banks's fiction, acknowledging his place within the Scottish and wider European literary traditions of the grotesque.

The reviewers of Banks's first novel *The Wasp Factory* (1990a, first published 1984) were often shocked by the depiction of the narrator Frank's acts of violence against children and animals and were divided in their judgements on the book's quality. While the *Daily Telegraph* and the *Financial Times* admired the work (albeit with some reservations), other newspapers and journals were not so impressed, as a review in the *Times Literary Supplement* attests:

> Unfortunately the novelist's satiric intention is *overwhelmed* by his relish for *exorbitant* brutalities. A literary equivalent of the nastiest

brand of juvenile delinquency: inflicting outrages on animals. (my italics)[1]

As the term 'exorbitant' signals, the reviewer evaluates the work in terms of a pre-established economy: the brutality goes beyond an acceptable level and the fine balance demanded by satire is 'overwhelmed' by Banks's excessive narrative.[2] The *Irish Times* review made a distinction between talent and the uses to which such talent is put:

> It is a sick, sick world when the confidence and investment of an astute firm of publishers is [sic] justified by a work of unparalleled depravity ... There is no denying the bizarre fertility of the author's imagination: his brilliant dialogue, his cruel humour, his repellent inventiveness. The majority of the literate public, however, will be relieved that only reviewers are obliged to look at any of it.

The effect of positing this distinction indicates how the reviewer's criticisms of the work move from aesthetic considerations to ethical ones, a similar trajectory to the one followed by Ruskin explored in Chapter 1 when he criticised architectural and sculptural grotesque in Venice. What both Ruskin and the reviewer imply is that the artist may have gifts but that such gifts are wasted when put to an ignoble or repellent use, with both the negative and more positive reactions to *The Wasp Factory* placing Banks's work firmly within the terms of the grotesque.

Textual economies and fiendish mechanisms: *The Wasp Factory*

One of the most prominent aspects of Banks's work in terms of its narrative control is the emphasis on what can be termed logical economy. This attention to the logical unfolding of narrative events underlies all of his fiction from his first published novel *The Wasp Factory* to his more recent mainstream works *The Steep Approach to Garbadale* (2007), *Transition* (2009) and *Stonemouth* (2012). This strategy can be loosely described as the 'how' of a narrative event: Banks typically describes how an event occurs by breaking it down into consecutive elements, and is often careful to distinguish between a character's relative perception of the event and the underlying process of causation. This can be seen in his novel about depressed rock star Daniel Weir *Espedair Street* (1990c first published 1987), where he includes descriptions of how elaborate visual illusions can be created by stage effects, such as 'The Great Contra-Flow Smoke Curtain' but also by the weather:

> [A]s we walked up that short hill between the dry banks, the breeze filled, and it shifted the tumbling leaves along with us, moving them slowly uphill like a strange stream backing up against the pull of gravity, spreading them and rolling them slowly up the slope at the same speed as we were walking, so that for a long and dizzying moment we seemed to walk and stand quite still together, travelling islands caught within that bright, chaotic flow, our ankles tickled by the brittle flood, our eyes tricked by the relative movement of those charging, rolling, whispering leaves.
>
> The effect lasted for only a few seconds before the wind blew stronger and the leaves outdistanced us, but for that brief time it was magical, and something so powerful and odd I could never express it. (Banks, 1990c, 98)

The narrative explicitly provides us with the explanation of the temporary effect created by the relative motion of the observers. This logical 'explanation' of a strange experience, however, does not dampen the lyricism of Daniel's description: in an example of what is a key feature of Banks's fiction the author simultaneously presents both the poetic effect and the prosaic cause. Such 'special effects' and careful outlines of their underlying origins, whether artificial or natural, have become a hallmark of the author's work, with detailed description creating a sense of possibility.

If Banks's texts often insist on the logical possibility of certain events occurring, then what we might, after Roland Barthes, call the semantic economy operating in his novels tends to be no less rigorous. In this scheme each textual element has a semantic value, that is to say each piece of information provided to the reader has a part to play in the overall semantic economy of the novel. My approach here is adopted in part from the terms used by Barthes in his book *S/Z* (1990, first published in French 1973), where he meticulously analyses Honoré de Balzac's short story 'Sarrasine'. Balzac's narrative of a sculptor's romantic obsession with someone he believes to be a woman but who turns out to be a castrato offers suggestive parallels to *The Wasp Factory* both in that it has a denouement involving mistaken sexual identity and that it shares many structural features with Banks's novel. In fact *The Wasp Factory* is in some ways a reversal of 'Sarrasine' since it is the fact of castration according to Barthes that causes the breakdown in the chain of signifiers and challenges all systems of difference in Balzac's story, whereas in *The Wasp Factory*, it is the very 'fact' of castration which turns out to be a fiction, and order (of a kind) is restored at the end of the novel.

The Wasp Factory ends in Frank's discovery that 'he' is in fact a she, resulting in a very obvious case of textual elements being retrospectively integrated into a semantic economy. Frank's father has brought him up to believe that he is a boy who lost his genitals when he was attacked by the family dog as a child, but Frank discovers that he was instead born with a female body, the development of which his father has sought to control with the surreptitious use of hormones. This fiction of castration has engendered a bizarre form of penis envy in the adolescent narrator, who carefully plots the destruction of those around him. Some of the explanation of the actions of Frank's father function so as to provide not only the mechanical explanation of how a narrative event occurred but to reinforce the internal consistency of the narrative being offered to the reader for inspection – i.e. its semantic economy. In particular, the details of Frank's father's behaviour collectively point to his act of deception: he has concealed Frank's existence from any social authority (no birth certificate or national insurance number exists for Frank) (13), he is a doctor of chemistry or biochemistry (14), he used to dress Frank's half-brother Eric up as a girl (66), he is reluctant for Frank to be examined by a doctor (94) and he has had medical training (108). Eric himself seems to be in on the secret, tapping his nose and winking slyly and on one occasion giving Frank a kiss on the lips (143). These pieces of information scattered throughout the novel have a limited semantic function until they are realigned by the revelation of Frank's sex at the end of the book.

The importance of these details is that they strengthen the consistency of the narrative of Frank's deception insofar as the elements can be viewed as mutually confirming, and they function within the overall semantic economy of the novel and authenticate the possibility of the father's secret project. Here Banks is not involved in a process of explaining each step but places elements early on in the narrative for later interpretation according to an overall scheme. The available details support, or at least do not tend to contradict, the possibility of the father's dishonesty and so have semantic significance and function in the overall narrative economy. As Barthes argues in relation to this aspect of 'Sarrasine':

> In other words, the discourse scrupulously keeps within a circle of *solidarities*, and this circle, in which 'everything holds together', is that of the readerly. As we might expect, the readerly is controlled by the principle of non-contradiction, but by multiplying solidarities, by stressing at every opportunity the *compatible* nature of circumstances, by attaching narrated events together with a kind of logical 'paste'. (Barthes, 1990, 156)

The details concerning Frank's father described in the above paragraph are exactly these types of solidarities. In this sense the semantic economy of Banks's work is 'readerly' in Barthes's formulation, i.e. it shares the set of features Barthes sees in the classic realist text. The fact that the solidarities are scattered throughout Banks's narrative strengthens this identification:

> [T]he greater the syntagmatic distance between the two data, the more skilful the narrative; the performance consists in manipulating a certain degree of impressionism: the touch must be light, as though it weren't worth remembering, and yet, appearing again later in another guise, it must already be a memory; the readerly is an effect based on the operations of solidarity (the readerly 'sticks'); but the more the solidarity is renewed, the more the intelligible becomes intelligent. (Barthes, 1990, 22–3)

Other examples of such solidarities can be seen in other enigma-driven books by Banks, where the narrative performs, in Barthes's words, a 'suspension of affinitive, already magnetised elements, before they are summoned together to take their place, economically, in the same *package*' (182). Thus the revelation of Alban Wopuld's paternity near the end of *The Steep Approach to Garbadale* casts a new light on his grandmother's earlier hostility to his romantic interest in his cousin.[3]

On a microcosmic level, this process can be seen at work in examples of estrangement where ambiguous descriptions of individual objects' appearances are followed by accounts of their nature and function; for example, the object Frank finds half-buried on the beach in *The Wasp Factory*:

> I touched the side of the tapered cylinder wonderingly, feeling something very calm and strong about it, though I didn't know why. Then I stepped back and looked again at it. Its shape became clear, and I could then guess roughly how much of it must still be buried under the sand. It was a bomb, stood on its tail. (Banks, 1990a, 68)

Banks describes what the object looks like before revealing what the object actually is, and The Factory itself is notable for being mentioned on the third line of the novel but only described in Chapter 8. The temporal gap in indicating what exactly something is or what exactly has happened runs through his work, both on the micro-textual level quoted above and on a larger scale. The chapter entitled 'What happened to Eric' in *The Wasp Factory* is a good example of temporal gaps working simultaneously on different scales, both in discrete descriptions and across the narrative as a whole.

Eric's unfortunate experience is first mentioned early on, 'I sat there and thought about Eric, to whom such an unpleasant thing happened. Poor twisted bugger' (16), but the precise occurrence is not described until Chapter 9, 'What Happened to Eric'. The narrative builds up the enigma of 'what happened' through these repeated veiled references that only give hints rather than any further information. To use structuralist terms, the temporal relation is a mixture of analepsis, in that the event Frank is narrating has happened in the 'past' of the narrative, and prolepsis, in that Banks is continually gesturing towards the future of his own narrative to the point where the enigma is revealed. This distinction can also be formulated as an event occurring in the past of the *histoire* but in the future of the *récit*. When the reader eventually reaches Chapter 9 of *The Wasp Factory*, Banks uses the same strategy:

> It was during that second year, when he was helping out in a big teaching hospital, *that it happened* ... He was doing that *the night he had his unpleasant experience* ... We got a letter explaining most of *what had happened* from a nurse who had been friendly with my brother. (Banks, 1990a, 139–40, my italics)

At this stage in the narrative, the reader is aware that what did happen was a profoundly disturbing experience for Eric and so comprehends that an unspecified horrific event has occurred in the *histoire* and may yet be presented in the *récit*. Having described Eric's actions that night, however, what Eric actually saw is postponed yet again as the narrative shifts from Eric's point of view to that of a hospital worker 'who heard Eric screaming and rushed into the ward brandishing a big spanner' (141).

Examples of enigma resolution of this kind (where the narrator claims a knowledge of the enigma but hints at it rather than revealing it) occur elsewhere in Banks's work, for example what happened to Davey in *Espedair Street*, to Frank in *The Wasp Factory*, as well as enigma resolutions of a more commonplace kind, for example, the identity of the murderous 'Radical Equaliser' in *Complicity* (1994, first published 1993) and what happened to the missing Uncle Rory in *The Crow Road* (1993a, first published 1992). As with the semantic economy described above, this structure of postponement and delayed disclosure functions to establish the possibility of truth so that 'expectation thus becomes the basic condition for truth: truth, these narratives tell us, is what is *at the end* of expectation' (Barthes, 1990, 76). The deliberate postponement of explanation found in Banks's narratives therefore itself generates the possibility of explanation, of 'truth' and the delays rhetorically establish the possibility of a truth or coherent logic adequate to the preceding events. As Barthes points out, this is again a feature of the classic, readerly text since, 'by participating in the need to set forth the *end* of every action (conclusion, interruption, closure, dénouement), the readerly declares itself to be historical' (52). This textual economy operates by establishing the 'truth', by regulating the enigma-disclosure process which itself can be reformulated as a promise-fulfilment equation in terms of the reader's expectations. One of the consequences of such narrative structuring is that the reader will find out later in the novel that the narrator's initial interpretation of specific narrative events, and thus their own reading, was incomplete. The reader, like the narrator, has been 'fooled' and their new understanding realigns the previous fictional events. As with the examples of Barthes's 'solidarities' discussed above, these reconfigurations of narrative events yield 'magnetised elements' which are only obvious on a rereading of the narratives in question, as Frank's confession that 'women are a bit too close for comfort as far as I'm concerned' (Banks, 1990a, 43) demonstrates all too clearly in retrospect.

Women are very close indeed, as Frank is later to discover. While *The Wasp Factory* is obviously an example of this reinterpretation, the same process also occurs in *Walking On Glass* (1990d, first published 1985) when Graham Park discovers that Sara ffitch, the girl he has been romantically pursuing, is actually having a secret sexual relationship with Bob Stock. What Graham interpreted as Sara's trip to the toilet, her wearing a Walkman in bed and an innocent conversation with her while she leaned out of her bedroom window, all turn out to be occasions when she was having sex with Bob Stock. Sara reveals that while talking to Graham from her bedroom window she was actually having intercourse with Bob Stock behind her, which leads to a humorous re-reading experience:

> He [Graham] thought suddenly how she must look, seen from inside the kitchen she was leaning out of; an ugly sexual idea occurred to him, and he looked about for the big black BMW bike [Bob Stock's motorcycle], but it wasn't there...
> 'Maybe,' she shrugged. Her eyes seemed to wander away from him, scanning the horizon. 'Ah,' she said, 'the Post Office Tower.'
> He turned round, looking south and west, though he knew he couldn't see the tall building from the street. (Banks, 1990d, 101)

Banks of course 'magnetises', to use Barthes's phrase, such a scene by hinting at a sexual event ('an ugly sexual idea occurred to him') and one might argue that his hand is too heavy for the 'impressionism' of Barthes's 'readerly' as the hint also involves the eventual 'co-respondent' Bob Stock. On the second reading, the reader is also aware of the later re-realignment produced by the further disclosure that 'Bob Stock' is in fact Graham's friend (and Sara's brother) Slater. This information leads to another set of ironic solidarities when re-reading the novel, including Graham having 'only ever met one of Slater's (supposedly many) lovers, at least as far as he knew' (15).

What these examples indicate is the coherence Banks *builds*, and I use the term consciously, into his books. We are presented with readerly texts in Barthes's sense, a quality only confirmed by the solidarities that are later integrated into the reader's understanding of the narrative and reconfirmed by re-reading when ironic elements are reinterpreted: 'I finely work my books, and construct them so that it should be possible and rewarding to read them again, and get more out of it' (Eggar, 1997, 21). The textual economies I have outlined help the text 'hang together' so in Barthes's words 'the readerly sticks'. A favoured narrative structure of Banks is where twin narrative strands are created through the ordering of sections or sometimes entire chapters in the novel so that two (or more) narratives alternate in sequence. My earlier example of the 'What Happened to Eric' chapter in *The Wasp Factory* is representative of this kind of narrative structure where there are two narrative strands moving forwards in time: one in the present (Frank waiting for Eric to return to the island) and one in the past (what happened to Eric, what happened to Frank). As the reader moves through the narrative present, they also move forwards through a narrative past 'adequate' to that present, that is, a past which does not contradict the present and which is in solidarity with the present. Michel Butor describes just such a structure in 'Research on the Technique of the Novel' (1970, first published in French 1964):

> When the episodes told by 'flashback' are also arranged in chronological order, there occurs a superimposition of two temporal sequences, like two voices in music ... Through the dialogue between these two 'voices' a 'density' or a psychological 'depth' is created. (Butor, 1970, 18–19)

The scare quotes employed by Butor signal a suitably sceptical attitude to the usefulness of 'density' and 'depth' in this context, and a suspicion of the physical register involved in such metaphors. What I wish to draw attention to is the extremely formal nature of these 'solidarities' that Banks creates: it is his adoption of the kind of structure that Butor describes that further allies Banks's fiction with the readerly in his creation (by formal means) of a 'density' or psychological 'depth'. The interweaving of narrative strands formally establishes the narrative past as having a bearing on the narrative present so that we journey through Frank's and Eric's pasts in order to find out why they commit their violent acts.

This structure of twin narratives is found in many of Banks's work, both mainstream (*The Wasp Factory*, *The Bridge*, *Complicity*, *The Crow Road*, *Espedair Street*) and science fiction (*Use of Weapons* (1992, first published 1990), *Against a Dark Background* (1993b), *Inversions* (1998)). This arrangement of narrative, by its form, offers the past as the logical origin of the present, and as the principal causal force in the story so that the past of the *histoire* offers the 'solution' to the present. What Butor's model offers is a means of appreciating how the formal structuring of Banks's novels creates a readerly effect in which textual details are integrated within an overall temporal and logical schema. This effect of cohesion is of a kind with the sense of authorial fabrication and the controlled flow of information to Banks's reader, including enigma-resolution and estrangement followed by revelation and anticipating second readings

Desiring structure: *The Bridge*

As has become clear in my discussion of the different textual economies operating in Banks's fiction, the author's attention to the details of specific mechanisms is a feature that runs through almost all his fiction. This attention is apparent both in terms of narrative detail and on a broader thematic level. To take an earlier example, Frank in *The Wasp Factory* describes all the various materials needed to construct a kite large enough to carry his cousin Esmerelda off the ground and out to sea. The logical economy can be seen as a drive to assert the logical possibility of something happening, and the role of mechanisms in Banks's work is often to support this drive by asserting the physical possibility of a specific object: in the example above, the scale and toughness of the materials necessary for a kite to be powerful enough to sweep the girl away. *The Wasp Factory* contains other physical descriptions of the mechanics of constructing objects such as the wasp candles (Banks, 1990a, 47) and the Factory itself (120–4), *Complicity* describes the method by which various mechanisms cause death, while characters in *A Song of Stone* (1997) end up being killed by the four elements. Such descriptions not only insist on the theoretical possibility of such devices but also emphasise the materiality of the objects involved, specifying how they are manufactured, how the individual elements are assembled and how they work in concert. Banks explores in detail the physical means by which something may be effected and this insistence on physical detail tends to reinforce the wider logical economy at work in the novels since the reader is given both the broad logic of the construction and its physical manifestation. When a constructed object is described in Banks's fiction, it is accompanied by the description of its mechanism and how it functions. His descriptions of manufactured objects, whether small- or large-scale, industrial or artistic, frequently attend both to their function and to their aesthetic beauty, and in fact signal the interpenetration of aesthetic and functional value-systems in how the objects are regarded. The protagonist of *The Bridge* struggles with an apprehension of a locomotive that is simultaneously aesthetic and technical:

> All he knew was that having seen that pounding, stationary engine, *anything* was possible. He had never been able to describe the original experience to his own satisfaction, and he had never tried to explain that feeling to Andrea, because he could never fully explain it to himself. (Banks, 1990b, 111)

This combination of sensitivity to technical power and difficulty in articulating emotion to his lover will become the key dynamic of the novel, and a shaping force in both the protagonist's real life in contemporary Scotland and his experiences in the fantasy world of the Bridge.

As well as codes and mechanisms, Banks's fiction also includes examples of different kinds of games. We have the various nasty games played by Frank in *The Wasp Factory*, the Black River game played by Prentice and his brother in *The Crow Road* (Banks, 1993a, 329–31), the fictional computer game 'Despot' played by Cameron in *Complicity* and the popular board game that is the source of the Wopuld family's wealth in *The Steep Approach to Garbadale*. One of Banks's most popular science fiction novels, *The Player of Games* (1988), involves a society where social and political status is decided by one's ability as a player of a complex game, similar to the game played by the quasi-monastic group in Hermann Hesse's *The Glass Bead Game* (1972, first published in German 1943). To broaden the issue somewhat, Banks's work often involves puzzles to which we are given clues, for example the name of Orr's real-world self (Alexander Lennox) in *The Bridge*, and the way Banks's texts offer ironic re-readings (as discussed above) can also be considered a game. The concept of games and of play therefore runs through this author's fiction, both in terms of invented games described in the books and in the operation of the narratives themselves. Recalling my earlier discussion of the grotesque, play figures in many ways as the master index of the grotesque for Ruskin as he attempted to divide the grotesque into subcategories according to the type of play (wise play, necessary play, inordinate play and absence of play) involved. The mechanisms of games in Bank's work can therefore be seen as part of the wider interest in mechanism, and as implicated in the discourse of the grotesque (with its tension between that which is serious and that which is playful). The awareness of being a pawn in someone else's game is a common one:

> For many of Banks's characters, the solution to the discovery that they have been trapped in such a game is to accept, themselves, the very role scripted for them – to play consciously and better the game which they did not realise they had been playing. (Craig, 2002, 20)

Indeed, an important narrative focus of many of Banks's first-person novels such as *The Wasp Factory*, *Complicity* and *The Steep Approach to Garbadale* centres on protagonists' growing realisation of wider, perhaps sinister, machinations surrounding them and their subsequent dilemma as to how to act on the basis of such knowledge.

At this stage in my discussion, it is clear that Banks's work is heavily concerned with structure both in terms of narrative structure and in terms of structure as a primary theme. The two most powerful examples of structure in Banks's work are the figure of the castle, which occurs throughout both his mainstream fiction and science fiction, and the figure of the bridge in the novel of the same name. I will begin by exploring the importance of structure in *The Bridge*, which opens with what appears to be the monologue of someone trapped in a car after a crash. What follows this opening section entitled 'Coma' is the story of John Orr, an amnesiac living on a structure called the Bridge that stretches across an ocean with no land in sight at either end. Orr is trying (with the help of a Dr Joyce) to regain his memory but has strange dreams involving what appears to be the barbarian hero of a sword-and-sorcery book who communicates in a Scottish accent. Orr also sees the image of a man in a hospital bed on his television screen. Mixed in with the narratives of Orr and the barbarian is a realist narrative dealing with the story of someone (who, we later find out, via two textual clues, is called Alexander Lennox) growing up in contemporary Scotland. How these three narratives are related is signalled by the opening section: Lennox is in a coma after a car-crash on the Forth Road Bridge and the subsequent narrative is his dreams while unconscious – dreams haunted by warped images of the adjacent Forth Rail Bridge.

The narrative is structured in geological periods (sections are titled Triassic, Eocene, and so on) and these geological terms are used in chronological order and so can be read as stages of consciousness which progress towards the present as Lennox progresses towards waking up in a hospital. Geological changes in rock are also used as a metaphor for human growth: 'we live the life of rocks; first igneous as children, metamorphic in our prime, sedimentary in our sedentary dotage' (Banks, 1990b, 211). As with Banks's other works, a clear logical connection shapes the links between the Bridge and the real world: because Lennox is an engineer with an interest in geology, the narrative sections are named after geological periods, and the society of the Bridge is a quasi-Victorian one in which engineers are accorded great respect. As well as permeating the novel's structure and themes this engineering, mechanistic view extends to the narrative's tropes as Lennox (in the realist narrative strand) likens his lover's body to a machine: 'He told her her aureoles were like pink washers, her nipples like little marshmallow bolts, and the tiny puckered slits at their tips like slots for a screwdriver' (208). As both Ronald Binns (1990) and Lucie Armitt (1996) note, the geologically labelled structure of the narrative mirrors the structure of the Bridge in the novel, which is the structure of the actual Forth Railway Bridge (near to where Banks grew up and now lives).[4]

The discourse of engineering also pervades Orr's description of his lover Abberlaine's clothing and body:

> Xs; that pattern within a pattern, covering her legs, another meshing beyond our own. The zig-zagging lace of her camiknickers, the criss-crossing ribbon holding the silk across her body; those straps and lines, the sheathed arms like stockinged legs themselves; a language, an architecture. Cantilevers and tubes, suspension ties; the dark lines of the suspenders crossing her curved upper thigh, under the knickers and down to the thick black stocking-top. Caissons, structural tubes, the engineering of these soft materials to contain and conceal and reveal that softness within. (Banks, 1990b, 175)

This lyrical description that blends the structural with the erotic evokes Orr's idiosyncratic blurring of these two domains, whereas his real-world counterpart Lennox, despite his professional and financial success, finds that his relationship to Andrea is a persistent course of anxiety and dissatisfaction. The technical expertise and the supposed control that he has exerted over his career do not extend to his emotions and love life, and Lennox's struggle both to articulate and to resolve such feelings produces a fantasy where he ends up talking to a machine because, as the machine tells him, he is not frightened of machines, while people are another matter (277). The disintegration of Orr's privileged status and comfortable life on the Bridge leads him to set out on a dangerous quest to find out his real identity, a journey that will eventually see Lennox wake up in his hospital bed.

There is a reciprocal movement in *The Bridge*, so that as well as the repeated emphasis on the human body as a structure or machine, the Bridge is compared to a body:

> There are small buildings and large ones; offices, wards, workshops, dwellings and shops, all stuck like angular limpets of metal, glass and wood to the massive tubes and interweaving girders of the bridge itself, jumbled and squeezed and squashed between the original structure's red-painted members like brittle hernias popping out between immense collections of muscles. (Banks, 1990b, 35–6)

Orr also notes the tendency towards grotesque machine–body hybrids in the artwork of the Bridge's inhabitants. The grotesque mixture of engineering and biological elements is reminiscent of Swiss artist H.R. Giger's *Biomechanoid* and *Biomechanical Landscape* series (see Giger 1996) as the extract below demonstrates:

> Worse than the poor execution, though, is the downright unhealthy preoccupation with distortions of the human form which all the artists appear to share. The sculptors have twisted it into a bizarre resemblance of the structures of the bridge itself; thighs become caissons, torsos either caissons or structural tubes, and arms and legs stressed girders; sections of bodies are constructed from riveted iron painted bridge red; tubular girders become limbs, merging into grotesque conglomerations of metal and flesh like tumorous miscegenistic eruptions of cell and grain. (Banks, 1990b, 74)

This grotesque is the grotesque of the hybrid, a grotesque and illegitimate (con)fusion of categories which Orr terms 'miscegenistic'. Metamorphosis is both theme and part of the structure of the novel since it is the title of the last of the three main sections of the novel. Banks ironically metamorphoses this word to create the names of the other sections: 'Metaphormosis' (the Bridge is a mysterious metaphor, as is the castle) and 'Metamorpheus', which suggests both Morpheus, the god of sleep and dreams, and 'Orpheus', the mythic hero who must journey to the underworld (in Orr/Lennox's case his unconscious) to find his love. Probably the most famous account of Orpheus's journey is given by Ovid in his collection of poetry *Metamorphoses*, from which Kafka borrowed the title for his grotesque short story in which Gregor Samsa wakes up as an insect.

As well as recalling Kafka's 'Metamorphosis', Banks's fiction through its interest in castles recalls Kafka's novel *The Castle* (1998, first published in German 1926). Like the strange *soi-disant* surveyor in Kafka's book who is always trying to get closer to the centre of the Castle's hierarchy, so at the outset the amnesiac Orr is a mystery (both to himself and to the reader) as he tries to navigate his way through the mysterious social and physical structure that is the Bridge. Both Victor Sage (1996) and Binns (1990) suggest the influence of Mervyn Peake's *Gormenghast* trilogy on *Walking on Glass* and *The Bridge*. Castles or their equivalents run through Banks's work, as Victor Sage notes (1996, 22–3) and the castle, Banks seems at pains to show us, is also the arch-symbol for the human psyche, something borne out by interviews and also suggested (twice) in *The Bridge*.[5] Banks's novel *A Song of Stone* (1997) explores the figure of the castle at length, specifically as the solidification of a particular intent, a song made into stone:

> Here is the house militant, a blocked-in enterprise huddled round a private, guarded void, its banners and its flags flown flagrant to the vulgar, following winds; a mailed fist prevailing against all levelling air. (Banks, 1997, 197)

The title of *A Song of Stone* had occurred earlier in Banks's work in a description in *The Bridge* of a prison composed of several buried cylindrical buildings that can be rotated so as to change the configuration of the interlinking corridors, confusing anyone trying to escape. An official asks Orr if he knows what the prison is an image of: 'A lock! He says triumphantly, eyes flashing. It is a poem; *a song in metal and rock*. A perfect, real image of its purpose; a lock, a safe, a set of tumblers; a safe place to store evil' (1990b, 223, my italics). The image of the prison is a perfect counterpart to the intention the structure embodies, that of locking people away. In the same way, in *A Song of Stone* the castle functions as both a physical and symbolic embodiment of the political intent behind its construction, in this case the elevation (physically and socially) of an elite over the commonality of people (the air is 'all levelling' but the castle resolutely asserts and defends its privileges). This fusion of form and function, and the interest in something whose formal structure 'embodies' a specific purpose as well as 'performing' it, is clearly emblematic of Bank's oeuvre as a whole. The interest in form and in objects is one also found in a particular form of European fiction, the *nouveau roman*.

The European and Scottish Banks

We can see a web of influences from writers outside literature in English such as Gunter Grass (particularly the grotesque images of *The Tin Drum*) Franz Kafka (*The Trial* and *The Castle* but also some of Kafka's shorter works) and Herman Hesse (*The Glass Bead Game*). We also have the interest in games and codes that recall the stories of Italo Calvino and Jorge Luis Borges. One literary tradition that may share affinities with Banks's writing is that of the *nouveau roman*, particularly when we consider the emphasis in Banks's work on the physicality of objects. Parallels between the work of *nouveau romancier* Michel Butor and Banks can be seen in their shared interest in geology: Butor's *Portrait de l'Artiste en Jeune Singe* (1967) has a chapter entitled 'Minéralogie', while Banks structures *The Bridge* according to geological periods. Orr, as *The Bridge* is unable to resist making explicit (Banks, 1990b, 233), can be seen as 'ore', an identity buried in geological strata. Butor's *L'Emploi du Temps* (1957) contains recurrent images of fire, air and water, just as Bank's *A Song of Stone* mobilises the four elements; the narrator Abel is morally soiled by his earthy childhood experience in a ditch, his lover is drowned in the Castle's moat, the lieutenant, through the ingenious use of a windmill, is destroyed by air and the castle is burnt down at the end of the book.[6] Banks's structuring techniques are thus reminiscent of this aspect of the *nouveau roman*, and we can also see *L'Emploi du Temps*'s motifs of fire, ash and sand in the recurrent motif of glass in *The Crow Road*. In *The Crow Road* it is glass, the product of sand and fire, which is the source of Uncle Fergus's wealth; Fergus lives in Gaineamh ('Sand') Castle; Fergus's gift of a necklace made from fulgurite (sand struck by lightning) to his niece is also glass, as are the table Prentice breaks when arguing with his father, the display case that the adolescent Fergus breaks with Lachy's head, Lachy's prosthetic eye, the paperweight Prentice is struck on the head with, the chandelier in Mrs Ippot's house, the crystal bowl which sings as Prentice and Ash make love, and the window through which a naked Prentice waves to Ash at the end of the novel (her very name forming part of the field of reference). *The Crow Road* was 'was something I wrote, fairly consciously, as a family book' (Bragg, 1997) and uses a single material, glass, to trace the complex variations that can issue from a common source.

Viewing Banks's work through the prism of Scottish national identity, as Thom Nairn does in his essay 'Iain Banks and the Fiction Factory' (1993) produces a different but in some ways complementary image to Banks as a writer obsessed with formal structure in the European tradition. Nairn points out that in *The Bridge* the fact that the semi-literate Scots-speaking barbarian is shackled to his RP-speaking familiar has as much to do with that state of the Union as it does with the inside of Lennox's head (Nairn, 1993, 133). Dorothy McMillan follows a similar track in regarding the use of glass in *The Crow Road* (discussed above) as evidence of Banks working through issues of national identity: 'Glass wonderfully figures the unity in diversity to which the idea of the nation aspires' (McMillan, 1995, 90). Berthold Schoene-Harwood attacks Nairn's approach to *The Wasp Factory* and accuses him of resuscitating 'the stereotyping myth of the Caledonian antisyzygy' and being 'insensitive to the possible gender-specificity of the *dopplegänger* motif' (Schoene-Harwood, 2000, 105). While Schoene-Harwood's gender-oriented reading of the novel is a valuable corrective to the possible univocal manner of Scottish criticism, his attack on Nairn itself seems univocal in underplaying how Nairn's essay also emphasises the affinities between Banks's novels *The Bridge* and *Walking on Glass* and work by writers such as Gunter Grass and J.G. Ballard, remarking that 'the antisyzygy, after all, is far from exclusively Caledonian' (Schoene-Harwood, 2000, 128). Shoene-Harwood makes much of Frank's reflections on dam building (Banks, 1990a, 25) as a metaphor for the adolescent's thwarted gender identity (his chapter on *The Wasp Factory* is entitled 'Dams Burst'). However, the influence of the grotesque cartoons of Charles Addams in this scenario is also clear, as can be seen by the resemblance of Frank's dam game to the cartoon of a boy filling a bath holding a toy town, from Addams's *Monster Rally* (1950).[7] Nairn also highlights the importance of Alasdair Gray's novel *Lanark*

(1982, first published 1981), which is a clear (and acknowledged) influence on the form of *The Bridge*.[8]

While *The Bridge* shares with *Lanark* its interweaving of fantastic and realist narrative and its re-visioning of a specific place (for Gray his native Glasgow, for Banks the Forth Railway Bridge near his home in North Queensferry), it is important for the purposes of this study to note the prevalence of the grotesque in both works, often as a quality associated with visual art. In *Lanark* the art student Duncan Thaw repeatedly meets with resistance to the grotesque in his paintings, both from his teachers (Gray, 1982, 229) and from a girl he desires, to whom he responds: 'I may have drawn them grotesque. Not many of us are as we should be, even in our own estimations, so how can we help being grotesque?' (280). Orr in *The Bridge* has a similar negative reaction to Abberlaine's painting of trains which 'are grotesque, gnarled things, like giant maggots or decaying tree trunks' (Banks, 1990b, 122). Banks's grotesque lending of mechanical aspects to the human body and vice versa, discussed above, finds its equivalent in *Lanark* in Thaw's reflections on his interest in the grotesque:

> Everyone carried on their necks a grotesque art object, originally inherited, which they never tired of altering and adding to. Yet while he looked on people with the cold interest usually felt for things, the world of things began to cause surprising emotions. A haulage vehicle carrying a huge piece of bright yellow machinery swelled his heart with tenderness and stiffened his penis with lust. A section of tenement, the surface a dirty yellow plaster with oval holes through which brickwork showed, gave the eerie conviction he was beholding a kind of flesh. (Gray, 1982, 228)

Here again the grotesque is the interpenetration and swapping of human and mechanical characteristics. While Gray and Banks thus share a focus on the grotesque in their work, this may not make Banks's work 'more Scottish' in some straightforward way. As I have shown throughout this study, the grotesque is both a long and a wide tradition in European art and literature and it is perhaps as much through their common interest in the grotesque, in elaborate structuring devices and in hybrid realist/fantasy narratives, rather than their Scottishness that the parallels between Banks and Gray should be understood. Gavin Wallace in 'Voices in Empty Houses: The Novel of Damaged Identity' (1993) seems wedded to the idea of Caledonian antisyzygy[9] and asserts that:

> In English novels, the deranged, the desperate, the neurotic and the variously addicted might provide the odd deviant diversion to emphasise the reassuring normality of everything else. In Scottish novels, they are narrators and protagonists, rarely, if ever, fully in control of their existences, and morbidly aware of the fact. (Wallace, 1993, 217–18)

The diversity and sheer volume of the grotesque in the work of Carter, Amis, McEwan, Self and Litt examined in this study, to say nothing of Patrick McGrath, Jeanette Winterson and others, undermine any such claim for the English novel, while work by writers such as Patrick McCabe, Dermot Bolger and Mike McCormack populate Irish fiction with the deranged, the desperate and the neurotic. Antisyzygy and its cognates can no longer be seen as a distinctively Caledonian phenomenon.

David Punter in the second volume of *The Literature of Terror* (1996) discusses *The Wasp Factory* under 'contemporary Gothic transformations' although his description of the book is brief and does not make explicit the links between Banks and the gothic. Victor Sage is more methodical and focused in his approach and identifies Mary Shelley's *Frankenstein* as the novel's gothic influence: 'Frank's is the story of Frankenstein's monster written ironically from the monster's deceived point of view, and set in the world of the 1980s' (Sage, 1996, 24). We might add to Sage's account that Banks makes this debt clear early on in the novel in Frank's description of his half-brother Eric's birth:

> The first Mrs Cauldhame, Mary, who was Eric's mother, died in childbirth in the house. Eric's head was too big for her; she haemorrhaged and bled to death on the marital bed in 1960. Eric has suffered from quite severe migraine all his life, and I am very much inclined to attribute the ailment to his manner of entry into the world. The whole thing about his migraine and his dead

mother had, I think, a lot to do with What Happened to Eric. (Banks, 1990a, 23)

This allusion to Mary Shelley's own birth, which caused the death of her mother Mary Wollstonecraft, helps develop the Frankenstein parallels and Frank, like Shelley's monster, is the result of an experiment to create an artificial man.[10] Sage's incorporation of Banks's book into the gothic tradition, however, does not address the important ways in which the novel invokes the gothic only to distance itself from it. Whereas Shelley's monster resembles Rousseau's natural man and is a Romantic being capable of sensitive feelings and virtuous actions, Banks's Frank takes his/her cue from the defiantly non-romantic *Lord of the Flies* and devotes him/herself to sadism, ritual and murder. While Sage argues that Frank's case reveals 'the paradox that (1) gender is socially not biologically determined; but that (2) if religion and the Law of the Father were proved to be historically unnecessary, they would have to be re-invented' (1996, 27), he may be over-emphasising the extent to which Frank's aggression and sadism occur in a vacuum, despite the island setting and the *Lord of the Flies*-style devotion to ritual.

Frank's self-fashioning may in fact owe more to imitation than invention and if we follow Judith Butler in thinking of gender as performance without an origin, then Frank's view of women becomes an indictment of wider cultural prejudices:

> Women, *I know from watching hundreds – maybe thousands – of films and television programmes*, cannot withstand really major things happening to them; they get raped, or their loved one dies, and they go to pieces, go crazy and commit suicide, or just pine away until they die. (Banks, 1990a, 147–8, my italics)

The Wasp Factory emphasises again and again that it is the wider culture that teaches Frank the sexist attitudes and the sense of loss that lead him to 'out-man' (183) those around him to compensate for the loss of his fictional manhood:

> Lacking, as one might say, one will, I forged another ... reciprocating in my angry innocence the emasculation I could not then fully

appreciate, but somehow – through the attitude of others perhaps – sensed as an unfair, irrecoverable loss ... and so I became the killer, a small image of the ruthless soldier-hero *almost all I've ever seen or read seems to pay strict homage to*. (Banks, 1990a, 183, my italics)

The social construction of gender is foregrounded in these reflections and the novel eventually shows that Frank is not a monster and is in fact a physically normal girl. We see another invocation of Romantic gothic in the killing of Frank's cousin Esmerelda (her name recalling Hugo's monster's love in *Notre Dame de Paris*). Having first disposed of her by creating a giant kite to carry her off the island and out to sea, Frank wonders what has happened to her:

I would like to think that she died still being floated by the giant kite, that she went round the world and rose higher as she died of starvation and dehydration and so grew less weighty still, to become, eventually, a tiny skeleton riding the jetstreams of the planet; a sort of Flying Dutchwoman. But I doubt that such a *romantic* vision really matches the truth. (Banks, 1990a, 95, my italics)

Banks holds out this pseudo-Wagnerian romantic vision, but only to reject it and while the (rewritten) gothic is one element of Banks's work, to overemphasise it risks ignoring the visceral nature of its images and events, its frequent hybrid mixture of realist and fantastic narratives and, the subject of the rest of this chapter, the tension in the books between the probable and the possible, the readerly and the bizarre, form and force.

Form and force

My analysis up to now has had as its central focus the textual economies and attention to structure and mechanisms exhibited by Banks's fiction. We have seen how the economies of the texts ally his work with Barthes's readerly text and how structure and geometry inform his writing. It is no surprise, therefore, to find that Banks's own descriptions of his work echo this conception of his fiction as constructed: '*The Bridge* is more intrinsically complicated [than *The*

Wasp Factory]. It's a much more complicated machine. I'm proud of having constructed it and the fact that it still works' (Furniss, 1996, 4). This concern with shape and form permeates his fiction, from the overall structure of the novels, to delayed disclosure, twin narrative strands, character motivation and the mechanics of strange events and contraptions. Banks's metaphor of the book as a machine encompasses this geometrical and economic approach to form. The author's narratives continually assert the possibility of the events depicted taking place and he has spoken in interview of his drive to produce detailed descriptions of sometimes unpleasant scenes:

> When I write the scenes it is a technical exercise. My emotional self is saying 'this is an awful, terrible, obscene thing', but as far as I'm concerned it is happening in the reality of the book, and therefore it has to be described as well as possible. The role of a novelist is never to compromise. (Eggar, 1997, 21)

As I have explored in relation to *The Bridge*, this idea of a tension between technical requirement and emotional response is an enduring one in Banks's fiction and raises questions about the limits of form and structure.

If we adopt *nouveau roman* pioneer Alain Robbe-Grillet's metaphor of a police investigation (1963, 21) for the logical structure of a novel, then each of Banks's mainstream novels, as a readerly text, according to Barthes:

> assumes the careful and suspicious mien of an individual afraid of being caught in some flagrant contradiction; it is always on the lookout and always, just in case, preparing its defence against the enemy that may force it to acknowledge the scandal of some illogicality, some disturbance of the 'common sense.' (Barthes, 1990, 156)

Banks's science fiction, on the other hand, does not, for generic reasons, have the same insistence on possibility but rather partakes in a generic emphasis on the plausibility of the events depicted. The distinction between the two strands of Banks's writing might therefore be made in the terms Aristotle uses to discuss probability and poetry in that Banks's science fiction deals with probable impossibilities while his mainstream fiction is in the business of improbable possibilities. To return to the *nouveau roman* for a moment, one common point of reference between Banks and the *nouveau roman* is the work of Kafka, as demonstrated by Robbe-Grillet, arguing in 'Du Réalisme à la Réalité' (in 1963, revised from 1955) against the tendency to label Kafka's fiction absurd:

> Le monde visible de ses romans est bien, pour lui, le monde réel, et ce qu'il y a derrière (s'il y a quelque chose) paraît sans valeur, face à l'évidence des objets, gestes, paroles, etc. L'effet d'hallucination provient de leur netteté extraordinaire, et non de flottements ou de brumes. Rien n'est plus fantastique, en définitive, que la précision. (Robbe-Grillet, 1963, 141–2)

> The visible world of his novels is actually, for him, the real world, and that which is behind it (if there is anything behind it) appears valueless, faced with the evidence of objects, gestures, speech, etc. The effect of hallucination comes from their extraordinary clearness, and not from hesitations or mists. Nothing is more fantastic, finally, than precision.(my translation)

This precision-created fantasy is a paradox, and it is the conflict between the precision of the narrative and the strangeness of the events depicted that McEwan also identifies with Kafka in the quote used as the epigraph to this chapter. What McEwan sees in Kafka is equally applicable to the improbable possibilities of Banks's fiction: a tension between a realist economic form on the one hand and the collection of strange events described on the other. If, in Barthes's readerly, 'everything sticks' then when we come to Banks's stories it is clear that things have become seriously unstuck: the reader encounters a vibrator-wielding attacker (*Complicity*), an exploding granny (*The Crow Road*), gender deception (*The Wasp Factory*), a hard-drinking dog (*Espedair Street*), death by lightning strike (*The Crow Road*), by windmill (*Song of Stone*) and by kite (*The Wasp Factory*), to name but a few of the oddities found along the way.

Contradiction, in Harpham's analysis, is the central characteristic of the grotesque, and my discussion of Banks's fiction has shown how approaching his work in terms of the grotesque draws out the central contradictions in his novels. Among these tensions between terms we have improbable possibilities versus probable impossibilities, the readerly versus bizarre events, control versus play and humour versus horror. McEwan's account of Kafka also suggests an important tension visible in Banks between form and content, or rather between a specific kind of form and a specific kind of content. Deleuze and Guattari in *Kafka: Toward a Minor Literature* (1986, first published in French 1975) describe Kafka's work as a 'rhizome' or burrow and refer to the 'sobriety' of his 'writing machine' (19). Drunkenness, as was discussed in the first chapter, was a characteristic of the grotesque for Ruskin, Baudelaire and many other critics. Seen from this perspective, Banks's writing is both sober and drunk: sober in its control, its dryness, its readerly economy, but drunk in its bizarre playfulness, its repellent imagery and its unlikely happenings. The apparent paradox of such a description of Banks's work, and its connection to the grotesque can be illuminated by a closer examination of the foundations both of form and of that which might exceed it.

Andrew Gibson in *Towards a Postmodern Theory of Narrative* (1996) uses the work of Jacques Derrida and Gilles Deleuze, among others, to launch an attack on structuralist narratology as exemplified by work by Gérard Genette and Tzvetan Todorov. Of central significance in his attack on this kind of narratology is its reliance on what he calls geometrical thought:

> The virtue of geometrical thought is that it releases us from merely linear models. But that virtue is compromised, because geometrical segmentations appear according to an irreversible and, above all, a univocal order. (Gibson, 1996, 20)

Narratology, then, as practised by critics such as Todorov and Genette, may end up imposing a pre-determined pattern on the texts being scrutinised, where the elements are integrated into an overall structural geometry of narrative. The challenge to the contemporary critic, therefore, is to 'seek to deconstruct the methodological procedure which moves from imbricated narrative text to its clear reformulation in geometric terms' (Gibson, 1996, 23). The fiction of Banks presents an interesting case for such an approach, exhibiting, as I have described, a use of geometry both in terms of narrative architectonics and in terms of textual images and figures. A useful parallel to this is discussed in Jacques Derrida's essay 'Force and Signification' (1978, first published in French 1963), in which he critiques Jean Rousset's book on Corneille *Forme et Signification*. The parallel lies in the fact that Rousset suggests that the reason for the geometrical nature of his analysis of Corneille lies in the dramatist's own preoccupation with symmetry, something to which Derrida draws attention:

> At the beginning of the essay entitled '*Polyeucte*, or the Ring and the Helix,' the author [Rousset] prudently warns us that if he insists upon 'schemas that might appear excessively geometrical, it is because Corneille, more than any other, practised symmetry.' (Derrida, 1978, 17)

Derrida goes on to criticise Rousset's reading of Corneille for subordinating Corneille's plays to a critical conception of 'the Corneillean movement' (19), a hypostasised form in which everything is symmetrical and unified. Rousset's pursuit of form, Derrida argues, means that the supposed triumph of Corneille's plays is actually the triumph of Rousset's excessively geometrised conception of them and so ultimately a (in Derrida's terms 'violent') triumph of form over force.

If we map Derrida's comments onto my earlier account of Banks's work it becomes clear that an account which pays attention *only* to the qualities of geometrical structure exhibited by his novels risks committing the same critical procedure. If, as Derrida claims, 'the relief and design of structures appears more clearly when content, which is the living energy of meaning, is neutralised' (5), then a critical assessment of Banks's work must go beyond an examination of the form and economy of the novels. To approach the grotesque in Banks's fiction is to attempt to discuss this content, so we must avoid neutralising the texts' energies. Derrida contends that within the Western, Classical tradition we have seen meaning as produced only by system, only by form and economy, whereas he now proposes that meaning is now to be seen as emerging not from form, but from that which exceeds it, namely, force, quality and duration. Derrida is working to open up narrative criticism to that which it had previously frequently ignored or sidelined i.e. force, that which resists form and which cannot be understood using Rousset-style narrative descriptions because it is not amenable to inclusion in formal, economic or geometric models.

Barthes's readerly form rhetorically establishes a 'truth' at the end of the reader's expectation, a 'coherent' logic adequate to the events described; however, while Banks's fiction frequently exhibits a readerly form, we might question whether a logic adequate to the events described in much of his fiction actually exists. In these texts paradoxically the formal rhetoric of the readerly may be experienced as exactly that, a *rhetoric* based on *form*. The combination of this rhetoric and economy on the one hand and the bizarre events on the other is what creates the odd effect one experiences on reading Banks's books. To return to my starting point, it is this quality that the reviewers of *The Wasp Factory* are responding to, in their attempt to read *The Wasp Factory* as a 'realist' work, to read its economy and its form when they encounter grotesque excess and overloading. This pattern of response is manifested in the economic discourse employed by many of the reviewers of the book: 'bizarre fertility', 'the novelist's satiric intention is overwhelmed by his relish for exorbitant brutalities', 'there's a potential here where the author has starved and wormed it'. Sage reads such reactions to the novel in another way:

> [T]here are signs in the reviews that the novel [*The Wasp Factory*] is often *misread*. Thom Nairn has complained about the way English reviewers have missed the jokes in the novel because they aren't Scots, but I think that the reason might also be that *they read it over-naturalistically*. (Sage, 1996, 24, my italics)

Sage posits his barbarian/culture dynamic (a 'central dialectic' in Banks's work) as an improvement on such 'over-naturalistic misreading', but his solution risks substituting one partial model of the text for another and tends to elevate the 'gothic Banks' over the 'readerly Banks'. Walter Benjamin's essay on Kafka (1969, first published in German 1955) is salutary on this point: 'There are two ways to miss the point of Kafka's works. One is to interpret them naturally, the other is the supernatural interpretation' (Benjamin, 1969, 127). As Réda Bensmaïa (1986) elaborates:

> Benjamin was one of the first 'readers' of Kafka to see and then try to show – to demonstrate – that Kafka's work was, from a certain point of view, to be taken literally: in a word, that it functioned on the surface of its signs and that the issue was not – at least, not *only* – to try to interpret it but, above all, to practice it as an experimental machine, a machine for effects, as in physics. (Bensmaïa, 1986, xi)

Applying Benjamin's approach to Banks suggests that Sage's cultural dialectic and the contrasting 'over-naturalistic' reviewers may be, through their partiality, the two ways to miss the point of Banks's works, the readerly form and the macabre and bizarre events of which constitute texts that are, like the works of Kafka, a grotesque mix of the naturalistic and the excessive.

This paradox within Banks's fiction arises from the contradictions of its formal qualities of clarity, economy and control and its persistent drive to violate such regulation. If we are to focus critically on Banks's work then our need to attend to the grotesque now becomes apparent:

> The force of the work, the force of genius, the force, too, of that which engenders in general is precisely that which resists geometrical metaphorisation and is the proper object of literary criticism. (Derrida, 1978, 20)

The critic's task then becomes the exploration of that which resists form in Banks's work, which is precisely the realm of the grotesque in his fiction: the violent deaths, the blurring of mechanical and organic and the macabre detailing of repellent events that populate his novels. Derrida's claim that Rousset thinks that the only form that is beautiful is 'the form that is aligned with meaning, the form that can be understood because it is, above all, *in league* with meaning' (20, my italics) recalls my earlier discussion of Barthes's *S/Z*, where Barthes writes of the solidarities of the readerly text causing the 'intelligible to become intelligent'. What Barthes is emphasising is that it is through form that the readerly establishes its realist credentials, that the readerly *rhetorically* establishes its 'truth', fulfilling the '(ideological) goal of this technique ... to naturalise meaning and thus to give credence to the reality of the story' (Barthes, 1990, 23).

Banks himself is quite open about the idea that the rhetorical form of his fiction is all that is important in making it appear realistic. Empirical research is not relevant to his 'realism'; for example, Banks revealed that the inspiration for the semen injection scene in *Complicity* was found in an old admiralty logbook, but that he had no idea what physical effect such an injection would have.[11] The insistence on materiality in Banks's work, on the supposedly empirical, is merely a rhetorical gesture signalling the 'realism' of the narrative, just as the economies of the novels help regulate the realism. It is this formal requirement that Banks described above as 'a technical exercise', even for an 'obscene event'. Thus to read Banks realistically or naturalistically is to attend to the form of the work, and to see his novels (as some of *The Wasp Factory* critics did) as displaying admirable control but as being fatally marred by the violent and disturbing images and events. However, far from acknowledging these tensions as key to Bank's literary practice, such privileging of order, economy and control in the responses marks a contemporary and perhaps unreflective addition to Ruskin's venerable discourse on the grotesque.

According to Derrida, Rousset 'decides that everything not intelligible in the light of a 'preestablished' teleological framework, and not visible in its simultaneity, is reducible to the inconsequentiality of accident or dross' (Derrida, 1978, 25). In Derridean terms, this is the idealist approach promoted by classical aesthetics, and the origins of such an approach are evident in Aristotle's injunction that anything not essential to the structure should be omitted from the work. Gianni Vattimo opposes such a classical aesthetic in his essay 'Ornament/Monument' in *The End of Modernity* (1988, first published in Italian 1985):

> What is lost in the foundation and ungrounding which is ornament is the heuristic and critical function of the distinction between decoration as surplus and what is 'proper' to the thing and to the work. The critical validity of this distinction today appears completely exhausted, in particular at the level of the discourse of the arts and of militant criticism. (Vattimo, 1988, 87–8)

This contemporary 'exhaustion' is of a piece with Derrida's argument: the distinction between what is 'proper' and what is 'surplus' – this critical pursuit of economic form which Chapter 1 showed was historically the key to distinctions between the grotesque and realism – is revealed to be based on outdated metaphysics. Therefore the contemporary critic's task, following Vattimo and Derrida, is to try to develop new critical models that can attend to contradictory aspects of the literary work without ordering them according to a pre-established hierarchy:

> Our intention here is not, through the simple motions of balancing, equilibration or overturning, to oppose duration to space, quality to quantity, force to form, the depth of meaning or value to the surface of figures. Quite to the contrary. To counter this simple alternative, to counter the simple choice of one of the terms or one of the series against the other, we maintain that it is necessary to seek new concepts and new models, an *economy* escaping this system of metaphysical opposition. (Derrida, 1978, 19)

I have therefore endeavoured in this chapter to resist a championing of content over form, or force over structure in Banks's fiction, but instead to show how these supposed alternatives frequently apparent in criticism of the author are themselves *metaphorical* models of grotesque texts.

As the previous chapter's discussion of early versus late McEwan outlined, my emphasis on the grotesque in the contemporary British fiction that this book explores is not intended to favour a single aspect or phase of a writer's work but instead to analyse both how their creative work has been shaped by the aesthetic tradition of the grotesque and how the critical responses to this literature sometimes fall back on arguably outmoded critical models. My focus on the discourse of the grotesque should, however, not be taken as a simple call 'to celebrate the transgressive', but should instead be seen as following Derrida's approach to such issues where 'If we appear to oppose one series to the other, it is because from within the classical system we wish to make apparent the noncritical privilege naively granted to the other series by a certain structuralism' (Derrida, 1978, 20). When reading Banks's work, to attend to its structure is to attend to the form of the text, and so is to read 'as a realist' and to effect the text's 'realism', as if one were faced with Barthes's classic, readerly text. However, such an approach tends to subordinate force to form whereas I have been attempting to think about Banks's fiction in terms of both form and force. To read Banks's books and focus on the detailed violence of their content is to attend to the grotesque force of the fiction, as my previous work on the grotesque as exorbitant, excessive and non-classical shows. What Derrida's and Vattimo's arguments suggest is that there is no 'real' Banks: neither the Banks of realist economy ('overwhelmed by exorbitant brutalities' as the reviewer quoted at the beginning of this chapter claimed) nor the Banks of grotesque force is the 'proper' Banks. One cannot read his work 'over-naturalistically', as Sage puts it, since his work is both naturalistic and grotesque, economic and excessive, 'sober' and 'drunk'. To privilege one aspect over the other is a metaphysical, rather than a critical, move and my exploration of the grotesque in Banks is intended to be a productive step towards a critical approach attuned to both force and form.

Notes

1 This quotation and all subsequent reviews of *The Wasp Factory* are taken from the blurb to the 1990 Abacus edition of the novel.
2 Banks in an interview with Stan Nicholls (1993) professes much the same puzzled reaction to the reviews of *The Wasp Factory* as Ian McEwan had to the negative reviews of his own early stories: '*The Wasp Factory* was a lot more bizarre than I thought it was. I regarded it as a fairly run-of-the-mill weird story; I didn't expect it to cause such a fuss, or to be pilloried and praised to the extent it was. I was slightly bemused by the extremity and the polarisation in the reactions to it' (Nicholls, 1993, 139).
3 For an exploration of incest in this novel see Duggan (forthcoming).
4 'The sections Coma and Coda represent the viaducts at either end, Triassic and Eocene the two linking sections between the main sections of the structure, and the three parts, Metaphormosis, Metamorpheus, and Metamorphosis, those main sections themselves (with four chapters each, just as the bridge's three main sections rest on four granite feet).' (Binns, 1990, 11)

5 See for example Cobley (1990, 26) and Bragg (1997): 'Castles have always had a deep psychological resonance with me. I think it's something to do with identity, with the security of the soul – in a non-religious sense – the concentricity of walls and of levels through which you let people and so on. It's all a defensive metaphor.'
   Dr Joyce suggests to Orr: ' [I]f we regard the human mind as – say – like a castle ... then all you've been doing for the last few sessions is taking me on a guided tour of the curtain wall.' (Banks, 1990b, 89)
6 M.C. Spencer in 'The Unfinished Cathedral: Michel Butor's *L'Emploi du Temps*' (1969) discusses Butor's use of the four elements and divides *L'Emploi*'s imagery into four categories: igneous, liquid, atmospheric and ocular.
7 Addams's *Monster Rally* contains a number of other cartoons reminiscent of *The Wasp Factory*, including a boy digging a grave on a beach (Paul's fate in *The Wasp Factory*), a sibling murder (Paul or Esmerelda), failed suicide bids (Frank's relatives) and a school report (with which his parents are pleased), accusing the boy of being 'perverse, crafty, and wanton' and of having 'an extraordinarily morbid ingenuity' (Addams, 1950, 16).
8 'I don't think *The Bridge* would be the way it is at all if it wasn't for *Lanark*.' (Banks quoted in Nairn, 1993, 129)
9 'Whether conscious or unconscious, for better or for worse, duality, division and fracture persist as the prevailing creative and critical tools in Scotland.' (Wallace, 1993, 218)
10 Alasdair Gray's novel *Poor Things* (1992) is another reworking of *Frankenstein* as a doctor called Godwin inserts a baby's brain into the head of a female suicide, creating a new person called Bella Caledonia. Continuing Gray's interest in the grotesque, the work begins: 'The doctor who wrote this account of his early experiences died in 1911, and readers who know nothing about the daringly experimental history of Scottish medicine will perhaps mistake it for a grotesque fiction' (Gray, 1992, 1).
11 'I thought that was the most horrible thing in *Complicity*. It's a very old idea from an admiralty logbook my dad had. I thought it was so offensive and unpleasant I couldn't imagine writing anything in which I could justifiably use it. But at the same time when I did use it, I had this feeling of glee.' (Banks interviewed by *The Observer*, 14 June 1988 Review p. 16)

Chapter 6

Will Self: under the influence

> In fact, Banks's success as a storyteller is largely based on a readiness and a capacity to assimilate such a diverse menu of already-existing literary techniques: modernism and postmodernism, dirty realism and surrealism, fantasy and science fiction, William Burroughs and Edgar Burroughs, all seem equally integrated in the various burrowings and borrowings of his imagination. (Nairn, 1993, 133–4)

Will Self has emerged as one of the most important and indeed most industrious of British authors of recent times, having written several novels, novellas and collections of short stories, to say nothing of the many volumes of collected journalism. His multifaceted career has included appearances on a television game show, book reviewing and working as the restaurant critic for *The Observer*. As well as discussing the significance of grotesque imagery in his work, this chapter will be looking at Self's treatment of areas that are key to the grotesque: perspective, vision and the human body. I will be investigating how these are related to Self's use of satire and of language, and also how they influence his presentation of drugs, psychiatry and capitalism.

Losing perspective: *The Quantity Theory of Insanity* **and** *Cock & Bull*

Self's first book, *The Quantity Theory of Insanity* (1994b), was published to general acclaim in 1991, winning the Geoffrey Faber Memorial Prize. The first story in the collection, 'The North London Book of the Dead', which describes the narrator's surprise in discovering that his mother despite her recent death continues to reside in London, came in for particular praise. The opening lines of the story, and so in a sense of Self's career as an author, convey a flavour of the grotesque qualities that would mark him out a significant contemporary writer:

> I suppose that the form my bereavement took after my mother died was fairly conventional. Initially I was shocked. Her final illness was mercifully quick, but harrowing. Cancer tore through her body as if it were late for an important meeting with a lot of other successful diseases. (Self, 1994b, 1)

This comparison occupies the uncomfortable space between the visceral and the comic that is the realm of the grotesque, and the subjection of the body of the mother both to disease and to the comparison manages to be both shocking and poignant. Its exuberance comes into even greater focus when compared to the first lines of Albert Camus's *The Outsider* (1961, first published in French 1942), which can be read as a 'sober' (in the sense Deleuze and Guattari use of Kakfa) antecedent of Self's opening: 'Mother died today. Or, maybe, yesterday; I can't be sure. The telegram from the Home says: *Your mother passed away. Funeral tomorrow. Deep sympathy.* Which leaves the matter doubtful; it could have been yesterday' (Camus, 1961, 13). When Self's narrator's mother dies and reappears, it turns out she has moved to Crouch End, which while fantastic is not a fantasyland, and he learns that when people die they simply move to another part of London to be among other dead people. The North London Book of the Dead itself rather than a volume full of mystical secrets is something of a let-down, being a bureaucratic and boring guide for the recently deceased:

> It was genuinely uninspiring, based entirely on fact with no prophecies or commandments. The introductory pages were given over to flat statements such as 'Your (dead) identity should hold up to most official enquiries. Dead people work in most major civil service departments ensuring that full records of dead people are kept up to date. Should you in any instance run into difficulties, call one of the Dead Citizens' Advice Bureaux listed in the directory.' (Self, 1994b, 13)

The banal incongruity of the scenario was to become an abiding theme of much of Self's future fiction and his later novel *How the Dead Live* (2000a) reworks and expands the short story into a novel about a Jewish American woman who bears similarities to Self's own mother, dying in London and joining the boring community of the city's dead in the perfectly named Dulston.

This peculiar mixture of the strange and familiar is a feature of another story in *The Quantity Theory of Insanity*, 'Understanding the Ur-Bororo', where the narrator meets an anthropologist who has been studying the eponymous tribe that, as their name hints, are the most boring group of humans ever encountered. Their prodigious capacity to irk other groups is at once uniquely exotic and unbearably dreary, and this ability of the outlandish and the commonplace to swap places indicates the potentially overlooked correspondence between supposedly sophisticated European anthropologists and the subjects of their study. Tellingly, Self brought a similar sensitivity to restaurant reviewing in Britain:

> Eating food may feel great from the inside, but witnessing its ingurgitation is never entirely free from the queasiness that dances attendance upon all of life's primary biological activities. Put bluntly: it occurred to me that the current obsession with public eating – which is, after all, what restaurant-going amounts to – is just another opportunity for our relation with the natural world to be mediated by rituals bordering on the perverse.[1]

It is against the background of Claude Lévi-Strauss (who discussed a tribe called the Bororo in his book *The Savage Mind* (1966, first published in French 1962)) and Mary Douglas (Self quotes from her book *Purity and Danger* in *My Idea of Fun*) that Self's peculiar satirical perspective is formed, where Swiftian grotesque is deployed to expose our animality and so undermine our vanity, defamiliarising contemporary British culture and society as if they emerged from a distant place and time. In Self's work it is not some 'Eastern' or 'primitive' society which is atavistic, but contemporary Britain which is 'orientalised', permeated by bizarre and impenetrable rituals, created on a peculiar scale, but recognisably homely. Like the China of Kafka's 'The Great Wall of China' and

'An Imperial Message' (Kafka, 1999), with its ponderous time scales and strange bureaucracy, Britain is for Self the proper site for 'anthropological' satire since ultimately it is the British people, not the Ur-Bororo, who are a peculiar, boring tribe living in a complex ritualised society among the strange and vast monuments of the past. An interrogation of anthropology's ethical dimensions is central to the surreal landscape of Self's 2008 novel *The Butt*, where a tourist infringing the local ordinance against smoking is forced to set out on a quest for restitution in an only partly recognisable Australia beset by indigenous insurgency and laws based on animist principles.

Self's next book after *The Quantity Theory of Insanity*, *Cock & Bull* (1993, first published 1992) consists of two narratives subtitled respectively 'A Novelette' and 'A Farce' that echo Franz Kafka's 'Metamorphosis' (1999, first published in German 1915) but in Self's two stories the transformations are ones of sexuality. In *Cock*, the protagonist Carol grows a penis of her own and sodomises and kills her alcoholic and sexually inadequate husband Dan. The story is framed by another narrator, an anti-Semitic Oxford don described as 'an ersatz ancient mariner', who tells the story to a Jewish fellow-passenger on a train trip and then rapes him. In *Bull*, the protagonist is a modern Englishman called John Bull who grows a vagina behind his knee and after a brief affair with his male doctor becomes pregnant and flees London to live a new life with his son. Bull's vagina behind his knee recalls the adventures on the moon of the hero of Roman author Lucian's *True History*, where he finds himself in an all-male society where the young gestate in the calf of the leg. Lucian, along with Voltaire, Swift, and Rabelais, was identified by Bakhtin as belonging to the grotesque tradition of the menippea, as discussed in Chapter 1.

The effect of these metamorphoses on Carol and John has been discussed by Janet Harbord (1996), where she uses Judith Butler's theory of gender performativity to examine the feelings of superiority and power Carol's penis gives her and the feelings of vulnerability and emotional turmoil Bull's vagina gives to him: 'Here the body is seen to be changed by, and informing, the social identity of the subject. Nature is not static but within history, changeable' (Harbord, 1996, 43). Harbord's approach usefully addresses how the sex/gender dyad is experimented with in the novel; however, her comment that 'the changing of Carol's body to incorporate a penis which then enables her to take control of and resolve the situation of her acrimonious marriage could be read as the definition of nature through culture' (43) seems to place an unlikely positive gloss on Carol's murder of her husband and framing of his best friend for the killing, to say nothing of her further transformation into the hermaphroditic anti-Semite who rapes the narrator. In light of Iain Banks's *The Wasp Factory*, we might instead regard *Cock & Bull* as an interrogation of the solidification of gender roles, and a play with the reader's expectations of the kind of behaviour likely to be shown by a man with a vagina or a woman with a penis. The role of national identity also seems relevant since Carol becomes the negative stereotype of an Englishman (aggressive, snobbish, racist, homophobic) while John Bull (whose name proclaims him an English national stereotype) seems to opt out of such a role and moves to Wales to live with his son.

A visit to Toytown: *My Idea of Fun*

Self's first novel, *My Idea of Fun* (1994a, first published 1993) is narrated by Ian Wharton, a boy who thinks he has special powers of perception, as he grows up under the malign influence of The Fat Controller, a strange and perhaps demonic figure who also seems to possess magical powers.[2] Self weaves together a story drawing allusions to figures as diverse as Swift, Berkley, Thomas De Quincey Aleister Crowley, Mary Douglas and Thomas the Tank Engine, and the book also includes scenes of shocking violence as a dog is tortured and killed and a tramp murdered and then his corpse sexually abused. The repellent description of someone's face below is even later mentioned (Self, 1994a, 296) as having actually happened in the manner described:

> It looked as if someone had stuck a ratchet into the crease at the top of John's neck and then twisted it. Somebody else – or maybe the same sadist – had then gently smoothed over the spiralled web

of fleshy folds with a soldering iron, or at any rate some implement that seared – but slowly. (Self, 1994a, 176)

Wharton, like Frank in *The Wasp Factory*, practises strange rituals in order to achieve special powers of vision; in Wharton's case he seeks to use his own brand of eidetic memory and vision whereby he can momentarily freeze time and perceive things not visible from his actual point of view. While one reviewer of Self's novel felt, like some of those faced by Banks's debut, that 'there was something of the adolescent boy' about the violent scenes, he also noted that Self's 'almost excessively articulate focus on the scuzziness of life has already been compared with Martin Amis' (Baker, 1993, 22), situating the book's queasy mixture of comedy and horror squarely within the contemporary British grotesque.

The malevolent Fat Controller is part of Wharton's circle of strange friends: 'my life hadn't exactly tricked me out with a gallery of amusing pals, only a gallimaufry of grotesques' (Self, 1994a, 288), as he ruefully reflects. The critical reception of this 'gallimaufry of grotesques' and their violence was not universally positive, as Self noted in his article 'B and I', a review of Nicholson Baker's *The Fermata*:

> I can conceive that many critics will recoil from some of these episodes, because at a gut level there is something obscene – for them – about the pollution of an allegedly 'literary' text by such 'filth'. This was the same kind of reaction that I received for *My Idea of Fun*. Somehow the description of the raw actuality of sex or violence in unashamedly high literary style strikes some people as the equivalent of attending Lady So-and-So's little soirée and taking a monumental dump in her teacup.
> Such a perspective is as ridiculous as it is hidebound. Literature has always been powered forward by these kinds of irruptions of sex and violence. (Self, 1996b, 145)

Self thus rejects any idea of separating 'literary' purity from 'filth' and indeed responds with another 'filthy' comparison. He was equally unequivocal when asked during a television interview whether he included physical details in his fiction simply because they were disgusting:

> The modernist project has always been saying damn it all, we've dragged the reader kicking and screaming into the bedroom, now let's yank them on through to the bathroom, and then conceivably let's try and stuff their head down the toilet bowl. It seems to me absolutely pointless to shove them back out of the bathroom, back out of the bedroom and down into the ante-chamber where they're going to get a tray of cucumber sandwiches served by Lady Bracknell. I mean nobody's going to buy it. We know what's going on. (Aaronovitch, 1998)

The two comments show Self placing himself in the contemporary literary world but at the fraying end of a long literary tradition. To use my earlier pre- and post-classical distinction: like Martin Amis, Self's grotesque is part of a post-classical aesthetic where the boundaries between 'high style' and 'low-life' have become blurred.

In *My Idea of Fun*, as Ian becomes adept at his chosen career of marketing, he becomes aware of money as the ultimate fetish and of its circulation without rest within contemporary society, his reflections recalling John Self's musings in *Money*:

> At this fag end of the millennium money had begun to detach itself from the very medium of exchange. Money was lagging behind ... Everywhere you looked you saw advertisements screaming: 'Value for Money'. That such an obvious *non sequitur* should have become a benchmark of credibility was beyond Ian's, and indeed anyone's, understanding. (Self, 1994a, 223)

While junkies discuss the status of drugs as 'product' and whether they can be marketed in the same way as other commercial goods (250–1), The Fat Controller describes a group of drug addicts and a group of marketing people as fundamentally 'engaged in the same activity' (297). He sees the two groups participating in an attempt to manipulate demand, trying to stimulate the need for a particular product. Addicts when they take drugs are trying to satisfy temporarily a desire, but the effect of this is to create desire for the drug, to harden dependence, just as marketing people attempt to stimulate further demand for their products. Jean Baudrillard makes much the same point in his analysis of the consumer society:

> [I]t is clear that the whole market and motivation research, which pretends to uncover the underlying needs of the consumer and the real demand prevailing in the market, exists only to generate a demand for further market opportunities. (Baudrillard, 1988, 39)

In Self's novel the connection between consumer acquisitiveness and substance dependence reaches its ironic conclusion when the kiosks developed for marketing the edible financial product developed by Wharton's company end up being used by addicts for injecting drugs.

The Fat Controller, whom Wharton initially knows as Mr Broadhurst, is a grotesque source of both threat and amusement, a quality enhanced by the infusion of a childlike perspective into descriptions of his behaviour and appearance. The supposedly incredible powerful entity who tells Ian that he controls 'all the automata on the island of Britain, all those machines that bask in the dream that they have a soul' (Self, 1994a, 75) reveals himself in a toyshop window displaying model train sets:

> Trying to ignore this assault on my fundamental antinomies I peered at the train set. A tiny, rotund figure was stamping up and down on the daubed green of the false ground, like a drunken redneck at a howdown, or an aboriginal at a corroboree. It was Mr Broadhurst – and he was Hornby-sized. (Self, 1994a, 75)

The character's resemblance to 'The Fat Controller' in the children's series of books and television programmes 'Thomas the Tank Engine' (Hornby is a company that makes model train sets) lends both a ludicrous and sinister edge to his claims. David Punter in *The Literature of Terror* (1996) tries to untangle the narrative of the novel:

> Perhaps the best hypothesis we can frame is that we have all the while been immersed in a monodrama, within which Gyggle, the Fat Controller and the various other bizarre characters we meet

have all been elements in Ian's tortured psyche, in an unending cycle of offence and cover-up, of which eidesis, with its helpless invasion of other people's lives, their reality, is one emblem, and the cycle of capitalist production, based on exploitation and corruption, is another. (Punter, 1996, 176)

Dr Gyggle, however, shows signs earlier on that he is outside Ian's neurosis (like Dr Joyce listening to Orr's dreams in Banks's *The Bridge*) when he comments on the childlike nature of some of Ian's revelations about The Fat Controller:

> 'Somewhere deep down, your idea of what it is to be a person, to truly engage in the world, has become critically interfused with childish fantasy. Your choice of iconography is of course highly significant in this context.' (Self, 1994a, 148)

It seems that as Ian Wharton travels through Self's 'semi-permeable membrane between "neurosis" and "psychosis"' (Self, 1996a, 144), Dr Gyggle and indeed every other character becomes drawn into the bizarre psychodrama going on inside Wharton's head.[3]

The banalisation of metaphor in Self's fiction is closely related to the theme of 'enfeebled affect' that recurs in his work, signalling the loss of sensation or the ability to feel. Moments of potential transcendence or exhilaration frequently turn out to be disappointments, and a dull iterative quality overtakes any attempt at *jouissance*. When The Fat Controller remarks that 'addicts are psychopathic, regressive, they have enfeebled affect' (Self, 1994a, 197), the reader is encouraged to view the people involved as simply an extreme case of a general condition of urban alienation within late capitalist culture. The enfeebled affect of drug users is also linked to a wider, in this case sexual, malaise:

> We're like coke heads or chronic masturbators, aren't we? Attempting to crank the last iota of abandonment out of an intrinsically empty and mechanical experience. We push the plunger home, we abrade the clitoris, we yank the penis and we feel nothing. Not exactly nothing, worse than nothing, we feel a flicker or a prickle, the sensual equivalent of a retinal after-image. That's our fun now, not fun itself, only a tired allusion to it. (Self, 1994a, 163)

Will Self: under the influence   191

Thrill-seeking in this context, whether in search of carnal or chemical pleasures, has become the jaded pursuit of increasingly threadbare bliss presided over by a law of diminishing returns. The addictive cycles of consumption of whatever kind within this bleak universe lead to a predictable routine of pleasure-seeking that militates against any idea of fun, a term increasingly identified with lost childhood innocence.

Narcotic economy: *Grey Area* and *Tough, Tough Toys for Tough, Tough Boys*

A productive route into the grotesque in Self's fiction is through focusing on the importance of perspective in his work, and the influence of Jonathan Swift's writing (also evident in Martin Amis's work, as I discussed in Chapter 3) is at its clearest in Self's novel *Great Apes* (1998, first published 1997) and in his short stories 'Scale', 'Mono-cellular' and 'Design Faults in the Volvo 769 Turbo: A Manual'.[4] 'Scale' in fact incorporates Swift's influence into its own narrative: the narrator, who writes poems in the genre of 'Motorway Verse', pretends to be a doctoral student writing a thesis on 'The Apprehension of Scale in *Gulliver's Travels*, with special reference to Lilliput' (Self, 1996b, 104). This pretence enables him to secure the lease on a bungalow next to a model village, where he can indulge his interest in changes of scale. There is also a passing reference to Rabelais, whose work forms with Swift's the most famous example of play of perspective and scale in European literature, when the narrator describes the introduction of his pet lizard into the model village: 'But whereas the *nouveaux riches* opt for the Pantagruelian spectacle of giraffes cropping their laburnums, and hippopotamuses wallowing in the sun-saturated swimming pools, I have chosen to domesticate the more elegant frill-necked lizard' (120). Instead of introducing large animals into a domestic environment, (and so producing a 'Pantagruelian' effect), the narrator opts for the opposite change in scale, the shrinking of the environment in the form of the model village to produce a 'Gargantuan' effect, reminiscent also of monster movies: 'The sight of this pocket Godzilla stalking the dwarfish environs, its head darting this way and that, as if on the look-out for a canapé-sized human, never fails to amuse me' (121).

As I outlined in the opening chapter of this study, the grotesque scatology of Rabelais and Swift is frequently founded on a play of perspective and scale, and it is Gulliver's diminutive size among the giants of Brobdingnag that renders the sight of The Maids of Honour's naked bodies grotesque and repellent to him and consequently to the reader:

> Their Skins appeared so coarse and uneven, so variously coloured when I *saw them near*, with a Mole here and there as broad as a Trencher, and Hairs hanging from it thicker than Pack-threads; to say nothing further concerning the rest of their persons. Neither did they at all scruple while I was by, to discharge what they had drunk, to the Quantity of at least two Hogsheads, in a Vessel that held above three Tuns. (Swift, 1973, 95, my italics)

Gulliver's attempt to quantify is an important factor in the description and the link between scale or perspective and the grotesque is made clear in his reaction to the sight of a frog in Brobdingnag: 'The *Largeness* of its Features made it appear the most *deformed* Animal that can be conceived' (97, my italics), thus it is when the familiar is magnified that it becomes repellent and grotesque. By including these references to Swift and Rabelais, Self is placing his own story in the tradition of the grotesque and the distorted and continuing the practice of making the reader question how far such magnification reveals an underlying grossness that our culture prefers to ignore. Self's Swiftian play of scale is also employed in humorous ways, for example in the story 'Design Faults in the Volvo 760 Turbo: A Manual', as the adulterous Bill contemplates being caught by his wife Vanessa *in flagrante delicto* with Serena:

> It is not unlikely that Vanessa will see Bill snogging with Serena, because Bill is – he acknowledges with a spurt of dread – at least sixty feet high. He bestrides the two lanes of bumpy tarmac, his crotch forming a blue denim underpass for the rumbling traffic. Vanessa will be able to see him – this Colossus of Roads – the very instant she jolts across the intersection of the Edgware Road. (Self, 1999, 156–7)

The quotidian solidity of London's Edgware Road, blue jeans and safety-oriented Swedish automobiles is warped but not broken by the intrusion of mythically sized adulterers in Self's distorted but still familiar world.

The link between childhood and changes in size is made in 'Scale' when the narrator talks of how his children no longer visit him at the model village:

> Ever since my loss of sense of scale, I have found it difficult to relate to my children ... It's true that when I sat, puffing on my pipe, watching my son and daughter move about amongst the four-foot-high, half-timbered semis, I would feel transported, taken back to my own childhood. It was the confusion in scale that allowed this. For if the model village was to scale, my children would be at least sixty feet tall. Easily big enough, and competent enough, to re-parent me. (Self, 1996b, 100)

The narrator's loss of scale, however, does not issue solely from his experience of growing up, but also owes much to his pipe being full of a morphine mixture. After his divorce the narrator's wife claims all the adult-sized household goods while he is left with the children's crockery, further enhancing his miniaturist environment and his retreat from wider society and responsibility into drugged solitude. This peculiar return to childhood, like Charles Darke's in McEwan's *The Child in Time*, is evidence of a mind becoming unhinged and playing with the idea of being 're-parented'. In his introduction to M. Ageyev's *Novel with Cocaine* (1999, novel first published in Russian 1983), Self's comments on the link between childhood perspectives on time and the changes in perspective caused by drug use echo McEwan's evocation of childhood:

> The drug addict craves, above all else, a release from time, an arrest of entropy. To be high is to experience the atemporal abandon of the child – or it should be. In truth adults can't have fun, are constitutionally incapable of having fun, and the doomed rituals of drug addiction are a macabre simulation of playground attraction. (Ageyev, 1999, xv)

Such clear-eyed analysis of drug addiction that acknowledges both the addict's sometimes poignant desires for pleasure and the impossibility of their fulfilment is typical of Self's accounts of narcotics, as – despite his frequent association with drug use – he is never less than critical of it and aware of its dangers.

As well as describing this scale model of a real village, 'Scale' also plays with the different connotations of the word 'scale', including the scales of the lizard's skin, the limescale in the narrator's kettle, the sequence of motorway signs which signal a driver's speed, the star sign Libra, the climbing the narrator does, the scales of justice and, most memorably, the bathroom scales on which the narrator's infidelity is comically recorded as the broken machine permanently registers the combined weight of the au pair and himself. The short story also makes a play of temporal scale as well as of spatial scale when the narrator plans to be buried in a replica of an ancient chamber tomb next to the M40 motorway, hoping it will puzzle archaeologists in a distant future:

> Will the similarities in construction between my tomb and the great chamber tombs of Ireland and the Orkneys lead them to posit a continuous motorway culture, lasting some 7,000 years? I hope so. It has always been my contention that phenomena such as Silbury Hill and the Avebury stone circle can best be understood as, respectively, an embankment and a roundabout. (Self, 1996b, 123)[5]

This peculiar play with temporal scale alters our usual perspective of both the present (our motorway culture) and humorously distorts the past (the Avebury stone circle roundabout). If J.G. Ballard, who is an acknowledged influence on Self's writing, showed in his novel *Crash* (1995, first published 1973) how the contemporary fascination with car accidents may conceal a more primitive or ritualistic fascination with sudden death, then Self's own fiction has repeatedly returned to scenarios where archaeologists in the distant future pore over massive earthworks and the traces of our 'motorway culture', prefigured by a 1993 newspaper article entitled 'Mad about Motorways' which is included in *Junk Mail* (1996a, first published 1995).[6] In the story 'Chest' (from *Grey Area*) the everyday objects of contemporary life are cast as future relics of a savage and superstitious culture when the protagonist's car is transformed into 'a lay-by burial ship. A Sutton Hoo of the psyche. The armour of mashed milk cartons and crushed cans, the beadwork of fag butts, the weaponry of buckled hub caps and discarded lengths of chromium trim' (Self, 1996b, 134). Such a formulation takes on yet another twist in the essay 'Multiplex of Middens' (2000b), where Self describes a protesters' camp as inadvertently restoring the site to its previous incarnation as a Bronze Age hill fort, setting up a puzzle for future archaeologists.[7]

The novella *The Sweet Smell of Psychosis* (1997, first published 1996) includes Self's by now characteristic grotesque juxtapositions and sexual transformation, and its links to caricature are evident in *Guardian* cartoonist Martin Rowson's illustrations. Like the hero of Alexander Mackendrick's 1957 film *The Sweet Smell of Success* in which Tony Curtis plays a reporter gradually drawn into the amoral newspaper world of his boss Burt Lancaster, Self's protagonist Richard Hermes is part of a media clique that includes the sinister Bell, an all-powerful mover-and-shaker in the media reminiscent of The Fat Controller from *My Idea of Fun*, and the beautiful Ursula Bentley, the object of Richard's desires. The group frequents the Sealink club in Soho (a club also seen in *Great Apes*) and Richard's mind is gradually deranged by his growing lust and burgeoning cocaine habit. During a taxi journey he tries to take his mind off his sexual excitement by listening to the taxi-driver's autobiographical story of oppression and torture:

> It was a tale of courage, warmth and fortitude in the face of craven, cold brutality ... The *juxtaposition* of this and the squealing, coked-up atmosphere that had prevailed among the clique since they left the Sealink was *grotesque*. (Self, 1997, 53, my italics)

This grotesque juxtaposition of bravery in the face of cruelty and drug-fuelled indulgence is echoed by the street scene that the taxi drives past: beneath a billboard on which a woman of 'bursting pulchritude' advertises lingerie sits a double amputee drinking extra-strong lager. The effect is heightened when Richard realises that he has been the only one really listening to the driver: Bell, intent on his own schemes completely ignored the driver, while Ursula, who listened to some of the driver's story, thinks Richard is 'sweet' for getting worked up about the injustice. The 'annihilation of affect' (19) within the clique has eroded the characters' capacity to empathise with anyone else, recalling Ian Wharton's experiences in *My Idea of Fun*. The metamorphosis occurs at the end of the novella, when Richard finally gets into bed with Ursula, and in order to avert premature ejaculation imagines Bell's head and body. But as they lie together something strange begins to happen to Ursula's body:

> Her features were transfigured ... No, not transfigured, *transforming*! They were changing, being replaced by other, stronger, more brutish features. Ursula's forehead was bulging, growing whiter, she was being instantly encephalicised. And the arms that held Richard, they too were changing, becoming thicker, more muscular, hairier.
> (Self, 1997, 87–9)

Ursula transforms into Bell, and as Richard screams, Bell tells him how pleased he is to have Richard 'on board'. As we are told early on, the arch-seducer Bell 'always got his man, or woman' (19). Richard's desire for Ursula is revealed as his desire for entry into Bell's clique, figured ultimately as a desire for Bell himself.

As my discussion of *My Idea of Fun* has outlined, drug addicts in Self's work form a peculiar link between the realms of madness and of capitalism, where drug use is linked to psychosis and paranoia on the one hand but also to the cycle of consumer capitalism on the other. Whereas in *Money*, Martin Amis explicitly links the sexual fetishism of pornography with the economic fetishism of capitalism (as I explored in Chapter 3), Self compares drug addiction to a kind of consumer addiction, and his story 'The Rock of Crack as Big as the Ritz' from the collection *Tough, Tough Toys for Tough, Tough Boys* (1999, first published 1998) develops the parallels between drug addiction and capitalism established in *My Idea of Fun*. In 'The Rock of Crack as Big as the Ritz' crack cocaine becomes the emblem of money in place of the diamond of F. Scott Fitzgerald's story 'The Diamond as Big as the Ritz' (1922). Again, the experience of drug use is represented as the creation of a need rather than its satisfaction when two brothers discover a large lode of crack cocaine underneath their house. One of the brothers, Tembe, goes out to do his usual rounds of drug dealing while indulging himself with some of 'the product':

> For the crack was on to him now, surging into his brain like a great crashing breaker of pure want. This is the hit, Tembe realised, concretely, irrefutably, for the first time. The whole hit of rock is to want *more rock*. The buzz of rock is itself the wanting of *more rock* ... And the awareness of this fact, the giant nature of the hit, became part of the hit itself – in just the same way that the realisation that crack was the desire for crack had become part of the hit as well. (Self, 1999, 21–2)

Narcotics in this sense are the paragon of consumer capitalism, the ideal product for which no army of marketing executives is needed, no fancy packaging, no marketing strategy since the satisfaction in the consumption of the product is itself the creation of the want for more product. As Self has it here, there is no satisfaction other than the renewed desire for more 'product', trapping the consumer in a recursive cycle. 'The Money Critic' chapter in *My Idea of Fun* is preceded by a quote from Mary Douglas's *Purity and Danger*, where the anthropologist states that 'the more we reflect on the richness of the metaphor[between money and ritual], the more it becomes clear that this is no metaphor. Money is only an extreme and specialised type of ritual' (1966, 70). In the same way, Self seems to assert, drug use is not a metaphor for consumer 'habits' so much as a specialised form of consumer capitalism. Drug use as presented in Self's work, especially in *My Idea of Fun* and 'The Rock of Crack as Big as the Ritz' tends not to be an exception to the general economy, but, on the contrary, such addiction to consumption is the general paradigm of the wider economy.

The major influence on Self here would seem to be William Burroughs, on whose work Self has written several times and whom he brings up in conversation with both Martin Amis and J.G. Ballard (Self, 1996a). Self also shares his description of the 'gallimaufry of grotesques' of Burroughs's *Junky* (Self, 1996a, 8) with Ian Wharton's description of his friends in *My Idea of Fun* (Self, 1994a, 288). Self's comments in an article entitled 'New Crack City' make clear his debt to Burroughs in his approach to writing about drug use: 'As William

Burroughs so pithily observed, smack is the only commodity that you don't have to sell to people; instead you sell people to it' (Self, 1996a, 13). Self also seeks to broaden the scope of Burroughs's insights into addiction in the course of a short review of his novel *Junky*:

> For in describing addiction as a way of life, Burroughs creates a synecdoche through which he can explore the being of man under late capitalism. His descriptions of the 'junk territories' of the cities his narrator inhabits are, in fact, depictions of urban alienation itself. (Self, 1996a, 9–10)

My Idea of Fun and 'The Rock of Crack as Big as the Ritz' display exactly this kind of synecdoche, as Self explicitly plays with the links between drug use and consumer capitalism so that Burroughs and Ballard, alongside Swift and Rabelais, form another significant strand of influence in Self's fiction.

Self's non-fiction collection *Sore Sites* (2000b) is composed of essays and drawings on architecture originally published in *Building Design*, and one of its essays 'Not to Scale' focuses on the author's interest in scale:

> One of my main preoccupations as a writer of Surrealist fiction is the conundrum that the very notion of scale presents us with – time and time again ... There seem to me to be several different complexes or gestalts bound up in the notion of scale. Firstly we have our entire sense of the world radically and speedily transformed by the alterations in scale which is growing up; secondly, we inhabit an environment where mechanisation has altered our basic, ergonomic relations; and thirdly, we live in an allegedly 'globalised' society, throughout which personal bonds are becoming increasingly attenuated. (Self, 2000b, 57)

Sore Sites, like Self's collection of essays, interviews and reviews *Junk Mail*, contains a number of cartoons which play with scale, and its four sections are divided like generic clothing sizes into S, M, L and XL. In a television interview on *The South Bank Show* while talking about this interest in variations of scale, Self repeats his focus on childhood as a primal experience of changes in size:

It's as basic as *Alice in Wonderland*, the first thing you get is an alteration in scale when you grow up. A rediscovery of a childlike perspective is also an obsession with the miniature or the large ... It's trying to uncork the meaning of something by using scale as the primary means of distortion indeed much as Swift did in *Gulliver*.(Bragg, 1998)

In both cases Self mentions the change in scale attendant on growing up, which acts as a catalyst for a changing awareness of self, environment and their interrelation. As indicated in the interview, the ur-text for such transformations in children is Lewis Carroll's *Alice's Adventures in Wonderland* and in an introduction to the novel Self has been clear about its importance in shaping his idiosyncratic writing style,

forming some of the fundamental antimonies that constitute my imagination: the juxtaposition of the quotidian and the fantastic; the transposition of irreconcilable elements; the distortion of scale as a means of renouncing the sensible in favour of the intelligible; and most importantly, abrupt transmogrification conceived of as integral to the human condition. (Carroll, 2001, xii–xiii)

Such a reference to the human condition might at first blush seem odd given contemporary culture's prevailing suspicion of such a universal category; however, the rest of the quote reveals what a strange Alice-like condition this is, involving sudden metamorphoses and faced with situations that blur logic and absurdity. If Self's aesthetic strategies are conceived of as an appropriate response to such a condition, their juxtapositions, reversals and inversions indicate the indispensable nature of the grotesque as a contemporary artistic mode adequate to such circumstances.

Simian satire: *Great Apes*

If Carroll's importance to Self's development as an author is considerable, the same seems true of the writer bracketed with Carroll in *The South Bank Show* interview, Jonathan Swift. The link between drug use and changes in perception lead us from 'Scale' to the opening of Self's most overtly Swiftian work, *Great Apes*. 'Scale' ends with the narrator reassuring the reader, 'It may be said of me that I have lost my sense of scale, but never that I have lost my sense of proportion' (Self, 1996b, 123), evident in the narrator taking the 'long-view' of 'motorway culture'. *Great Apes* begins with the artist protagonist Simon Dykes reflecting on a similar theme: 'Some people lose their sense of proportion, thought Simon, but what would it be like to lose your sense of perspective?' (Self, 1998, 1). Here Self signals a move away from scale and to perspective as the central focus, for Simon wakes up after a night of indulgence in drugs and alcohol to find that everyone in London (including himself) has turned into a chimpanzee. He is treated as mentally ill by the ape establishment and struggles to come to terms with his 'chimpunity' under the tutelage of maverick psychoanalyst Zack Busner, the figure whom Self (as Balzac did in his *Comédie Humaine*) writes into several different works, including 'The Quantity Theory of Insanity' (1994b), 'Grey Area' (1996b) and *Dr Mukti and Other Tales of Woe* (2004). In fact, many of characters of *Great Apes* – including Dykes and Busner – first appeared in 'Inclusion®', a story about a psychiatric drug trial from *Grey Area*.[8]

The narrative begins with Dykes's evening out in London and his reflections on the human body, so central to his art and to his own life. Simon seems preoccupied with the human body and the distortions wrought upon it by twentieth-century urban living and he is also struck by what seems to him the grotesque physicality involved in sexual and domestic intimacy:

> And how that intimacy was then broadened, given further substance, by a willingness to include the other's shit and piss and furtive secretions. It all reached a climax with childbirth, with her swollen vagina stretched to tearing, voiding a half-gallon of what appeared to be won ton soup on to the plastic sheeting. And the placenta, organ-that-was-hers and not-hers, maybe even partly his. But no, they didn't want to fricasse it, or any of the three snacking opportunities, with onions and garlic, so it was removed for incineration, borne in a take-away, cardboard kidney dish. (Self, 1998, 11)[9]

This grotesque combination of childbirth and Chinese take-away, of voiding and ingestion, gives way to Simon's grotesque vision of a giant ape defecating on London's Oxford Circus:

> This pantagruelian pongid then paced around the block, kicking up cars like metallic divots, eating double-deckers as if they were Double Deckers, and then finally squatting in the very centre of the Circus itself to strain, push and deliver a turd the size of a newspaper kiosk, which wavered, lengthened from stub to cigar, before plummeting fifty feet from Kong's arsehole on to the shaven heads of a posse of style-victim cycle couriers, who, like cattle in a thunderstorm, had taken shelter in the open. (Self, 1998, 26–7)

This overtly Rabelaisian scene, which forms another instance of Self's running juxtaposition of the oral and the anal with its cigar-turd, recalls Gargantua's repayment for the hospitality of the people of Paris in *Gargantua and Pantagruel* (1955, first published in French 1532–47):

> The people so pestered him, in fact, that he was compelled to take a rest on the towers of Notre Dame; and when from there he saw so many, pressing all around him, he said in a clear voice: 'I think these clodhoppers want me to pay for my kind reception and offer them a *solatium*. They are quite justified, and I am going to give them some wine, to buy my welcome. But only in sport, *par ris.*'
> Then, with a smile, he undid his magnificent codpiece and, bringing out his john-thomas, pissed on them so fiercely that he drowned two hundred and sixty thousand, four hundred and eighteen persons, not counting the women and small children. (Rabelais, 1955, 74)

In *Great Apes* the target of Rabelais's satire, the pretentious and arrogant Parisians, have been transformed into the 'style-victims' of contemporary London, as Self continues Swift's and Rabelais's play of scale and perspective with the consequent grotesque of the scatological human (and alarmingly simian) body. *Great Apes* is thus firmly in the mould of Swift's *Gulliver's Travels*: a man is thrown into a fantastic world where the social forms of his own society (or in Self's case, of his species) will be viewed from an alien perspective. Self has described the novel as an attempt 'to look at humanity through the lens of ethology', that is in the manner of the scientific study of animals, and has said that the book, like a lot of his fiction, 'is about extreme transmogrification' (Bragg, 1998). Dyke's paintings that previously depicted children in various destructive environments now depict young chimpanzees in the same scenarios. As Patrick Gale points out in his review of the novel: 'Self leads one to look beyond the surface grotesquerie to assess the chimp ways – of raising children, of cherishing hierarchy, of cultivating an extended family group' (Gale, 1997, 6). However, as well as looking at humanity from an ethological perspective, Self's novel also considers the interest humans have had historically in their closest relations in the animal kingdom, and the inverted narrative reflects on the twin roles apes have occupied in human discourse, from dangerous brute animals to the benign chimps of the PG Tips television adverts: 'The human was held to be the most bestial of all the animals because it was the most chimp-like ... The human thus had a readymade niche of demonisation waiting for it to occupy' (Self, 1998, 186). In this inverted world, humans occupy apes' ambivalent position of being both the most bestial and threatening of animals and also a source of humour.

Great Apes draws from and alludes to the various 'ape' narratives in European literature, from Swift's *Gulliver's Travels* (1726) to Thomas Love Peacock's *Melincourt* (1927, first published 1818), to Kafka's 'A Report to an Academy' (1999, first published in German 1917), from which one of *Great Apes*' epigraphs is taken (and which is also the source for Ian McEwan's short story 'Reflections of a Kept Ape', as discussed in Chapter 4). In *Great Apes* we also have reversed depictions of apes in mass media: PG Tips advertisements where humans are dressed up as apes and a film called *Planet of the Humans*. Self, however, goes to great lengths to build a whole inverted society and culture for the chimps of *Great Apes*: the chimpanzee Freud explores the psychological damage done to the young females if their male parent does not mate with them (Self, 1998, 142), Chomsky's simian counterpart develops theories on the superiority of sign language over purely verbal speech (298) and Self parodies a popular song (130) and a Philip Larkin poem: 'They may not fuck you – your mum and alpha' (142). Self has even gone through his text changing all human descriptions to ape-oriented ones: Dykes has gone 'humanshit', bedrooms are 'nestrooms', furniture 'muzzles' rather than faces the wall of the room, chimps say they have no 'image' rather than no idea, and so on. There are Jewish chimps, chimps of African origin and Japanese chimps wandering around this transformed but still familiar London.

It is the similarities between the two worlds which form the centre of Self's satire and he explores humanity's need to distinguish itself from other species, for apes to be demonised as purely bestial or else treated as cute in their resemblance to us. Before Simon's transformation into a chimp, his partner Sarah observes men propositioning her in a London club:

> Other men's propositioning was a Bayreuth production, complete with mechanical effects; great flats descending, garishly depicting their Taste, their Intellect, their Status. The men were like apes – she thought – attempting to impress her by waving and kicking things about in a display of mock potency. (Self, 1998, 15)

Such comparisons are grotesque in the sense of crossing boundaries, in this case between human and animal in order to show simultaneously disturbing and comic similarities that suggest our own animality. The uncomfortable reassessment of human status and privilege, whereby complex social rules and etiquette begin to seem much less sophisticated in the light of 'instinctive' primate behaviour, is also connected to issues of embodiment. Dykes and Busner both suspect the simian Dykes's 'illness' of being related to his difficulties in the perception of his own body or 'proprioception' (137) as Busner puts it. From the *Alice*-like changes of scale and proportion in the early fiction to the simian alterations of *Great Apes*, Self's work creates a rich textual landscape in which both the disorientating personal experience of metamorphosis and the more far-reaching ethological satirical insights it can produce are explored in grotesque detail.

Literary form and intoxication

The grotesque, as well as being present in Self's descriptions of violence and sex, in his extensive treatment of the theme of transmogrifications and in his literary (and in relation to his cartoons, artistic) strategies of skewing scale and perspective, is also clearly present on a micro-scale in his use of language. The texture of Self's prose, both fiction and non-fiction, is embroidered with highly wrought metaphors and similes, as the following comparison from *My Idea of Fun* demonstrates:

> For the world has always smelt of Mummy as far as I am concerned. By this I mean that if bacon isn't frying, tobacco burning or perfume scintillating, I am instantly aware of the background taint. It's something milky, yeasty and yet sour, like a pellet of dough that's been rolled around in a sweaty belly button. (Self, 1994a, 19)

This simile shows the grotesque body not simply in terms of a visceral image but in grotesque juxtaposition to that which it describes, a juxtaposition that is grotesque because we do not expect the object of the simile, the body of the mother, to be referred to in this way. The same grotesque juxtaposition occurs when Self describes the body in its visceral aspect in an unexpectedly artistic way, as happens in 'Chest':

> The pavement outside Marten's the newsagent was streaked with sputum. In the outrageously dull light of a mid-afternoon, in midwinter, in middle England, the loops and lumps of mucus and phlegm appeared strangely bright, lurid even, as if some Jackson Pollock of the pneumo-thorax had been practising Action Hawking. (Self, 1996b, 127).

In addition to the unexpected equivalence, there is something of the humorously baroque about these similes, the playful and elaborate nature of their unfolding which complements the wide and baroque range of Self's vocabulary evident in his use 'gallimaufry', 'proprioception', 'hierophant' and 'transmogrification'. We can also see the connotation of energy in these metaphors, a kind of violence of action that is evident too in the short story 'Tough, Tough, Toys for Tough, Tough Boys' when 'the whisky went off like an antipersonality mine somewhere in the rubble-strewn terrain of Bill's forebrain' (Self, 1999, 131). Here we are not only dealing with the grotesque body, subject to strange transformations, but with a kind of grotesque juxtaposition in metaphor of object and epithet. Self has commented:

> That image that unites one complete perspective on things with another perspective on things, often in a grotesque and frequently morbid way, I suppose is a defining characteristic of my style. (Bragg, 1998)

Thus we can see that perspective goes to the heart of Self's approach to his fiction, both in terms of a recurring thematic and in the composition of his descriptions.

One factor in the specific grotesque effect Self produces is the peculiar familiarity of some of the metaphors. To take my earlier example from the 'North London Book of the Dead' where the cancer tearing through the mother's body is like an important disease hurrying to a meeting with other successful diseases, it is this link between a killer disease and that most prosaic and in some ways anodyne event, a meeting of business executives, that creates the 'friction' between the two perspectives. It is the very banality of the business meeting that drives the juxtaposition and helps create the grotesque effect. The same domesticity in the terms of the comparison can be seen in *My Idea of Fun* when the reader learns that a character's 'frustration was strained through the colander of his personality, until all that was left was a stock of watery pretension' (Self, 1994a, 209). A strange kind of defamiliarisation occurs, where the object is described from a different perspective that is familiar and banal in itself but grotesque when placed in conjunction with its object.

A self-reflexive deployment of metaphor near the beginning of *Great Apes* contributes to a sense of banality in a fashion typical of Self's writing, as Dykes meditates on his loss of belief in the 'genre of sex', with this loss of affect being cast in aesthetic or perhaps philosophical terms. Self extends this loss from sex to time:

Now things speed up. Time is a battered old accordion, abused by a sozzled busker; haplessly it wheezes in and out, bringing events into tight proximity, and then dragging them far, far apart again. And, of course, time is also like this metaphor itself, formulaic, flat, and ill contrived. Time flirts with us in this fashion, entertaining all of us with an inductive peepshow, where cause's coin invariably produces the same routine of cheap effect. (Self, 1994a, 203)

The dullness and flatness of experience and the lost ability to be excited by something is furthered by comparisons to tawdry 'lowlife' scenes of down-at-heel street performers and peepshows. Such a conception is close to what Fredric Jameson in *Postmodernism or the Cultural Logic of Late Capitalism* terms 'the waning of affect', a quality he sees as characteristic of the postmodern era (1991, 11). Such a contemporary loss of affect seems to be more acute than it was for any Romantic figure, as the narrator of 'Scale' makes clear when comparing Coleridge's drug vision in 'Kubla Khan' to his own: 'Well I mean, it's pathetic, this DIY addiction. No wonder that there are no pleasure domes for me, in my *bricolage* reverie. Instead I see twice five yards of fertile ground, with sheds and raspberry canes girded round. In a word: an allotment' (Self, 1996b, 100). The grandeur of a Romantic hallucination has been reduced to a disappointingly limited and commonplace scene, producing a deflation that has a good deal of comic value. In terms of comedy, Self has cited Woody Allen as an influence who has grown, remarking that 'as I grew older I began to appreciate the way Allen's humour both anticipates the evolution of late-twentieth century comedy – the crystallisation of the absurdity of urban alienation' (Self, 1996a, 154). Allen's famous and prolific use of the 'bathetic let-down' (158) would seem to be the one-liner equivalent of the comically deflating effect that Self so often builds up at length in his writing. One particular story by Allen, 'The Kuglemass Episode' (Allen, 1980) – where a Jewish academic is transported into the world of Emma Bovary and his textual appearance is witnessed by people reading Flaubert's novel – comes in for particular praise from Self, who argues that 'this kind of conceit goes far further than the simple schemas of Allen one-liners, creating a *reductio ad absurdum* of fantasy/reality, reality/fantasy, that is the hallmark of true satire' (Self, 1996b, 159). Exactly this kind of conceit is used in Self's own novel *My Idea of Fun* when The Fat Controller appears in the texts of library books Wharton consults, one of which is De Quincey's *Confessions of an English Opium-Eater* (1907, first published 1821). In Self's narrative, The Fat Controller usurps the place of De Quincey's Malayan visitor and turns up at the Romantic writer's house demanding opium (Self, 1994a, 127–8). In this conceit, the real and the fantastic take on each other's characteristics, and we get a strange co-mingling of fantasy and realism, a co-mingling which was apparent from Self's earliest work, especially 'The North London Book of the Dead'.

Self's appraisal of Woody Allen's '*reductio ad absurdum* of fantasy/ reality, reality/fantasy that is the true hallmark of satire' may be taken as a useful indication of how Self's own satire tends to operate. Having said that satire 'depends on comic exaggeration and on stereotyping', Self was then asked by Martin Amis whether he considered himself a satirist, to which he responded:

> Unquestionably, yes. I mean, when critics say – well, one critic said about *Quantity Theory*: I don't think Self is interested in character, or in narrative, he's interested in conceits and language – and I took this on the chin. I read this when I was writing *Cock & Bull*, which is, of course, an elaborate joke about the failure of narrative. It's true, I'm not really interested in character at all. Indeed, I don't even really believe in the whole idea of psychological realism. I see it as dying with the nineteenth-century novel. (Self, 1996a, 381)

So, for Self, satire in a sense frees him from the strictures of the nineteenth-century novel (as he sees it); he is similarly trenchant about the decline of the nineteenth-century novel as a viable form in his interview with J.G. Ballard in *Junk Mail* (Self, 1996a, 349–50), while Ballard's comments are almost identical to his own 1995 introduction to *Crash*. In this way Self might be regarded as using in his fiction that perhaps oxymoronic quality, an 'orthodox grotesque'. His ubiquitous allusions to Rabelais and Swift continually stress how his work relates to a literary tradition of satire that has become sanctioned with the passage of time, and that is closely associated with the machinery and preoccupations of the grotesque. One of the effects of writing in the Swiftian tradition of satire is facing accusations of what Self terms 'a lack of sympathy' (Self, 1996a, 350), where critics suggest that the author is misanthropic and as a consequence of such misanthropy has created repellent narratives and characters. As Martin Amis explored in *Money*, the force of 'character' and 'motivation' as concepts inherited from nineteenth-century realism seems to be exhausted, and Self in his conversations with Amis and Ballard takes care to concur with their rather polemical views concerning the novel's turn away from realism.

One historical source of ideas about satire and the grotesque that may help us place Self's work in relation to realism is Wyndam Lewis's writings in *Men Without Art* (1934). Lewis, a modernist writing specifically against Romantic approaches to art and literature and against the nineteenth-century novel, provides a useful template to consider Self's work. Like Self, Swift is the major figure in the tradition within which Lewis places his own work and which he seeks to defend (Lewis uses a long quote from the passage describing the Maids of Honour of Brobdingnag in his discussion). As far as the coincidence of satire and the grotesque is concerned, Lewis sees them as inextricably linked:

> There is a stiffening of Satire in everything good, of 'the grotesque', which is the same thing – the non-human outlook must be there (beneath the fluff and pulp which is all that is seen by the majority) to correct our soft conceit. This cannot be gainsaid. Satire is *good*!
> (Lewis, 1934, 121)

Thus, for Lewis, satire and the grotesque are intertwined in their mutual dependence on different perspectives, and Lewis's 'non-human outlook' might be said to anticipate the ethological and 'anthropological' perspectives used by Self in his work, as well as the 'Martian' and global perspectives of Martin Amis and the childhood and adolescent perspectives of Ian McEwan.

Lewis's examination in *Men Without Art* of Hazlitt's distinction between Shakespeare's characters (in Hazlitt's terms 'men') and Ben Jonson's ('more like machines, governed by mere routine, or by the convenience of the poet whose property they are') has parallels with Self's own fiction. Lewis defends Jonson on the grounds that it is *because* the characters are like machines that they are suitable for satire, but Self's rejection of a 'sympathetic character' is more radical, as shown by his comments on *My Idea of Fun*:

It's not that I demand that a character be 'sympathetic' in any commonly understood way – indeed, the wish to show the impossibility of achieving this in the contemporary novel is what lay behind my creation of Ian Wharton – but I do want his lack of sympathetic qualities to point to some wider issue, whether social, psychological or metaphysical. (Self, 1996a, 145–6)

The background to Self's comments lies in the conversations with Ballard and Amis, where the writers argue that traditional realism and its concomitant concepts of character and motivation are unsuited to contemporary concerns and worldviews. The wider issues Self describes his work pointing to, in the above quotation, can be considered the reason why the characters cannot be sympathetic: our 'social, psychological or metaphysical' understanding of the subject, post-Douglas and post-Lévi-Strauss, post-Freud and post-Darwin, may well be unconducive to 'sympathy' in Self's sense. The human subject as the neurotic descendant of apes, mired in ritual, and far less rational that it thinks it is, is positioned within a kind of fiction (the grotesque) which does not veil characters' sexualities, addictions, neuroses or biological natures and so is less likely to preserve the reader's 'sympathy' as its nineteenth-century fictional counterpart may have done.

Lewis and Self, however, concur on another aspect of satire, which is its relation to a moral framework. The first chapter of *Men Without Art* is entitled 'Why the Greatest Satire is Non-Moral', and Lewis goes about arguing his case by asserting the universal applicability of laughter (1934, 109–14). Self proceeds from a different starting point but seems to reach a similar conclusion when he declares in interview that 'a modern satire cannot necessarily be a satire with even a hidden moral message, but rather a modern satire has to have the message 'think for yourself' beneath it' (Bragg, 1998). For Self, it is in the acutely morally relativised contemporary epoch that the role of the satirist changes. In his conversation with Amis, Self suggests that Amis has accepted 'the loss of objective moral correlatives', to which Amis responds:

I am very interested in where my characters stand morally. And in that sense I'm not in a moral vacuum. But on the other hand, I don't feel any urge to convert them, or punish them, or bring them round. Or even to make them see what they're doing. Because that doesn't square with how I see the world. (Self, 1996a, 399)

In that both writers share (with Ballard) a recognition of the inadequacy of the novelist-as-judge for characters, this kind of comment depicts Self as a specifically modern satirist of the rituals of contemporary culture.

When considering Self's multiple literary influences, one can identify a certain strand of drug-related writing in the references to Burroughs and Kerouac, and to De Quincey's *Confessions of an English Opium-Eater* and Coleridge's 'Kubla Khan'. Such works are famous (or infamous) for their spirit of intoxication and for the abandon with which they spin out their bizarre visions or stories, and collectively form part of a tradition that disobeys normative forms of narrative economy. Self's own stories seem to partake in this excess and overloading of narrative and, as I have outlined, the prominent features of his work include his gloriously vast vocabulary, the 'stretched' metaphors, the grotesque sex and violence. Chapter 1 of this study discussed how the grotesque in art and literature has frequently been identified with intoxication by critics such as Ruskin. The relationship between intoxication and economy has historically been defined on two interrelated levels: on the one hand we have the metaphor of intoxication used by critics to signal a disregard of narrative economy and decorum. It is this metaphor of intoxication which Northrop Frye, in *Anatomy of Criticism* (1957), puts in scare quotes when he notes that: 'The metaphor of "intoxication" is often employed for the breakdown of rhetorical control' (1957, 328). On the other hand we have the metaphor of intoxication, not used as a self-conscious term in literary criticism, but referring to the disposition of the author. Here the intoxication found in the text is not so much a metaphor for the poor craftsmanship of the writer (which is the sense Frye uses it in when describing a kind of rant) but is a metaphor for the writer's state of mind during the text's production.

A famous example of this in action is Walter Scott's review of E.T.A. Hoffmann's stories, outlined in Chapter 1. As I described, Scott seems at least as interested in Hoffmann's person as he is in the writer's work, and he gradually builds a picture of a writer inured to intoxication. We can see here the displacement of concerns over Hoffmann's writing, over its bizarre events, its excess which breaks up narrative economy, to concerns over Hoffmann's habits of intoxication. In Scott's discourse, disruptions in narrative economy are understood to issue from disruptions of the bodily economy of the writer, since the author, addled by nightmares and abuse of wine, tobacco and very possibly opium, can hardly be expected to produce any kind of coherent (and disciplined) prose. Wordsworth, in stark contrast, had a 'virtuous, manly, and well-regulated disposition' which is why his poetry produces 'pleasing, tender, and consoling reflections' (Scott, 1835, XVIII, 305).

The metaphor of intoxication in Scott's discourse loses Frye's scare quotes and for him intoxication is no longer a useful way of describing prose but is a way of explaining it so that the writing itself stands less as a metaphor, and more as a synecdoche of the author's intoxication and his disturbed mental state. If we apply this to Self's work, then the irruption of sex, violence and the grotesque in his fiction now takes on a symptomatic edge so that attention is turned not to vagaries of style but to the symptoms of an unstable mind, perhaps overturned by substance abuse. The incident when Self smoked heroin on the prime minister's aeroplane, his subsequent dismissal from *The Observer*, and his numerous newspaper and television articles on the subject of drugs and drug addiction has sometimes led his writing to be viewed principally through the prism of his past drug use. This risks creating the perception that, as with Scott on Hoffmann, features of Self's writing should be understood not as a metaphor for drug taking but as a synecdoche of drug taking and the artistic consequence of intoxication.

Against such a risk, it is important to attend to how such a collapse of metaphor into synecdoche works to reassert a particular kind of aesthetic economy where well-regulated and sober prose becomes naturalised and legitimised by the link between narrative economy and bodily health. Social and chemical deviancy in the form of intoxication and of excessive indulgence in mind-altering substances in this view results in artistic deviancy, in the disregard for artistic norms and decorum and the disruption of the aesthetic economy of realism, as I explored in Chapter 1. At its most extreme, this discourse seems to abolish other artistic modes and reduce all art to the level of natural representation – Hoffmann, Self and the others, according to this argument, are describing realistically the flotsam and jetsam of their drugged minds, so that they are not creating so much as reflecting. However, as I have discussed above, Self's work presents drug use not as an exception to the wider economy and an activity and lifestyle separated off from the rest of consumer capitalism, but as a particular and specialised part of it. Unlike Scott on Hoffmann, Self's fiction and criticism suggests that in contemporary consumer society drugs do not marginalise the artist and his work but may on the contrary make his work a synecdoche of the wider culture. The view of Self's work in the media, though, is usually closer to Scott's view of drug taking as a social perversion and, using a metaphor of economy, the cause of his artistic 'perversion' and 'aberrant' aesthetic practices, than it is to Self's projected relationship between capitalism and drug use.

As Self's career as a writer has developed and he has moved further away from his time as an addict, the close association of his fiction with drugs has diminished. This maturity, *pace* my discussion of Ian McEwan, has not led to a more conventional mode of writing, and Self continues to be conspicuous in his willingness to trace the extreme transmogrifications of everyday life in his fiction's heady mix of the fantastic and the prosaic. Later novels such as *The Book of Dave* (2006) and *The Butt* (2008) have extended the range of Self's grotesque idiom by increasing by several magnitudes the distortions and flights of imagination he fictionally wreaks on contemporary society. In *The Book of Dave* a divorced London taxi-driver's feelings of resentment and marginalisation lead him to write a seething rant of a book that centuries later has become the holy scripture of a future civilisation living an Early-Modern-level existence in an England transformed by floods. In this novel, which is subtitled 'A Revelation of the Recent Past and the Distant Future', Self's longstanding interest that I delineated above in what people in the future will make of the objects that survive our civilisation becomes an imaginative leap into the future that is also a penetrating inquiry into the contemporary. *The Butt* is set in a fantasy of contemporary Australia, but as its subtitle 'An Exit Strategy' hints, there is a strong nightmarish atmosphere of post-occupation Iraq, beset by sudden insurgent attacks and controlled by adherence to ritualistic laws putatively based on 'native tradition'. The protagonist's voyage into the heart of the 'wild zone' in an act of contrition reveals the contradictory and destructive nature of the West's attitudes to its 'others', fed by a toxic combination of cultural supremacy and patronising orientalism.

Instead of Self's fiction being explained by the author (or more precisely by his drug use) we should regard it as being an example of Barthes's description of the text 'made up of multiple writings, drawn from many cultures and entering into mutual relations of dialogue, parody, contestation...' (Barthes, 1977, 148). In Self's fiction, the tradition of grotesque satire in Swift and Rabelais meets the approaches of Lévi-Strauss and Mary Douglas, and the European tradition of Kafka and Céline meets the American Beat writers and drug users Burroughs and Kerouac. The profusion of influences that Thom Nairn sees in the work of Iain Banks (quoted at the beginning of this chapter) can also be traced in the 'burrowings and borrowings' of Self's fiction, which – like the grotesque body of Frankenstein's monster – is made up of diverse elements. In the same way that Self incorporates a profusion of literary sources, his fiction shares a number of family likenesses with the other writers examined here: the sexual transformations and theatrical characters of Angela Carter can be found in his work and, like Martin Amis, Self frequently presents the human body as grotesque and depicts an endless empty cycle of consumer capitalism with an exuberant, hyperbolic use of language and the play of perspective. In common with the work of Ian McEwan, Self's fiction uses childhood perspectives on the mysterious world of adults and prowls the border between madness and sanity, and Iain Banks's work shares with Self's an appetite for grotesque violence and psychopathic paranoia, together with careful juxtaposition. As we have seen, Self's fiction draws together a number of strands of the grotesque and from them weaves a very individual and distinctive contemporary voice of considerable intellectual energy.

Notes

1 Self quoted in 'Self Love', a supplement (undated) with *The Observer* which includes a selection of Self's restaurant reviews for the newspaper.

2   See M. Hunter Hayes's *Understanding Will Self* (2007) for a discussion of the parallels between *My Idea of Fun* and James Hogg's *Confessions of a Justified Sinner* (2002, first published 1824).
3   The childish connotations of these scenarios also recur in 'Tough, Tough Toys for Tough, Tough Boys' – the story detailing Bill's car journey from the Scottish Highlands to London takes its title from a Tonka toy advertisement (Self, 1999, 144).
4   'Scale' is from the collection *Grey Area and Other Stories* (1996b, first published 1994) and was originally published in 1993 in a limited pictorial edition and subsequently in an abridged version in *Granta*. 'Mono-cellular' is from *The Quantity Theory of Insanity* (1994b, first published 1991). 'Design Faults in the Volvo 769 Turbo: A Manual' is from *Tough, Tough Toys for Tough, Tough Boys* (1999, first published 1998) and was originally published in a limited edition by Penguin in 1998.
5   See also in 'Scale' the narrator's drug vision where he visits the motorway chieftains 20,000 years from now (Self, 1996b, 96–8).
6   '[I]t is my contention that the motorways of today are our pyramids, our ziggurats, our great collective earthworks. Perhaps 10,000 years from now, when they are grassed over, the archaeologists of this distant era will be puzzled by the harmony between the motorways, with their sweeping curves, banks and revetments, and neolithic monuments such as Silbury Hill and the Avebury stone circle. Possibly they will advance the theory of the existence of a continuous motorway culture lasting some 7,000 years' (Self, 1996a, 133, first published in *The Times* 25 September 1993).

The influence of works by J.G. Ballard such as *The Day of Creation* (1987) and especially *Crash* (1995, first published 1973) – with its stylised and ritualised encounters between human and machine, sex and technology – can be seen in both this preoccupation and in Self's interest in cars (see especially 'Tough, Tough, Toys for Tough, Tough Boys' (Self, 1999)).
7   'The idea that in some distant future Crystal Palace might be excavated, revealing successively: the remains of a Bronze Age hill fort; the remains of a multiplex cinema; the remains of an iron and glass palace; and then far far deeper the remains of another Bronze Age hill fort, brings a twitch to my jowls. Will the disputatious archaeologists of the distant future be led to posit an interregnum, a dark age between their civilisation and our own? I certainly hope so.' (Self, 2000b, 177)

8 See M. Hunter Hayes's *Understanding Will Self* (2007) for a detailed account of Self's use of characters across multiple texts.
9 In contrast to this description, Self in a review described the fictional birth scene in the hospital television drama programme *ER* and its 'gunk-free' baby as 'a falling off in verisimilitude for the show's otherwise ghastly *verité* (*Independent on Sunday* 12 March 2000 Review p. 14).

Chapter 7

Toby Litt: haunted by the grotesque

> Self's work contains striking contradictions at times, demanding that readers believe in the veracity of his fictional world while intentionally undermining the very processes that would make such consideration possible. (Hayes, 2007, 4)

Toby Litt's first collection of stories, *Adventures in Capitalism* (2003) was first published in 1996 and immediately created a critical stir around its inventive approach to the world of branding and consumerism. The book's playful combination of actual brand names (including HMV, Wagamama and Mr Kipling) with intertextual homage to Michel Foucault marked it out as signalling the emergence of a new talent in British fiction. Since its publication, Litt has written eleven books, the titles of which proceed in alphabetical order up to his 2010 novel *King Death*. This chapter will examine the development of Litt's work and how it is informed by the grotesque in terms of its consistent use of distortion and humour and in relation to its complex fusion of the prosaic and the fantastic. The discussion of a selection of Litt's fiction will show how his literary career has been shaped by an arguably postmodern approach to contemporary culture but one that is also based on a contemporary form of the literary grotesque. Looking beyond the grotesque bodies (and component parts) scattered through his fiction, Litt's tendency to subvert genre is perhaps one of his most prominent qualities, as noted by Fiona Tolan (Tew, Tolan and Wilson, 2008, 84), apparent in his appropriation of and play with Beat fiction in *Beatniks* (1998, first published 1997), crime thrillers in *Corpsing* (2000), 'chick lit' in *Finding Myself* (2004a, first published 2003), ghost stories in *Ghost Story* (2005, first published 2004), medical drama in *Hospital* (2007) and science fiction in *Journey into Space* (2009), in addition to *deadkidsongs* (2001) and its complex relation to Romantic literature explored below. So, while his writing certainly exhibits some of the abiding concerns of literary postmodernism, including scepticism regarding narrative truthfulness and an acute awareness of the power of mass media and advertising in shaping human behaviour, it does so through tapping into the rich tradition of jarring comparisons, the grotesque body, physical transformations, warped mentalities and black comedy of the grotesque.

Adventures in postmodernism

Adventures in Capitalism (2003) is divided into two sections, 'Early Capitalism' and 'Late Capitalism', and the collection's various forays into the apparently mundane world of shopping and consumption are performed in a humorous but sometimes darkly comic vein. If the chronological division of contents might suggest a dry and perhaps academic approach to current economic affairs, the stories themselves are a far more loose collection bound up with delusory consumption of various kinds, starting with the opening story 'It Could Have Been Me and It Was', which plays with the National Lottery's slogan 'It Could be You'. The narrator of the tale has won the lottery and decides to act for a 'fairytale year' on every advertising exhortation he encounters, leading to an orgy of purchasing, with all brand-names italicised, in a catalogue of cars, food and services including joining *Weight-Watchers* and the *Territorial Army*. The punishing schedule of obeying advertisers and buying their wares leads the hapless narrator to China in a bid to preserve himself in a zone of illegible signifiers but even there he struggles to escape a globalised system of branding, eventually ending up back in the UK and finishing the story in a clinic where he is denied access to any media and confined to reading *Bleak House*. Dickens's classic novel of thwarted desire for an inheritance used up by a bureaucratic Chancery Court serves as a suitable echo of the story's unhappy lottery winner whose decision to take at face value advertisements familiar to most British readers is driven to comically absurd levels where the unwanted and apparently useless items pile up until they threaten the narrator's very survival. The willingness to push an idea to comic and disturbing – that is, grotesque – extremes is a quality that became apparent in the stories that followed in this collection and to a significant degree in Litt's later writing.

In her review of this collection Mary Scott notes that 'Toby Litt's short stories will no doubt be compared to those of Will Self, who is brilliant, imaginative and under-endowed with human warmth' (1996, 48) and indeed *Adventures in Capitalism* does share a number of qualities with Self's oeuvre, not least the grotesque combinations of the fantastic and the banal. In Litt's world, as in Self's, there are strange metamorphoses as a sunflower grows out of a character's cheek in 'The Sunflower', while in 'Launderama' a ghost is found haunting that most unromantic and utilitarian of spaces, a launderette. Scott's point about the lack of human warmth seems to fulfil Self's prediction that contemporary novelists who eschew the role of moral arbiter are often accused of 'a lack of sympathy' (Self, 1996b, 350) although this charge has not been quite as prominent in the reception of Litt's work as it has been in Self's case. As I showed in the last chapter, Self's fiction imaginatively explores the territories of late capitalism and the ways in which drug taking comes to represent an extreme example of a general cultural condition. The cultivation of consumer desire through marketing and advertising is a key theme for both Self and Litt, and 'It Could Have Been Me and It Was', although not depicting drug use, might perhaps best be understood as presenting an addiction to consumption that is produced through the often unremarked rhetorical power of advertising. This same rhetorical power is evident in 'Please Use a Basket', where the Boots shop assistant whose image is used in stores to encourage shoppers to use baskets (which themselves encourage shoppers to buy more items) is dismayed that her former visibility as an advertising icon is of no use in her new war against capitalism as a member of the Socialist Worker Party, trying to sell party newspapers outside a Boots shop.

Brand consciousness is a recurrent motif in *Adventures in Capitalism*, as the characters negotiate a contemporary world saturated with real brands that will be familiar to many British readers from their own experience. The comic speculation of the deluded narrator of 'Mr Kipling' about the fictitious person behind the real brand of cakes has fun by pointing out the absurdity of the narrator's impression of the 'real' Mr Kipling, whose Anglo-Catholicism is apparently manifested in the cinnamon of his cakes, according to the narrator, which leads local people to doubt his sanity. The story, however, goes beyond this to alert us to the wider absurdity of the use of an invented person and retro packaging to sell the mass-produced cakes of a modern manufacturer. From this perspective, just as Self situates drug addicts within a capitalist matrix of supply and cultivated demand, the credulous or 'mad' narrator of Litt's story may not be as divergent from the media-formed general perception of Mr Kipling as might be at first supposed. The *reductio ad absurdum* of quasi-subliminal ad copy in these two stories is therefore both a source of humour at the narrators' expense while also serving as an uneasy reminder of the sneaky techniques of modern marketing. In 'Fluffy Pink Bunny Rabbit' the tribulations of an actor working as a charity collector while dressed as a rabbit yields the following Arcimboldo-like image of a taxi-driver:

> I glanced back at the back of the cabbie's head. For a moment, it seemed to me that he was completely constructed from the thousands of Full English Breakfasts he had eaten. The back of his neck was streaky bacon. His ears were huge mushrooms. His hair was an accumulation of every hair I'd ever picked out of my food. In the rear-view mirror, I saw his fried bread forehead, his grilled tomato mouth, his black pudding chin, his pork sausage nose. (Litt, 2003, 80)

This description is remarkably similar to a passage discussed in Chapter 3 from Martin Amis's story 'State of England', which was first published in the *New Yorker* the same year that *Adventures in Capitalism* came out, and demonstrates Litt's interest in grotesque humour and presentation of the human body. While this shows an affinity with Amis, the opening of 'Flies II' seems to burlesque the macabre early fiction of Ian McEwan:

> It was the flies. It was the flies, you see, that first led me to suspect that the man living in the end flat of my block had murdered his mother. They hung about all last summer. (Litt, 2003, 175)

The air of decay and suspicion of hidden corpses recalls 'First Love, Last Rites' and *The Cement Garden*, but these elements are handled in Litt's far more comic mode as the elderly narrator provides an increasingly comic and unhinged account of his quarry's actions. Viewed in this light, Litt's first collection is situated at a point in contemporary literature where the grotesque as embodied by the work of established authors is becoming a mode that new writers can draw on in their creation of emergent literary forms.

In an interview with Clare Dwyer Hogg in *The Independent* in 2003 entitled 'Adventures in Postmodernism', Litt expresses an antipathy to the label 'postmodern', claiming that the term might be 'off-putting' and that 'I've never written anything in the hope that it would be postmodern, because as far as I'm concerned, that's something historical' (Dwyer Hogg, 2003, 22). Despite this resistance it is clear that Litt's playful approach to the lack of reality behind advertising is an often-identified concern of postmodern thought:

> Because, somewhere, *someone*, must be living life as advertised. They *have* to be, or else take me out and shoot me *now*. If not, then why do the rest of us even bother to buy? Life as advertised, life as it *should* be, has to be available somewhere. *Maybe*, it's a *rare* metal, *of course* it's an expensive and precious ore, but *please God*, don't let it be a *radioactive* element. (Litt, 2003, 110)

This suspicion that nothing may lie behind the superficial blandishments of advertising leads Litt to an intertextual engagement with poststructuralist philosophy that has seen his work aligned with experimental postmodernist fiction (see, for example, Greaney, 2006), and the story 'When I Met Michel Foucault' is perhaps the most obvious example of this aspect of his writing. The narrative tells of the sometimes erotic dream encounter the narrator Toby has with Foucault, and is interspersed with quotation from and comments about scholarship on the French theorist. The story continues the collection's focus on advertising with a sequence of slogan-bearing badges, and a slightly disturbing climax set in a San Francisco S&M club where the term 'branding' moves from being a trademark and a metaphor for ownership to becoming literal painful physical torture with a hot iron. Litt brings into view this often overlooked etymological connection between retail branding and the punishment inflicted on criminals and embeds it in Foucault's rumoured sexual practices and famous work on prisons *Discipline and Punish* (1991, first published 1975). This punning approach is also apparent in the epigraph to Litt's novel *Corpsing* (2000), listing the two connotations of 'corpse' as a dead body and an actor's blunder. More generally, this interplay of the literal and metaphoric is a fundamental characteristic of Litt's fiction, which tends to elaborate fanciful scenarios in a lucid and concrete way.

Adventures in Capitalism's fragmentary epigraph from Samuel Johnson, 'if the world be promiscuously described ...', situates Litt's writing within eighteenth-century debates around what is fit to be represented in literature, debates which emerged around the new genre of the novel and which often involved the invocation of the grotesque, as I explored in the first chapter of this study. Johnson's point in the *Rambler* of 31 March 1750 from which the fragment comes is that fiction should render virtue attractive and vice disgusting and that this consideration should take precedence over the defence of novelistic description on the grounds of mere verisimilitude. For Johnson, if the new kind of literature is to be worth reading, it must exhibit 'discrimination' rather than 'promiscuously' describing life to the hordes of vulnerable readers (Johnson, 1837, 18). Given the proliferation of real brand names in the collection, Litt's inclination to supply such a discriminating eye seems doubtful and one should perhaps instead look to the grotesque combination of banality and fantasy in his stories as indicating a grotesque approach to realist narrative that manages to be almost prosy in its surreal presentations of often dysfunctional people.

The importance of the eighteenth-century novel as an inspiration for Litt's developing form of the grotesque is made clear in an interview with the author entitled 'The New Bawdy', where he responds to a question about contemporary fiction:

> Things are quite stylish and quite dry. There's not a lot of sweat. There are quite a lot of bodies but they're curiously disinfected bodies. If you look at eighteenth-century fiction, or fiction that comes out of the humours, of grotesque personality, even through Dickens who is not a favourite writer of mine, there's more bustling. One of the things you don't see now is bawdy. If anyone tries bawdy now it becomes embarrassing almost immediately. But it used to be a huge register. (Marshall, 2003a)

The presence of the gross, sweating body and the citation of Dickens attest to the significance of the literary tradition of the grotesque for Litt, and certainly there are frequent eruptions of the grotesque, biological body throughout his oeuvre and a mingling of slapstick humour and repellent physicality. *Corpsing*'s slow-motion, detailed medical descriptions of what each bullet of a gun attack does to the protagonist's internal organs as it penetrates his body are an extended visceral demolition of 'disinfected', 'dry' treatments of the body. *Adventures in Capitalism*'s tension between a quasi-realist attention to quotidian detail and the collection's variety of bathetic oddball characters led one early reviewer to opine: 'One just hopes he'll settle down to something more serious' (Seaton, 1996, 39). Such comments, however, serve to relegate the playful and multifaceted to subordinated artistic value and continue the long tradition that this study has sought to critique of rejecting the grotesque for its supposed failure to separate the serious from the comic. In fact, Litt's subsequent long novels as well as shorter prose pieces have preserved this vital feature of the grotesque and have developed into strange hybrids of fantasy and realism, humour and horror where children's toy models are used to commit murder and women are haunted by lost children.

The grotesque distortions of *deadkidsongs*

If *Adventures in Capitalism* in its pursuit of a comic grotesque bears comparison with the work of Amis and Self, then *deadkidsongs* is an ambitious novel that enters similar terrain to Ian McEwan's disturbing stories of childhood and Iain Banks's *The Wasp Factory*. Litt's frequently observed penchant for comedy is mostly held in abeyance in this story of acts of cruelty and violence perpetrated by a gang of 1970s schoolboys, some of which recall Frank's work in Banks's novel. The militaristic rituals of the four boys in the fictional town of Amplewick become something more dangerous when one of them, Matthew, dies of meningitis and the remaining members, Andrew, Peter and Paul, decide to avenge his death by persecuting his relatives. The novel's title is a loose translation of the *kindertotenlieder* collection of poems written in the 1830s by Fredrich Rückert on the death of his two children, which was turned into a song cycle by Gustav Mahler at the beginning of the twentieth century, and the song cycle provides some of the structure of Litt's book. *deadkidsongs* is divided into four seasonal sections, with each boy taking a turn narrating part of each section, but despite the SUMMER-AUTUMN-WINTER-SPRING banner at the very beginning of the novel, the seasonal cycle finishes with 'Winter (also)' rather than 'Spring'. This formal departure from the expected structure is one aspect of a complex pattern of distortion within the novel, a distortion that takes in Romantic source material and themes but also includes conflicting accounts by the different narrators and their written records.

Employing the time-honoured technique of a frame narrator, Matthew, who has found some secret papers that belonged to his deceased father, the main body of the narrative opens with the boys hanging upside-down in a tree and describes how the world looks from their inverted perspective, an image that Litt has said was one of the starting points for this book about boys.[1] As this study has shown, inversion and play of perspective have been important features of the grotesque tradition, from Rabelais and Swift to the present day, and the sense that the Amplewick boys, who call themselves simply 'Gang', live in a world turned upside-down is gradually developed during their adventures. When Andrew begins to punish Matthew's grandparents for their supposed negligence in failing to prevent his death, he effects a destructive inversion of a helpful bob-a-job:

> He took the handyman skills he had learnt from his father and turned them upside-down. Safety devices were converted into death-traps. The substitution of inadequate, or overadequate fuses, was only the first of his endangerments: throughout the house screws were loosened by a turn or two, or three, and nails pulled a quarter inch from flush; the stair carpet was made to slide back and forth, and the dining-room door to scrape against the lintel. (Litt, 2001, 247)

The cruel ingenuity shown by the boys in their pursuit of revenge is pushed to almost comic levels in the long description of Andrew's actions and the novel exploits the uneasy zone between potentially funny practical jokes and ludicrous childhood games on the one hand and more threatening behaviour and physical danger on the other. Black humour is never too far away and Litt is not above making jokes about gouged eyes (404). Chapter 8's Courier-typeset 'Official Archives of the Gang' are full of amusing spelling mistakes and gaffes (e.g. 'she became histerical and needed to be seduced by a fireman' (218)). However, there is an underlying seriousness to many of the boys' thoughts and feelings and their attempts to exploit each other's weaknesses in pursuit of power show an adult side to their personalities. The disturbed but amusing old man persona of 'Flies II', with his National Service background, balaclava and 'trusty catapult', holed up in his flat with 'tea, cake and evaporated milk' (Litt, 2003, 178) has metamorphosed into a group of young boys singing anachronistic war songs and wearing army surplus, admiring Andrew's physically abusive 'Best Father' and who seem to be steadily transformed into violent killers as the narrative unfolds.

The reason why this transformation into animal cruelty, mutilation and a deadly assault on an elderly women with Airfix models is apparent rather than manifest is that, as the boys take it in turns to narrate the plot, certain discrepancies between their accounts gradually emerge. Different records of Andrew almost drowning after being thrown in water by his father, and different versions of which boy was sleepwalking and who carried Matthew's coffin are the early signs of a narrative instability that increases until doubt is cast on whether there are in fact four individuals involved, with at least one reviewer convinced that the different narrators are memories in the schizoid psyche of a single adult mind.[2] The two competing Chapter 13s, each of which begins on a different p. 375 leave the reader in a dilemma as to which incoherent narrative to trust, and certainly Paul's reflections late on in the novel provide evidence for such a reading:

> All at once, something strange happened. I began to know the *exact* things Andrew had done before I'd even seen them. It was as if I were in two places and times at once, both with myself here now and with Andrew at the moment of killing. (Litt, 2001, 403)

While it remains unclear if the more gruesome acts of violence have been committed or were prevented by timely police intervention, nonetheless the air of calculated sadism is not wholly dispelled. The above quote's sense of being possessed by another person is something that is developed by Litt at greater length in *Finding Myself* and *Ghost Story*, as discussed below.

Mahler's *kindertotenlieder* provides the title and some of the structure for *deadkidsongs*'s seasonal cycle of narrative sections, and fragments of the five Rückert poems used by the composer as the libretto for his song cycle feature as epigraphs to the narratives of the Evangelist-sounding quartet of Andrew, Peter, Paul and Matthew. Litt reproduces the German original in heavy gothic type, with English translations below. Asked in interview whether these were his own translations, Litt replied 'Yes. They're quite distorted' (McCrum, 2001, 17), but this hardly does justice to his changes. In place of the high-culture Rückert elegies mourning two children who died of scarlet fever, Litt has introduced argot including 'kids', 'koochy-koo face' and 'diddy daughter' into his English versions. As the novel progresses, the translations become more distorted until the epigraph to 'Chapter 13 (also)' departs even further from its Romantic precursor through the addition of killing to the translation, in the form of the children committing 'Matricide', 'Patricide' and 'Fratricide'. This semantic sleight-of-hand functions as a grotesque distortion of a Romantic tradition of childhood innocence in which children were, in Litt's words, 'incredibly sentimentalised' (McCrum, 2001, 17). Against the mute shadows that haunt Rückert's poems, who do not speak or display much individuality or anti-social impulse, Litt pitches his violent, power-obsessed but active Amplewick boys, who 'Live to Kill, Kill to Live' (Litt, 2001, 285). The Romantic and indeed gothic commonplace of an evil father-figure mistreating an innocent child is almost reversed, since although Andrew's violent father functions as a gothic 'dark father' whose domestic abuse has warped Andrew, the children end up launching a secret war against Matthew's vulnerable grandparents, whom they nickname the Dinosaurs.

The adoption of an anti-Romantic view of childhood in *deadkidsongs* has been remarked by a number of critics and Litt has been open about his intentions in interview: 'It seemed to me far more interesting to satirize say, Nature in *deadkidsongs* – a view of Nature that is Wordsworthian, and says we learn positive values from nature, that we are improved by it' (Tew, Tolan and Wilson, 2008, 80). In this satirical cause Litt has placed the boys in the notionally idyllic English countryside of Amplewick, but this beautiful natural landscape does not seem to act as a humanising force in their lives. One of the book's potential titles was 'Descriptions of the English Countryside', and the narrative contains a great deal of detail on the local environment that the boys explore and make their home, meeting at various outdoor 'camps' to develop their nefarious plans. While much of the novel is narrated in the first person plural, the unity of this collective 'we' or 'us' is not harmonious, and after Matthew's death Paul and Andrew struggle over the direction of Gang, in effect the compliance, or perhaps allegiance, of Peter. Gang's frequent isolation from other people and its group mentality and internal power struggles have led to comparisons with *Lord of the Flies* (e.g. McCrum, 2001, 17 and Tew, 2004, 131), a work that continues to cast a shadow over much recent writing on children, including *The Cement Garden*, as discussed in Chapter 4. However, although *deadkidsongs* might be firmly aligned with Golding's novel in terms of its anti-Romantic treatment of boys, Litt's work does not follow the quasi-Christian allegorical approach perceived in *Lord of the Flies*. Litt has also sought to distinguish his novel from the earlier book in terms of his use of a realist and specifically English setting, rather than Golding's desert island:

> I didn't want to isolate the boys in the way that island novels like *Lord of the Flies* or *Robinson Crusoe* isolate their characters in order to make a point about society – because the isolation creates a distance. You can say with *Lord of the Flies* that there is barbarism because there is a lack of adult supervision; because they're in a barbarous place; because boys will be boys when conditions are right. *deadkidsongs* doesn't say that: it says, if you ruthlessly follow the logic of power, this is what happens. (Tew, Tolan and Wilson, 2008, 79–80)

Although this description of the important influences on the boys' growth holds true for *deadkidsongs*, the issue of isolation raised here is quite a complex one, as Litt's fiction repeatedly deals with small groups of characters who are detached from their surroundings in a variety of ways, from *Exhibitionism*'s 'The New Puritans' to *Finding Myself* to *Journey into Space*. Many of his plots begin with an apparently predictable set of relationships between a limited group of people that later breaks down under a combination of both internal and external factors, including sexual disenchantment ('Alphabed' from *Exhibitionism*), deceit (*Finding Myself*) and bereavement (*Ghost Story*).

The significance of the semi-rural territory around the boys' homes in Amplewick and their sense of ownership of it is tied up with the characters' exaggerated patriotism and a background though persistent threat of imminent Soviet attack. Gang's activities are viewed by its members as a kind of preparation for a Russian invasion and the boys see War, which is always capitalised in their discourse, as man's highest calling (with the gender-typing this implies). The hallowed nature of warfare to the boys is made clear by Paul's reflections:

> If pressed, Paul would say that he found War exciting. What he meant by exciting was that he understood the total importance of War, for making human life, all life, what it is. Life is War. Life is conflict. And to sit down all pretend-friendly at the kitchen table and act as if it wasn't ... Well, that was the behaviour of someone afraid of conflict. And this was how Paul knew his father to be a coward. (Litt, 2001, 85)

War in the boys' minds takes on the ambivalent status of a potential national disaster that may destroy them and a longed-for opportunity to engage in open violence and display discipline and heroism against a dehumanised enemy. The mythic quality of warfare shapes their attitude to people in uniforms, including medical staff, although the unwelcome attentions of a local policeman earns him the title of 'SS-Kommandant'. This slippage between Germany and Russia and the apparent interchangeability of Nazi foes and Soviet ones are part of an atmosphere of ongoing endless war, in which Englishmen must forever be vigilant. As Philip Tew observes, by the end of the novel 'the wartime aspects of the imaginary, mythic past subsume the co-ordinates of the map' (2004, 132), as the boys try to elude the 'foreign forces' that have invaded their English hometown. Litt has claimed in interview that *deadkidsongs* is 'the most political thing I've written' (Tew, Tolan and Wilson, 2008, 80), and the book's political edge comes from the illuminating connections it establishes between the boys' acts and the wider contexts both of the Cold War and of contemporary masculinity. Just as Frank's understanding of gender differences is drawn from the contemporary social milieu in Banks's *The Wasp Factory*, so Gang's sense of group identity is not self-generated in a desert island vacuum such as the one used in *Lord of the Flies* but rather is consciously constructed by them from existing models of national and gender identities which they select from their environment. As Paul's thoughts on War show, the idea of conflict takes on an almost religious significance for the boys and is contrasted with his parents' desire to inculcate a different set of values to those of Andrew's father, a violent man idolised by Gang as 'Best Father' who abuses Andrew and his mother (Litt, 2001, 340–2). The boys' participation in military-style games under his tutelage dominates the very closed and secretive network of their relationships and makes them resistant to attempts by others to alter their views.

Paul's parents' despairing attempts to change their son's perception of Andrew's father are unsuccessful at least in part because of the correlation the boys perceive between their lifestyle in Gang and the wider historical and political context of 1970s England. Andrew's father has fostered a sense of power worship and bullying in the group and his mistreatment of Andrew is key to Andrew's leading role in Gang and controlling influence over the other boys. Gang consistently view such mistreatment as a kind of preparation for the wider world awaiting them after school and regard other grown-ups as desiring the boys to be well-behaved and 'weak' (187). Aware of the tension between Paul's parents and Andrew's father, Paul chooses the Best Father based on the future value of the hardships he imposes:

> It was a conflict in which one of the sides was fighting against the very idea of conflict itself. Paul's parents, under their political delusion, were trying to make the world a better, less violent place, by bringing their son up in what they saw as a better, less violent way. Paul, like all of Gang, saw beyond his immediate circumstances, and out into the wider world, a world which was not improving, which, if anything, was becoming worse. (Litt, 2001, 85)

In support of his Gang 'training' and activities Paul cites persistent global conflict that can only be resolved through state violence and the uncompromising cultivation and use of power. The naturalness of violence is shown not as a product of the boys' independence from adult supervision, as Golding's book might indicate, but to issue from the political views fostered by Andrew's father, views which have some popularity in the wider world. The idea that the essence of life is conflict and that conflict should be constantly anticipated and practised, and that those who seek to avoid it are cowards, is thus revealed as a particular political construction that paradoxically is rooted in the particular moment while also already archaic, like the First World War songs sung by Gang, who, according to Litt, 'are being true to beliefs held by 50-year-old men in club chairs' (Tew, Tolan and Wilson, 2008, 79). *deadkidsongs* stages the elevation of such right-wing political sentiments into an adolescent lifestyle of domination and obedience with its concomitant hierarchies and plotting. The Best Father is shown to create both a home-life of violent domestic abuse and a vision of world affairs as continual warfare and it is out of this overlapping territory that the dysfunctional Andrew will emerge.

In discussing the novel's setting, Litt has specified 1979 as a key year (Tew, Tolan and Wilson, 2008, 79) and the Conservative Party victory under Margaret Thatcher in the general election of that year has been seen as introducing a new right-wing neo-liberal agenda into British politics. Having launched policies of deregulation and privatisation of state-owned businesses and regularly confronting unions, the Conservative government was soon languishing in the opinion polls, but was boosted by the British victory in the Falklands conflict in 1982 and elected with a large majority the following year. The emphasis during this period of economic and social reorganisation was frequently on the importance of competition, particularly through market-based solutions, as a force for positive change and a means of delivering better and more efficient services to the public. The enshrinement of competition as a desirable and perhaps natural feature of social and economic life was sometimes thought to reflect the supposedly 'Darwinian' nature of historical progress, with competition producing a more advanced species and civilisation. The boys' focus on Darwin in *deadkidsongs* is therefore more than simply a common interest in dinosaurs often exhibited by young boys but the extension of a nominally evolutionary approach to social relations. As Peter reads from his textbook *The Death of the Dinosaurs: A Scientific Investigation and Explication* to the other members of Gang (Litt, 2001, 196–9) they perceive the death of large dim-witted dinosaurs and the subsequent pre-eminence of small mammals and *homo sapiens* as the story of their own struggle against adults in general and Matthews' grandparent guardians in particular. The use of Darwin's theory in this way radically alters the boys' view of the natural world and the natural order of things and the textbook's mantra that 'Extinction is not only Nature's way, it is Nature's very self' (199) turns Romantic Nature as a force of sometimes agitated but ultimately balanced harmony into a zone of renewal through endless destruction. Gang's motto of 'Live to Kill, Kill to Live' and Paul's reflection that 'Life is War' are revealed by Litt to be not so much a sociopathic aberration as the grotesque exaggeration of extinction as 'Nature's very self'. The boys' faith in the naturalness and perpetuity of conditions of conflict can therefore be read not as a sign of dysfunction on their part due to isolation but on the contrary their careful integration of a specific political vision. This politics embraces nationalist sentiment and is based on competition and destruction, embodied both in the Cold War competition for supremacy in destructive potential through nuclear weapons stockpiling and in emergent right-wing support at the end of the 1970s for the application of competition as a solution to social problems.

The division in opinion as to how to interpret the demise of the dinosaurs in relation to their own lives is suggestive, with Andrew claiming that Gang is the catastrophic event that destroyed the dinosaurs while Paul argues that they have to be *homo sapiens*, 'the thing that survives' (200). Andrew has gradually emerged as a leader whose appetite for violence could wreck the futures of all the boys, so Paul's pragmatic approach eventually trumps Andrew's self-destructive one but they are united in their rage against Mr and Mrs Dinosaur, or Bert and Estella, their real names only revealed by Paul when he has decided to try to protect them from Andrew's attacks. *deadkidsongs* is notable for its lack of names, with only a very few characters designated by real names (e.g. Miranda, Matthew's sister, and Alma, the social worker), and Gang habitually use their compass point code names as surnames, increasing the claustrophobic atmosphere of the narrative and the focus on the immediate and local. Conflict is now seen by the boys as a central engine of progress, and success viewed as survival in a competitive environment, so it does not come as a complete surprise to the reader that despite the boys' code of loyalty Gang become riven by divergent plans and a power struggle emerges. Their use of quasi-sexual blackmail, subterfuge and violence against one another is part and parcel of their existence in a world they regard as structured by tight control and the ruthless use of power and in this regard is a synecdoche of the darker aspects of adult life, not adolescent resistance to it.

The novel finishes with a second Chapter 13 followed by a coda by the frame narrator. 'Chapter 13 (also)' is ostensibly narrated by 'Peter (Paul)' and describes Gang's apprehension at the hands of 'the authorities', represented by the professional triumvirate of headteacher, social worker and police officer. In this version the killings of Miranda, Bert and Estelle and Andrew's suicide in the first Chapter 13 have not taken place, and Paul has revealed Gang's activities to the grown-ups and blamed Andrew for their misbehaviour, a symbolic betrayal. Peter (or Paul) is in 'temporary exile in the still-free land of Canada' (399) and presents a final vision of the English countryside he misses:

> The hedgerows leave their benign temporary grid upon the fields of wide, ungarnered wheat. A hawk is hovering above one of these mice-sparse fields, like the hand of a child told it may select only one chocolate from the Christmas box. In an adjacent field, on emerald grass, sheep are complying with the zigzag of a border collie – itself obedient to the whistles of a humble shepherd ... A myxomatosized rabbit, using the last of its strength, falls down into the darkness of its home warren. (Litt, 2001, 399)

Litt here carefully constructs what his description through a subtle simile suggests is a self-consciously attractive 'chocolate box' image of pastoral England, but has grotesquely distorted such a Romantic image by showing how it is structured by humanity's mastery of nature. Images of peace achieved through the exercise of power and control define this natural scene in which certain species are unwanted rodents that need to be destroyed. 'Natural' hierarchies of obedience define the natural order: hawk over mice, human over dog over sheep and parent over chocolate-choosing child. The scene's 'Englishness', what marks it out an *English* countryside, is seen to reside in this system of deference and subordination. Litt's final 'Descriptions of the English Countryside' do not recall the wild places of the Lake poets but a human-dominated countryside in which the disease of myxomatosis is emblematic of the deployment of human power against the natural world in the cause of agricultural efficiency. The grotesque juxtaposition of the rabbit inadvertently killing its colony with pleasant images of sunshine over fields shows how far Litt has distorted Romantic sensibilities in his novel.

This final patriotic image of an English countryside finishes with a political flourish looking to a positive future:

> Believe it or believe it not: the Spring will come, and England shall be free once more. I can but hope that I myself will have the posthumous satisfaction of knowing that, in some small way, I helped to bring utopia to pass. (Litt, 2001, 400)

This hoped-for Spring, redolent of the end of Percy Shelley's 'Ode to the West Wind' (1820) will bring political liberation and social regeneration to England. Shelley's poem was written in Italy shortly after the death of his three-year-old son William and so may be placed in a Romantic tradition of mourning children that includes Rückert's *kindertotenlieder*. The melancholy grandeur of the ode and its hopes for radical change in far-off England, imagined from a difficult present and to occur perhaps long after the poet's death, is transformed into a grotesque cliché of conformity in *deadkidsongs*. In place of Shelley's Romantic and nature-mediated dream of the liberal and progressive England to come, Litt offers a similarly nature-inflected twentieth-century one that turns out to be a twisted fascist vision based on exploitation and patriarchal violence.

The 'myxomatosized rabbit' of the novel's final pages is the second time this diseased creature has appeared, the first being in Chapter 5. In this earlier episode, Gang find a dying rabbit and are told by Andrew's father to try and dump the body down a warren to kill the colony. Having been told by the Best Father that myxomatosis is like cancer for rabbits, Matthew – who narrates the chapter – begins to think of his grandfather's illness that he calls 'the Big C' (131) and notices that the rabbit's eyes look a little like his grandfather's. This identification with vulnerability is in stark contrast to Andrew's behaviour:

> Andrew was very happy to be doing two of the things he most enjoyed in the world: obeying his father and killing animals. He dumped the rabbit in the biggest of the holes and cleaned his hands off on his back pockets. 'Our crops are safe,' he said. (Litt, 2001, 131)

The toxic convergence of filial obedience and animal cruelty is a welcome development for Andrew, and is an early indication of the obscene lengths to which he will go in order to act on such desires. His portentous declaration is slightly premature, however, as the rabbit, earning Matthew's admiration, tries to run away: 'With some last strength that it had bravely gathered, the rabbit tried to lollop away from the warren. Maybe it was trying to save its brother and sister rabbits' (132). This *Watership Down*-like moment is short-lived as Andrew kicks the escaping animal and kills it, frustrating his original plan, and he tells the rest of Gang not to mention this 'failure' to his father. This is the disappointing reality, mixed with feelings of anthropomorphic pity, that the description of a better England at the end of the novel wants to put right by having the rabbit enter the warren, symbolising the simultaneous satisfaction of a craving for violence and a deep desire for paternal approval and a final victory over the capacity of nature to inspire tender feelings.

Exposing the body: *Exhibitionism*

Litt's next book after *deadkidsongs* was the collection *Exhibitionism* (2002) that includes 'Of the Third Kind' where two secretive schoolboys live like the boys of Gang in Amplewick in the 1970s but play Space, having given up playing War, and the kind of surreptitious sexual experimentation hinted at in *deadkidsongs* seems to take place. The collection's stories alternate between those focused on sex and another strand devoted to 'other matters', with the sex stories frequently dealing with the grotesque side of carnal matters. Litt's established interest in experimentation with genre is much in evidence, with stories in the form of a newsgroup posting, a film script, an audioguide and a 'book-in-a-box' piece entitled 'Alphabed', a story of jaded sexual desire alternately narrated by an unnamed 'he' and 'she'. 'Alphabed' is divided into 26 alphabetically labelled short paragraphs 'to be read in any order other than the printed' (179). Sexual familiarity has bred a degree of mutual contempt, and the grotesque physical body is much in evidence:

> What he'd always wanted, he thought, was not a woman but an alabaster statue that would come alive when he wanted to fuck it. Skin, close up, was about the most disgusting thing he could think of. There were moles on her shoulders – some of them little brown cauliflowers that he wanted to bite off. (Litt, 2002, 198)

This cinematically aligned 'close up' is a modern film-influenced iteration of Swift's play of perspective with grotesque Brobdingnagian bodies. The man's desire for the woman is periodic, leading to disgust with her now grotesque body and a sexist fantasy of a 'classical' body (in the Bakhtinian sense) that would become human and penetrable on command. The male surveillance of, and exasperation with female corporeality staged in Swift's 'The Lady's Dressing Room', a touchstone for Martin Amis's *Rachel Papers*, is transformed by Litt into a more equal but still grotesque reciprocal disenchantment in the shared bedchamber. The characters seem isolated in a bower of bliss that is grotesquely inverted and transformed into a foul-smelling den, but the collapse of the passion between the couple and their bored repetition of sexual congress threatens the very fabric of their being:

> This is the state that they are themselves heading towards: deliquescence. A few more days of this, he thinks, and they will flow off either edge of the bed; they will seep into and through the colourless carpet; they will stain the floorboards and wet the wiring; they will drip from the nicotine-brown ceiling of their downstairs neighbours' flat, they will obey gravity all the way down into the ground. (Litt, 2002, 206)

This deliquescence is a distant end since although their desire for one another has dissolved and this should spell the end of their relationship; their reluctance to part despite growing mutual loathing sets them on a path to slow entropic decay. Experiment is now impossible where spontaneity has been reduced to the mechanical repetition characteristic of primitive computer code: 'Once, each touch was pure exploration and improvisation. Now, preprogrammed sub-routine, Basic or C++' (199). Despite the alphabetically printed order, these brief passages of short sentence fragments express a chronic lack of progress and the impossibility of neat closure, with the characters' repeated futile attempts to 'reshuffle' their sexual repertoire unlikely to lead to anything fresh, anticipating the reader's failure to find a happy ending through sequence changes.

The best known of the stories in this collection is 'The New Puritans', which first appeared in and provided the title for the anthology *All Hail the New Puritans* (2002) edited by Nicholas Blincoe and Matt Thorne that included a ten-point manifesto calling for a 'return' to textual simplicity and attention to contemporary life and abstinence from play with narrative temporality and authorial intrusion. The fifteen short stories by different writers included in the anthology were to abide by this set of principles, inspired partly by the Dogme 95 film movement in Denmark and its rejection of special effects. Thorne has claimed in interview that the work of Martin Amis and Salman Rushdie in particular and magical realism in general were targets for the New Puritan project (Marshall, 2003b). While meeting with a mixed critical reception and with only a very small number of works explicitly conforming to its guidelines, the New Puritans, as some of the contributors became known, are perhaps more productively understood as a moment rather than a movement in contemporary literature. What Litt shares with this manifesto, however, is a predilection for a stripped-down prose style that is open to the influence of popular genres, including film and television, and that is willing to reference existing commercial brands. 'The New Puritans' deals with Jack and Jill's encounter with the odd behaviour of their new neighbours while they secretly work on copying extremely violent pornographic videos for a criminal, only to discover at the end of the story that despite their nursery-rhyme names they have been deceived by both the neighbours and their criminal boss and are to become the unwilling 'actors' in a disturbing film of their own. Litt's handling of secrets between and within romantic couples, evident in much of his writing, is here deployed in the context of exploitation and suffering and might be read as offering an ironic warning about the contemporary desire for 'authentic' cultural products based on 'real' human experiences.

Litt's enduring interest in deforming established literary genres and film- or television-generated cultural codes is a key factor in his oeuvre's sustained engagement with the grotesque, an engagement that comprises startling generic mixtures and narrative reversals and inversions as well as the grotesque body and taboo or extreme subject matter. As this study has shown, the contemporary literary grotesque is composed of fiction that deforms and distorts existing inherited aesthetic norms through exaggeration, caricature, symbolic inversion and reversal, combinations of humour and horror and an emphasis on the body. While hyperbolic Swiftian aspects are evident in Litt's writing, the frequent flatness and deadpan quality of his prose, even when dealing with horrifying subject matter, can produce a different kind of grotesque, one that is 'dry' and under-developed rather than decadent and overdrawn. Litt's work can combine these different strands of the grotesque, mixing plainly presented rawness with flights of ludicrous absurdity. It is noteworthy that in the interview where he laments the absence of the bawdy and Dickensian grotesque in contemporary fiction quoted above, he immediately makes the move to describing his approach in writing 'The New Puritans', uniting two apparently distinct aesthetic approaches:

> I think that in the *Puritans* story that I wrote I was writing a deliberately dead prose certainly in relationship to the people it was describing. It was deadpan prose which is making no moral judgements ... I don't think the novel of politeness in that way, the novel of polite form, is something that's worth me writing. (Marshall, 2003a)

What is significant here is that the bawdy and the deadpan are both, *in their different ways*, deviations from what Litt calls 'the novel of polite form' – that is, a kind of fiction that does not transgress aesthetic norms and that observes generic conventions and economies

– and so the opposite of the grotesque. Viewed from this perspective, the very different styles employed by Litt in his work, from the deadpan 'The New Puritans' to the Rabelaisian energy of the lengthy *Hospital* (2007), can be understood as different manifestations of a desire to distort and render grotesque familiar literary modes, defying expectation through both over and under-writing. The 'happy medium' of an uncomplicated realism that advocates sobriety of practice and abstemiousness in description is not an area that seems to interest Litt, and his literary career includes works where he by turns under- and over-loads the descriptive economy of his text.

Litt's attention to distortions of generic conventions applies both to the diverse genres with which each individual book engages and to the textures of the prose of which they are composed. This can be seen in the trademark skilful development of unexpected comparisons in his work, where the child's perspective of *deadkidsongs* yields 'when the breeze struck our cheek, it was like the sloppily affectionate lick of a dog you secretly hate' (Litt, 2001, 176) and the blackly humorous 'the Doctor had finished describing how quietly and peacefully Matthew had died, as if death were an athletic event in which points were awarded for style' (171). 'Unhaunted' from *Exhibitionism*, by contrast, is narrated by lesbian online dater Daphne, whose domesticity is pushed towards bathos by her extensive line in creatively banal metaphors that runs from consumerism '[it] lit me up like the Disney Store on Xmas Eve' (Litt, 2002, 143) to the humdrum-existential 'just one more speck of dust in the Hoover bag of existence' (149) to the melodrama of being jilted 'she packed as efficiently as a nurse boxing up the few bedside belongings of someone dead during the nightshift' (148). These startling, or in 'Unhaunted' deliberately underwhelming, metaphors manage to create a strange lyricism while remaining firmly rooted in everyday life and avoiding obvious poetic effects. Such accomplished descriptions can hardly be described as workmanlike but they do help to create the impression of down-to-earth solidity in his prose, a solidity that can then be played off against the unusual or perhaps supernatural. 'Unhaunted' is a sophisticated reworking of a ghost story where the messiness Daphne thinks has been caused by her ex-lover Chloë sneaking into her home while she is out is revealed to be Daphne's own doing: 'I didn't want her to have disappeared from my life as completely as she seemed to have done;

and neither did I want entirely to have vanished from her life' (154). This distress-induced attempt is a false haunting or unhaunting in the hope of prolonging some kind of ghostly contact with her former partner.

The hauntological grotesque

The experience of being haunted or possessed is one that has preoccupied much of Litt's fiction, evident from the early short stories of *Adventures in Capitalism*. The dream encounter with the deceased Michel Foucault in that collection is matched by the preternatural experience of the narrator of 'Launderama', who thinks he has seen the ghost haunting a launderette. The narrator's behaviour seems increasingly peculiar to his neighbours and he becomes obsessed with this ghostly figure that only he can see. When he attempts to rescue her from drowning in a washing machine, only to find no one inside, he is forced to acknowledge the girl's absence, but in a manner that attests to her persistence as a figment of his imagination:

> I might not have seen a girl murdered, but I'd seen one disappear. The fact that she seemed never to have existed didn't make her any less desirable, or any less missed once she'd gone. (Litt, 2003, 128)

The description holds onto the affect of an encounter that the narrator suspects has not really taken place but which has an emotional hold over him nonetheless. The girl's phantom existence does not prevent her emerging in the story as the romantic rival to his girlfriend Sarah, with the narrator confessing that looking across the road at the Launderama 'where I thought I'd seen a ghost ... was the nearest I came be being unfaithful to Sarah' (2003, 139–40). The desire for this nonexistent and nameless other girl cannot fully amount to infidelity but the story cleverly dwells on the emotional betrayal the narrator's infatuation with what he calls 'the ghost-girl' ultimately represents. Having found a black hair wrapped around his ring finger, and placed it in his copy of *The Turn of the Screw* (2003, first published 1898), the narrator has undergone a form of spectral marriage. Despite moving in with Sarah and planning a future with her he still displays signs of ambivalence regarding his supposedly happy relationship and is 'already a little nostalgic for bachelordom' (140). His return to the now-deserted launderette, site of the dormant but perhaps still potent romantic fixation, ends with the exposure of such 'unfaithful' behaviour when, much to Sarah's horror, a dead body materialises in the washing machine of their new flat in Richmond.

Having played with the notion of a self-created false haunting in 'Unhaunting', Litt's country-house novel *Finding Myself* in which 'chick lit' novelist Victoria About spies via hidden cameras on her group of guests in a rented holiday home is also the occasion for strange hauntings that disrupt the generally comic tone of the book. Edith, a teenage guest in the house, becomes convinced she is in communication with the ghost of the dead child of the house owners which, in self-reflexive but confusing fashion, appears in the form of a child dressed up in a sheet playing at being a ghost. This haunting is ended by the local vicar performing an exorcism, much to Edith's distress. In keeping with Litt's penchant for genre-bending and his satirical fun with Victoria's literary aspirations (she plans to use her spying to write a book entitled *From the Lighthouse* that functions as a comic reversal of Virginia Woolf's *To the Lighthouse*), the events in the house drift away from modernist models and show the hallmarks of other less reputable country-house genres. Aspects of haunted house, murder-mystery, upstairs-downstairs and bed-hopping farce modes come crowding in, including tabloid intrusion, pervert vicars and even nods to Victorian gothic in Victoria's temporary imprisonment in the house's attic and to James's *The Turn of the Screw* in her speculation about the haunting being a symptom of young woman's sexual hysteria (Litt, 2004a, 167). The novelist's hopes to seal the group off from the world are repeatedly frustrated and she ends up hoodwinked when her guests become aware of her electronic surveillance and decide to put on performances for her benefit. Victoria's spying has created the sense of the house being 'doubly haunted – by the dead and by the living' (259) as the novelist's sister puts it. The text itself is 'haunted' by the handwritten marginalia of Simona, the writer's devious editor, whose emendations and cutting comments further break up any sense of 'natural' unity to the work. The reader is at points aware of the provisional nature of Victoria's perspective on events (despite her technological mastery and spying) and rather than giving the effect of univocal coherence the text instead becomes a polyphonic space of antagonistic viewpoints.

The theme of spying, topically reminiscent of the television series *Big Brother*, which features hidden camera footage of game show contestants who live together in a house isolated from the outside world, is connected in *Finding Myself* to the hypothesis (theorised by Foucault in *Discipline and Punish*) that people aware that they are bring spied on begin to act 'unnaturally' for the benefit of the camera. This forms part of a wider concern in Litt's fiction to do with the ways in which people model their behaviour on cultural norms, in particular the influence of cinema and television on how people understand the world, as he has described in interview:

> As a writer ... I have to deal with the fact that the people I'm writing about are put together out of this other medium [film] and are film-haunted subjects and television-haunted subjects, which is probably what was going on in *Finding Myself*. (Litt, 2004b)

Along with these different forms of spectral presence there is a different but perhaps more serious order of haunting going on in Victoria's relationship with her devout sister Fleur. While a lot of fun is being had in the holiday home, the reader discovers that Fleur, having had an abortion after a positive Down syndrome's test some years ago, 'is haunted by the idea of this child that she could have had' (Litt, 2004a, 198). This revelation creates a shift in tone away from the comic escapades and towards the exploration of personal suffering. In doing so, *Finding Myself* extends and deepens the problematic inaugurated by 'Launderama'; that is, the difficulty of dealing with feelings of loss generated by the absence of something that did not exist. In Fleur's case her termination has become the unbearable loss of an unborn child, and the loss of potential life this represents will become the central theme of Litt's next book, *Ghost Story*.

One of the first things to strike the reader of *Ghost Story* is the great difference in genre and tone of its two main sections, 'Story' and 'Ghost Story'. 'Story' begins the book and has two short pieces of previously published fiction: 'The Hare', about a researcher resembling Litt who is obsessed with a hare that appears to him periodically, and 'Foxes' about a man whose wife gives birth to foxes.

In between these fairytale-like pieces of prose, however, is a series of short autobiographical descriptions of Litt's experience of his partner Leigh Wilson's three miscarriages. 'Ghost Story' is the main narrative body of the work that follows these introductory fragments and tells the story of Paddy and Agatha and their son Max's move into a new house and the aftermath of Agatha's miscarriage. The family's grief and Agatha's increasingly disturbed behaviour form the core of this novel's exploration of a particular kind of bereavement and its embodiment as haunting. The atmosphere of claustrophobia and introspection intensifies as 'Ghost Story' progresses and Agatha hears strange noises in the house and is reminded of her lost baby as well as the daughter of the house's previous drug addict inhabitants. This conjunction of lost baby and lost daughter is an echo of *Finding Myself*, albeit one that operates in a very different register as Paddy and Agatha struggle to articulate to themselves and each other their feelings of loss, and to find an appropriate means of expressing their shared but asymmetrical grief. When Agatha is informed that the foetus she is carrying is dead, she feels she has become 'the most grotesque parody of motherhood' (Litt, 2005, 163), a terrible reversal of all her hopes.

The difficulty in ascribing a form to what has been lost is the principal challenge for the bereaved couple, and this challenge includes linguistic as well as conceptual dimensions. Paddy and Agatha are striving to invent a form of language that can adequately bear witness to their grief and this produces a concentrated, sometimes almost congested prose, where the divergence between thoughts and words is repeatedly emphasised. When Paddy's father dies near the end of the novel, he is struck by how different mourning someone he has known for many years is to the mourning of their miscarried child:

> 'But how can you mourn something that hasn't lived? You can't, logically. You haven't known it – and so you're mourning a possibility, or you're mourning all the possibilities it could have contained, which are infinite, as far as you can see them.' (Litt, 2005, 220)

The lack of form of the lost baby and its status as the loss of a lifetime's potential, defies the couple's capacity to provide a shape, either mental or linguistic, to mourn. Paddy's speech is part of a crucial conversation at the end of the novel that inaugurates a period of frank communication and reconciliation between him and his partner, and this ability to put at least some of their feelings into words is the achievement of hard-fought endeavour in the narrative. Just before *Ghost Story* was released, Litt wrote a newspaper article about miscarriages in which he explored the apparent absence of a public language involving miscarriages:

> [A]s well as the lack of a public language, I feel that although a private language of grief does exist it remains just that, private. It exists almost exclusively within and between couples who are dealing with this particular kind of loss. (Litt, 2004c, 10)

In this sense, the central drama of 'Ghost Story' can be seen as Paddy and Agatha's struggle to establish just such a private code through which mourning can be channelled.

The decision to write on the subject of his partner's miscarriages is addressed by Litt in the autobiographical section of *Ghost Story* when he asks 'in fact, writing about the subject, the incident, at all: isn't this merely grotesque and absurd?' (Litt, 2005. li). His use of the term grotesque is bound up with the mixture of pain and horror created by miscarriage and an aversion to the disclosure of private suffering, particularly of the intimate and gynaecological kind. However, the term in this context also connotes a kind of ontological confusion as to the status of what has been lost. Litt's question thus shares with Paddy's question quoted above a preoccupation with the paradox of mourning something that never fully came into being. The miscarried embryo or foetus occupies a grey area between life and death, complicating any quick attempt to rationalise its non-arrival in the world, an ambiguous state that most resembles that of a ghost. Indeed, calling it 'it', as Litt reflects, exacerbates the bitterness of loss, of the absence of even female or male identity. The unknown entity suspended between presence and absence is the traditional place of the ghost or spectre and *Ghost Story* dramatises how the loss of something, or better some*one*, that never came into existence can become a haunting ghostly presence overpowering the living. The ontological puzzle posed by this specific form of bereavement to which Litt and Paddy allude resembles what Jacques Derrida in *Specters of Marx: The State of the Debt, the Work of Mourning and the New International* terms 'a hauntology' (1994, 10), a logic of haunting that problematises the division between presence and absence, being and non-being, living and non-living so fundamental to ontology and Western philosophical thought in general. In this 'virtual space of spectrality', conventional temporality is challenged by the spectre that 'begins by coming back' (11) and in Litt's novel this is played out in the confused feelings of parents mourning not only what will never be but what never was. *Ghost Story* therefore brings to a point of crisis the theme of being haunted by the loss of what never existed that was addressed in different ways in 'Launderama', 'Unhaunting' and *Finding Myself.*

The juxtaposition of 'Ghost Story' with the autobiographical accounts and 'The Hare' and 'Foxes' of the 'Story' section produces an uneven reading experience where the reader is challenged to make connections between the different parts. The narrator of 'Foxes' is an author who has fled his home after his wife gives birth to foxcubs, and who upon his return to the family home some time later sees three foxes counting to themselves devouring the cooked body of a man. This forms the conclusion to 'Story' and as Leigh Wilson argues:

> The repeated counting brings together the miscarriages described in the previous sections, the fairy-tale grotesque of the narrator's experience, and the horrific glee as the foxcubs devour human flesh. (Wilson, 2006, 112)

Three is the magic number, the 'law of three' as it is described in 'The Hare' (Litt, 2005, xvii); three miscarriages are the threshold for more medical attention as to possible causes and three months is the amount of time Litt wants to elapse before telling friends of the pregnancy. 'The Hare' and 'Foxes', with their tales of male flight and fairytale transformations perhaps express the magical thinking induced by feelings of powerlessness, that are for Litt the defining emotions produced by the experience of repeated miscarriages (Litt, 2004c, 10). The combination of fantasy, realism and autobiography within *Ghost Story* does not form a comfortable unity; however, this kind of uncomfortable reading experience might be regarded as an artistically valuable one. Through it Litt's book leads the reader to question what is possible in our world, and what we are capable of as people, which can be regarded as fundamental features of horror and ghost stories: 'I want the two parts to haunt each other. I want people to read the directly autobiographical section in the context of 'The Hare' and 'Foxes'' (Litt, 2004b). The book's refraction of autobiography through different realist modes of varying and sometimes questionable verisimilitude produces a grotesque and 'hauntological' novel that, like the marginalia of *Finding Myself* and different accounts of *deadkidsongs*, tends to destabilise its own brand of realism.

In addition to its mixture of genres, *Ghost Story* is notable for its modernist-influenced focus on subjective experience and the complex play of memory in the present. Visual descriptions are avoided and the reader has little sense of what Paddy and Agatha and their house look like. The emphasis in the main narrative is more aural than visual and, in keeping with the formless nature of their grieving, the haunting that Agatha experiences is in the form of a scraping noise that she hears at intervals, the source of which she cannot identify. Standing in opposition to the 'private' language Paddy and Agatha have begun to assemble with great effort at the end of the book, the haunting sound of the house lacks definition, its origin unknown and consequently threatening. Unlike *The Turn of the Screw*, with its unclear sightings of strange people, the spectral aural manifestations of *Ghost Story* are sinister because of their lack of specific form and Litt has carefully arranged their manifestation in the text in Chapter 16 to coincide with the top of each verso page (Litt, 2005, 116–30). Each time Agatha, and the reader, try to digest the nature of this 'scrape' or 'sound', a new occurrence unexpectedly appears as the reader turns the page, disrupting the chain of thought and causing confusion. This attention to the reader's material experience of the printed book, like his creative use of different typefaces and marginalia in previous works, is a sign of the skill with which Litt plays games with the reader. Litt's play with Henry James's *The Turn of the Screw* and its ambiguity as to whether its hauntings are manifestations of forces internal or external to the governess, is aided by the resemblance between his child characters' names and those used by James, as Dennis Flannery has noted:

The torturing impact of Litt's novel and the particular pain and grief it articulates come from making the second child – who has a name, Rose, which semantically echoes the Flora of James's story, just as her brother's name 'Max' phonetically echoes Miles – present but stillborn, inanimate but endowed with a power to confer life on the house. Litt's 'turn' inheres in making the second child not a child at all. (Flannery, 2005, 299–300)

The climax of *Ghost Story* brings this intertextual relationship into sharp relief as Agatha bathes her son Max in the bath and imagines pushing his head under the water. The reader may well fear that, like Miles, whose 'little heart, dispossessed, had stopped' in the governess's tight embrace at the end of *The Turn of the Screw* (James, 2003, 217), Max may be in great danger, but Max is saved just in time when pulled from the water by Paddy. When the reader discovers that 'Paddy wasn't there, and the hands which had saved Max seemed to have been hers alone' (Litt, 2005, 215) they are faced with a beneficent possession that has the power to reverse the fatal pattern set by James. Litt's last lines form an apostrophe requesting that the reader remember his fictional family and 'forget them slowly', with the final word appearing on an otherwise blank verso (226). It is in the tiny gap while the page is turned by the first-time reader that the moment of doubt and possibility so essential for a ghost story is conjured.

Ghost Story may represent something of a milestone in the growth of Litt's particular kind of literary grotesque, a form of the grotesque that can incorporate fantastic, realist, fairytale, modernist and autobiographical literary modes within itself while maintaining artistic coherence and the capacity to evoke affect in the reader. The reason why, though well regarded, it is not a culmination of Litt's aesthetic lies very much in the provisional nature of each work in his oeuvre, where the author is forever looking to innovate within different genres rather than trying to perfect a particular voice or style. Having said that, the very willingness to overstep and blur boundaries and idioms, to stretch specific forms almost to breaking point and to reflect on the limits of different kinds of literary discourse, is itself conducive to the realm of the grotesque, with its juxtapositions, deformations and subversions. The syncretic lack of a 'master principle' at work in this writer's diverse fiction is testament to its engagement with the often radical dissection of and experiment with literary and cultural traditions in ways that open up their contradictions to his readers.

Since *Ghost Story* Litt's work has continued in its exploration of different genres, including medical drama and romance (*Hospital* (2007) and *King Death* (2010)), rock-star memoir (*I play the drums in a band called* okay (2008)) and science fiction (*Journey into Space* (2009)). The lengthy and baroque *Hospital*, subtitled 'A Dream-Vision' is most clearly indebted to the tradition of the grotesque as a London hospital in thrown into chaos when entropy goes into reverse and patients are spontaneously healed, sometimes despite the best efforts of themselves and others. Full of Rabelaisian energy, throwing together dozens of characters and generic elements from medical romance, satanic cults, voodoo and fetishist erotica and containing many bizarre physical metamorphoses, Litt has described *Hospital* as 'an attempt to be unreasonable at novel length' (Richards and Sellars, 2007). When *Hospital*'s boy protagonist is 'fascinated and disgusted, fascinated by his disgust and disgusted by his fascination' (Litt, 2007, 33), he approaches Amis's comment in interview that 'in my writing, yes, I am fascinated by what I deplore, or I deplore what fascinates me: it's hard to get it the right way round' (Haffenden, 1985, 4). The world turned upside-down of the hospital where nobody dies and where the less desirable aspects of bodily regeneration soon become apparent is a fitting enough monument to Litt's commitment to excess and to grotesque violations of narrative economy that simultaneously draw on the canonical dream-visions of *Piers Plowman* and on low-status contemporary pulp romance. However, as this chapter has shown, in addition to the clear influence of modernist writers, including James and Woolf, there is strong evidence for the importance of the grotesque as having a decisive influence on the development of Litt's writing, in its singular fusion of exuberant fantasy and deadpan, almost hallucinogenic banality. It is from the fertile literary tradition of the grotesque that Litt has fashioned a contemporary approach to genre-bending prose and from the grotesque's drive to flout convention and violate aesthetic economies that he continues to wage his long, alphabetically ordered campaign against what he has called 'the novel of polite form'.

Notes

1. 'I have known I was going to write a book about childhood for at least 10 years. The first idea I had was called The Childhood Novel. It started with some boys hanging upside down in a tree and the alternative title was Descriptions of the English Countryside. It was going to be to do not just with the boys themselves but with everything around them. The countryside. Where they were. The time they were growing up in.' (McCrum, 2001, 17)
2. 'But, by this stage, the reader has come to suspect that Gang's several narrators are not reliable, and not even several. Hidden behind a series of masks, one of the boys has grown up and has never been able to leave his childhood behind.' (Frehilly, 2001, 55)

Conclusion

This study has focused on the grotesque in contemporary British fiction from a number of different perspectives, and from the discussion of the grotesque in Chapter 1 onwards I developed a set of qualities of the grotesque drawn from approaches that were formal, thematic, psychoanalytic and discourse oriented in nature that became the critical framework for a re-evaluation of contemporary British fiction. As the first chapter showed, the grotesque as a set of features is extremely resistant to simple description and part of my aim has been to preserve the diverse and contradictory nature of the grotesque rather than subdividing the category in order to dispose of an unwanted 'tendency', something that, as I have discussed, has been a frequent aspect of much writing on the grotesque. Bearing this in mind, I have approached the term historically and from a number of theoretical positions in order to produce an account of the grotesque that can illuminate key aspects of contemporary British writing.

The theoretical approaches used to discuss the six writers' novels and short stories have shifted as this study moved from one writer to another but the focus has always moved within my initial outline of the grotesque. Metamorphoses, inversions, reversals, parodies, plays of scale and perspective, hyperbole, narrative 'diseconomy', mixtures of humour and horror, an interest in the 'biological' human body – the grotesque in this study has revealed itself in the complex interplay of all of these aspects. Having examined the work of Carter, Amis, Banks, McEwan, Self and Litt in detail and having placed their work within the tradition of the grotesque, the 'family resemblances' between the works are now quite clear. Each writer's oeuvre exhibits the grotesque in a different but related way, and my discussions have produced examples of the grotesque such as play of perspective that run across these authors' works. Inversions of expectation are a frequent feature of the fiction examined here, where the reader feels amused and disturbed at the same time, as well as inversions of relationships, for example between adults and children, or between humans and apes or robots. Temporal inversion or reversal is of course another feature of the grotesque fiction I have focused on in this study, particularly in Amis and McEwan.

Taking this fiction as a group, it becomes clear that grotesque inversion or reversal is not only a trope in these narratives but is frequently a structural feature of the novel form itself for these writers. Amis's play with the form of the novel, his interest in 'the murderee', the unmotivated confidence trick, the amnesiac narrator, the suicide that doesn't make sense, all point to a picture of the contemporary novel as grotesque. Much of the subject matter of the fiction discussed tends towards the repellent, including murder, addiction, pornography, sadism, psychosis, addiction and sexual abuse. Sibling incest as a theme features in the work of no fewer than five of the writers examined in this study (Will Self being the exception) and the tone of the fiction moves between the humorous and the horrible, combining the two sometimes in a single image; such combinations go to the heart of the grotesque as hybrid and contradictory.

The first chapter of this study was devoted to outlining a tradition of the grotesque in European art and literature of which the contemporary works under discussion are a part. Writers such as Swift, Rabelais, Dickens, Kafka, Lewis and Burroughs are in this sense inheritors of the grotesque who turn it to their own particular requirements, whether these requirements are regarded as being determined personally (Spilka (1969) on Dickens and Kafka, for example) or historically (Bakhtin (1984b) makes this point repeatedly while discussing the menippea). The six contemporary authors, by the same measure, reconfigure and bequeath their grotesque that pervades so much contemporary fiction and criticism, often in unexpected ways, as this study has shown. Contemporary British fiction draws on this tradition of the grotesque in multiple ways and although there are important differences between the authors' works, they do share a coherent set of features central to the grotesque that are also central to these writers' fiction. The six writers taken as a group and analysed in terms of the grotesque reveal the diverse ways that the grotesque permeates their distinctly contemporary preoccupations, whether involving consumer society, cinema, addiction, the influence of pornography, sexual politics or our understanding of gender and subjectivity. Theirs is a contemporary grotesque that is oriented towards the present and the aesthetic modes of which are modern while at the same time evoking the qualities of the grotesque as it has been articulated historically in European art and literature. To return to Gombrich's terms, this contemporary grotesque is both pre- and post- in its temporal orientation.

The writers discussed here are, of course, not alone in their preoccupation with the grotesque, and if we were to look outside the group there are many other British authors whose work could also be considered grotesque. Alasdair Gray's *Lanark* (1981) and *Poor Things* (1992) are remarkable works of fantastic transformations and the squalid trials and tribulations of Irvine Welsh's characters in novels like *Trainspotting* (1993) and *Filth* (1998) have their fair share of the grotesque. The Dog-Woman with her Rabelaisian dimensions and capacities in Jeanette Winterson's *Sexing the Cherry* (1989) is another obvious manifestation of the grotesque and Patrick McGrath returns again and again to the grotesque in his novels *The Grotesque* (1989) and *Spider* (1991). There is also a grotesque aspect to much of contemporary Irish writing: Patrick MacCabe's disturbed and murderous narrators in *The Butcher Boy* (1992) and *Winterwood* (2006) both recount narratives that are simultaneously humorous and disturbing and Martin McDonagh's gruesomely funny play *The Lieutenant of Inishmore* (2001) might also be considered grotesque. The comically dysfunctional but also disturbing subjects of David Foster Wallace's collection of short stories *Interviews with Hideous Men* (2000, first published 1999) or Jennifer Egan's time-scarred characters in *A Visit from the Goon Squad* (2010) show the continued importance of the grotesque in American literature beyond its strong association with Southern writing; these grotesque novels, whether they be in Irish, American, European or other literatures, exhibit intriguing and suggestive parallels to the fiction I have investigated. However, it is not possible within the confines of this study to trace in sufficient detail the ways in which the grotesque takes on different aesthetic, political and social resonances within different cultural contexts. Evident in the famous example of the totem pole, the often-puzzling grotesqueness of which to European eyes belies its narrative capacity for indigenous people in North America, the grotesque (like cuisine) soon alerts us to the temporal and geographical localism of many of our aesthetic norms.

Looking away from the grotesque for a moment, the current popularity in sales and on prize shortlists of historical novels, particularly those dealing with real historical figures, is testament to the reading public's appetite for literature of a serious, realist bent (see de Groot, 2010). The attractiveness of works that deal with periods when Britain was a key site of 'world events', such as Tudor England, mid-Victorian London or British experiences during two World Wars, is perhaps less surprising. So while the grotesque may be seen as a powerful force in contemporary culture, demonstrating British fiction's capacity for renewal, it by no means has become a dominant one. Paradoxically, despite the commercial and critical success of many contemporary writers of the grotesque, including the ones examined in detail in this book, the general aesthetic standards through which their work is read have continued to remain remarkably resistant to the challenges to normative aesthetic standards embodied in their fiction. J.G. Ballard argued that:

> The notion of the novelist as moral arbiter has gone for good. The idea that the novelist can sit like a magistrate above his characters, who are figures in the dark, or a collection of witnesses, or the accused in a shabby scandal – the notion of the novel as a moral structure in which the novelist can acquit some of his characters and sentence others, let others off with a stern warning – this Leavisite notion of the novel as moral criticism of life doesn't belong in the present world. This was the world of the past. A world of static human values. We now live in a huge goulash of competing appetites and dreams and aspirations and activities. (Ballard interviewed in Self, 1996a, 349–50)

He was perhaps premature in seeing such literary expectations as redundant. As I have shown, contemporary writers whose work engages with the grotesque face many of the criticisms their nineteenth- and eighteenth-century precursors received, from a lack of taste and discrimination to more personal accusations of immaturity and a lack of empathy. This 'goulash of competing appetites' that characterises the contemporary world for Ballard, however, is likely to serve as a conducive Petri dish for the cultivation of grotesque culture(s).

This book has framed the contemporary British grotesque as being both at the end of a long literary and artistic tradition *and* at the beginning of one. Chapter 1 explored how the grotesque's status as non-classical results in a paradox where it comes both before and after the establishment of classical norms. This dual temporal orientation helps account for the confusing feeling that British fiction is moving both forwards and backwards at the same time, simultaneously evolving into something bold and vibrant and new, and devolving into the incoherent mess of a squalid and potentially dubious past. The grotesque cannot serve as a new template for some yet-to-be-discovered mode, but the conditions of aesthetic 'slackening' and the decline of 'grand narratives' that together define postmodernity for Lyotard provide perfect conditions for the grotesque whereby the strength of old norms is weakened but they are not decisively supplanted by new ones. If we are in accordance with such a view of the contemporary moment then the coexistence of 'weak' forms of normative aesthetics together with an array of both established and emerging writers keen to pull at the edges of such norms in the cause of literary innovation makes the grotesque likely to be a paradoxical healthy sign of decay. The contemporary literary practice of the grotesque is itself productive of the de- and re-formation of normative aesthetics, as writers persistently probe the borders between valued forms and the artistically illegitimate and question the foundations of such distinctions. Of course, for the grotesque to be apprehended as such it must exist against the background of some kind of decorum, and it seems unlikely that we are heading for the complete dissolution of normative standards. Rather, in the absence of such a revolutionary *telos* in taste, the grotesque seems set to endure as an ambiguous sign of both growing pains and death pangs in the arts.

As I have endeavoured to show, contemporary British fiction that is grotesque is often perceived, especially by reviewers, within the narrow terms inherited from the realist novel. The negative criticism of these authors' works itself frequently follows the outline of the grotesque in its various aspects, with reviewers berating the authors for their inappropriately mixed tone, formal 'eccentricities', disturbing subject matter or sometimes for all three. This book has worked to illuminate the economies and 'classical' nature of the aesthetics of realism, and the strength such economies still hold is demonstrated by the tenor of much of this contemporary criticism. My research has continually sought to reflect critically on criticism relating to the grotesque, from Horace to Ruskin to Bakhtin, and to interrogate the operation of aesthetic categories and the discourses at work in their formation. The result has been to show the surprisingly similar aesthetic presuppositions present in areas of eighteenth-century, nineteenth-century and contemporary criticism of the grotesque in art and literature, despite the huge social and cultural changes that have taken place. One result of the approach I have taken is that it entails a reconsideration of the emergence of the realist novel and its relationship to the grotesque, and, viewed from the perspective of the grotesque, the 'classical' nature of realist aesthetics, viewed both historically and formally, is highlighted. With this in mind, it may be said that the grotesque fictions of Carter, Amis, McEwan, Banks, Self and Litt are engaging with the problematics of realism on several different levels and in several different areas. The grotesque, therefore, as I discussed in relation to the work of Amis, is less an aesthetic 'solution' to problems thrown up by classicism, or realism, or modernism, but rather a way of mediating and working through these issues of form, of register, of theme and of affect.

Finally, this book has examined a particular strand of the grotesque in contemporary writing, and the signs are that the grotesque is becoming more, rather than less, evident in literary and artistic culture in Britain and elsewhere. In its deployment of different theoretical perspectives, historical discussion, cultural criticism and textual analyses, this study is intended to interrogate received critical and aesthetic categories in providing a means of framing the intricate webs of influences and traditions within contemporary writing.

Bibliography

Primary texts

Carter, Angela

Carter, Angela (1967) *The Magic Toyshop* London: Heinemann
—— (1969) *Heroes and Villains* London: Heinemann
—— (1972) *The Infernal Desiring Machines of Doctor Hoffman* London: Rupert Hart-Davis
—— (1977) *The Passion of New Eve* London: Gollancz
—— (1979) *The Sadeian Woman: An Exercise in Cultural History* London: Virago
—— (1985) *Nights at the Circus* London: Picador (first published 1984)
—— (1987) *Love* London: Chatto & Windus (first published 1971)
—— (1992) *Wise Children* London: Vintage (first published 1991)
—— (1994) *Shadow Dance* London: Virago (first published 1966)
—— (1995) *Several Perceptions* London: Virago (first published 1969)
—— (1996) *Burning Your Boats: Collected Short Stories* London: Vintage includes *Fireworks* (1974), *The Bloody Chamber* (1979) and *American Ghosts and Old World Wonders* (1993)
—— (1997) *Shaking a Leg: Collected Writings* Harmondsworth: Penguin

Interviews with Carter

Appignanesi, Lisa (1987) *Writers in Conversation: Angela Carter* ICA Video
Evans, Kim (producer) (1992) 'Angela Carter's Curious Room' *Omnibus* broadcast BBC1 15 September 1992
Haffenden, John (1985) *Novelists in Interview* London: Methuen pp. 76–96
Harron, Mary (1984) 'I'm a Socialist, Damn It! How Can you Expect

me to Be Interested in Fairies?' *The Guardian* 25 September 1984 p. 10

Katsavos, Anna (1994) 'An Interview with Angela Carter' *Review of Contemporary Fiction* 14:3 (Fall) pp. 12–13

Martin Amis

Amis, Martin (1979) 'Point of View' *New Statesman* 14 December 1979 p. 954

—— (1982) *Other People: A Mystery Story* Harmondsworth: Penguin (first published 1981)

—— (1984a) *The Rachel Papers* Harmondsworth: Penguin (first published 1973)

—— (1984b) *Dead Babies* Harmondsworth: Penguin (first published 1975)

—— (1985a) *Money: A Suicide Note* Harmondsworth: Penguin (first published 1984)

—— (1985b) *Success* Harmondsworth: Penguin (first published 1978)

—— (1988) *Einstein's Monsters* Harmondsworth: Penguin (first published 1987)

—— (1989) *London Fields* London: Jonathan Cape

—— (1991) *Time's Arrow or The Nature of the Offence* London: Jonathan Cape

—— (1995) *The Information* London: Flamingo (an imprint of HarperCollins)

—— (1997) *Night Train* London: Jonathan Cape

—— (1998) *Heavy Water and Other Stories* London: Jonathan Cape

—— (2000) *Experience* London: Jonathan Cape

—— (2001) *The War Against Cliché: Essays and Reviews, 1971–2000* London: Jonathan Cape

—— (2003) *Yellow Dog* London: Jonathan Cape

—— (2006) *House of Meetings* London: Jonathan Cape

—— (2010) *The Pregnant Widow* London: Jonathan Cape

—— (2012) *Lionel Asbo: State of England* London: Jonathan Cape

Interviews with Amis

Bigsby, Christopher (1992) 'Martin Amis Interviewed by Christopher Bigsby' in Malcolm Bradbury and Judy Cooke (eds) *New Writing* London: Minerva

Flusfeder, David (1997) *Esquire* 7:8 (October) pp. 23–33

Fuller, Graham (1995) *Interview* 25 (May) pp. 122–5
Haffenden, John (1985) *Novelists in Interview* London: Methuen pp. 1–24
Self, Will (1996a) *Junk Mail* Harmondsworth: Penguin (first published 1995, interview first published 1993)

Ian McEwan

McEwan, Ian (1979) *In Between the Sheets and Other Stories* London: Picador (first published 1978)
—— (1980) *The Cement Garden* London: Picador (first published 1978)
—— (1981) *The Imitation Game: Three Plays for Television* London: Jonathan Cape
—— (1982) *The Comfort of Strangers* London: Picador (first published 1981)
—— (1986) 'Schoolboys' in John Carey (ed.) *William Golding: The Man and his Books* London: Faber and Faber
—— (1988) *The Child in Time* London: Picador (first published 1987)
—— (1989) *A Move Abroad: Or Shall we Die? and A Ploughman's Lunch* London: Pan Books
—— (1990) *The Innocent or The Special Relationship* London: Picador
—— (1991) *First Love, Last Rites* London: Picador (first published 1975)
—— (1992) *Black Dogs* London: Jonathan Cape
—— (1995) *The Daydreamer* London: Vintage (first published 1994)
—— (1998a) *Enduring Love* London: Vintage (first published 1997)
—— (1998b) *Amsterdam* London: Jonathan Cape
—— (2001) *Atonement* London: Jonathan Cape
—— (2005) *Saturday* London: Jonathan Cape
—— (2007) *On Chesil Beach* London: Jonathan Cape
—— (2010) *Solar* London: Jonathan Cape
—— (2012) *Sweet Tooth* London: Jonathan Cape

Interviews with McEwan

Grimes, William (1992) 'Rustic Calm Inspires McEwan Tale of Evil' *New York Times* 18 November 1992 www.nytimes.com/books/98/12/27/specials/mcewan-grimes.html (accessed 2 August 2000)
Haffenden, John (1985) *Novelists in Interview* London: Methuen pp. 168–90

Hamilton, Ian (1978) 'Points of Departure' *New Review* 5:2 (Autumn) pp. 9–21

Hanks, Robert (1998) 'Flashes of Inspiration' *The Independent* 12 September 1998 Review p. 14

Katz, Ian (2012) Guardian Open Weekend interview with Ian McEwan www.guardian.co.uk/books/video/2012/apr/03/ian-mcewan-innocent-video (accessed 15 April 2012)

Ricks, Christopher (1979) 'Adolescence and After' *The Listener* 12 April 1979 pp. 526–7

Walter, Natasha (1997) 'Looks like a teacher. Writes like a demon.' *The Observer* 24 August 1997 Review pp. 2–3

Iain Banks

Banks, Iain (1989) *Canal Dreams* London: Macmillan
—— (1990a) *The Wasp Factory* London: Abacus (first published 1984)
—— (1990b) *The Bridge* London: Abacus (first published 1986)
—— (1990c) *Espedair Street* London: Abacus (first published 1987)
—— (1990d) *Walking on Glass* London: Abacus (first published 1985)
—— (1993a) *The Crow Road* London: Abacus (first published 1992)
—— (1994) *Complicity* London: Abacus (first published 1993)
—— (1995) *Whit* London: Little, Brown
—— (1997) *A Song of Stone* London: Abacus
—— (1999) *The Business* London: Little, Brown
—— (2002) *Dead Air* London: Little, Brown
—— (2007) *The Steep Approach to Garbadale* London: Little, Brown
—— (2009) *Transition* London: Little, Brown
—— (2012) *Stonemouth* London: Little, Brown

Banks, Iain M. (1988) *The Player of Games* London: Macmillan
—— (1992) *Use of Weapons* London: Orbit (first published 1990)
—— (1993b) *Against a Dark Background* London: Orbit
—— (1998) *Inversions* London: Orbit

Interviews with Banks

'Nasty but Nice' *The Observer* 14 June 1988 Review p. 16

Bragg, Melvyn (1997) *The South Bank Show* broadcast ITV 16 December 1997

Cobley, Michael (1990) 'Eye to Eye' *Science Fiction Eye* 2:1 (February) p. 26

Eggar, Robin (1997) 'The Dark World of Iain Banks' *The Times* 14 November 1997 p. 21

Furniss, Olaf (1996) Interview with Iain Banks *Cyberia* online journal reproduced on Culture Shock website http://lucid.cba.uiuc.edu/~rkeogh/banks/text/banksint08.html (accessed 26 October 1998)

Nicholls, Stan (1993) *Wordsmiths of Wonder* London: Orbit pp. 137–42

Will Self

Self, Will (1993) *Cock & Bull* Harmondsworth: Penguin (first published 1992)

—— (1994a) *My Idea of Fun: A Cautionary Tale* Harmondsworth: Penguin (first published 1993)

—— (1994b) *The Quantity Theory of Insanity* Harmondsworth: Penguin (first published 1991)

—— (1996a) *Junk Mail* Harmondsworth: Penguin (first published 1995)

—— (1996b) *Grey Area and Other Stories* Harmondsworth: Penguin (first published 1994)

—— (1996c) 'My Generation' *The Observer* 21 January 1996 Life Magazine pp. 32–3

—— (1997) *The Sweet Smell of Psychosis* London: Bloomsbury (first published 1996)

—— (1998) *Great Apes* Harmondsworth: Penguin (first published 1997)

—— (1999) *Tough, Tough Toys for Tough, Tough Boys* Harmondsworth: Penguin (first published 1998)

—— (2000a) *How the Dead Live* London: Bloomsbury

—— (2000b) *Sore Sites* London: Ellipsis

—— (2002) *Dorian: An Imitation* London: Viking

—— (2004) *Dr Mukti and Other Tales of Woe* London: Bloomsbury

—— (2006) *The Book of Dave* London: Viking

—— (2008a) *Liver: A Fictional Organ with a Surface Anatomy of Four Lobes* London: Viking

——(2008b) *The Butt: An Exit Strategy* London: Bloomsbury

—— (2010) *Walking to Hollywood* London: Bloomsbury

—— (2012) *Umbrella* London: Bloomsbury

Interviews with Self

Aaronovitch, David (1998) *Booked* broadcast Channel 4 2 May 1998

Bragg, Melvyn (1998) *The South Bank Show* broadcast ITV 5 July 1998

Toby Litt

Litt, Toby (1998) *Beatniks: An English Road Movie* London: Vintage (first published 1997)
—— (2000) *Corpsing* London: Hamish Hamilton
—— (2001) *deadkidsongs* London: Penguin
—— (2002) *Exhibitionism* London: Hamish Hamilton
—— (2003) *Adventures in Capitalism* London: Penguin (first published 1996)
—— (2004a) *Finding Myself* London: Penguin (first published 2003)
—— (2004b) talk at Warwick Arts Centre 20 October 2004 www2.warwick.ac.uk/fac/arts/english/writingprog/archive/writers/litttoby/201004 (accessed 25 March 2011 (audio file))
—— (2004c) 'An Agony Shrouded in Silence' *Sunday Times* 26 September 2004 p. 10
—— (2005) *Ghost Story* London: Penguin (first published 2004)
—— (2007) *Hospital* London: Hamish Hamilton
—— (2008) *I play the drums in a band called okay* London: Hamish Hamilton
—— (2009) *Journey into Space* London: Penguin
—— (2010) *King Death* London: Penguin

Interviews with Litt

McCrum, Robert (2001) Interview with Toby Litt *The Observer* 11 February 2001 Books p. 17
Richards, Gwyn and Simon Sellars (2007) '"The Stuff of Now": Toby Litt on J.G. Ballard' *Ballardian* www.ballardian.com/the-stuff-of-now-toby-litt-on-jg-ballard (accessed 25 March 2011)
Tew, Philip and Fiona Tolan and Leigh Wilson (eds) (2008) *Writers Talk: Conversations with Contemporary British Novelists* London: Continuum

Secondary Texts

Addams, Charles (1950) *Monster Rally* New York: Simon and Schuster
Ageyev, M. (1999) *Novel with Cocaine* Michael Henry Heim (trans.) Harmondsworth: Penguin (first published in Russian 1983)
Allen, Nicola (2008) *Marginality in the Contemporary Novel* London: Continuum

Allen, Woody (1980) 'The Kuglemass Episode' in *Side Effects* New York: Random House (story first published 1977)
Amis, Kingsley (1954) *Lucky Jim* London: Victor Gollancz
Armitt, Lucie (1996) *Theorising the Fantastic* London: Arnold
Austen, Jane (1985) *Northanger Abbey* Harmondsworth: Penguin Classics (first published 1818)
Babcock, Barbara (1978) *The Reversible World: Symbolic Inversion in Art and Society* Ithaca, NY: Cornell University Press
Baker, Phil (1993) 'Tutorials from Hell' *Times Literary Supplement* 10 September 1993 p. 22 (review of Will Self's *My Idea of Fun*)
Bakhtin, Mikhail (1981) 'Discourse in the Novel' in Caryl Emerson and Michael Holquist (trans.) *The Dialogic Imagination* Austin: University of Texas Press
—— (1984a) *Rabelais and his World* Hélène Iswolsky (trans.) Bloomington: Indiana University Press (first published in Russian 1965)
—— (1984b) *Problems of Dostoevsky's Poetics* Caryl Emerson (trans.) Minneapolis: Minnesota University Press (first published in Russian 1963)
Ballard, J.G (1995) *Crash* London: Vintage (first published 1973)
Banks, J.R. (1982) 'A Gondola Named Desire' *Critical Quarterly* 24:2 (Summer) pp. 27–31
Barasch, Frances K. (1971) *The Grotesque: A Study in Meanings* The Hague and Paris: Mouton
Barthes, Roland (1977) 'The Death of the Author' in Stephen Heath (trans.) *Image-Music-Text* London: Fontana (essay first published in French 1968)
—— (1986a) 'From Work to Text' in Richard Howard (trans.) *The Rustle of Language* Oxford: Basil Blackwell (essay first published in French 1971)
—— (1986b) 'The Reality Effect' in Richard Howard (trans.) *The Rustle of Language* Oxford: Basil Blackwell (essay first published in French 1968).
—— (1990) *S/Z* Richard Miller (trans.) Oxford: Basil Blackwell (first published in French 1973)
Bataille, Georges (1985) 'The Big Toe' in *Visions of Excess: Selected Writings, 1927–1939* Minneapolis: University of Minnesota Press (essay first published in French 1929)
Baudrillard, Jean (1981) *For a Critique of the Political Economy of the Sign* Charles Levin (trans.) St Louis: Telos Press (first published in French 1972)

—— (1988) *Selected Writings* Mark Poster (ed.) London: Polity Press
—— (1993) *Symbolic Exchange and Death* Iain Hamilton Grant (trans.) London: Sage (first published in French 1976)
Benjamin, Walter (1969) *Illuminations* H. Zohn (trans.) London: Fontana (first published in German 1955)
Bensmaïa, Réda (1986) 'The Kafka Effect' Terry Cochran (trans.) foreword to Gilles Deleuze and Félix Guattari *Kafka: Toward a Minor Literature* Dana Polan (trans.) Minneapolis: University of Minnesota Press (book first published in French 1975)
Bettelheim, Bruno (1976) *The Uses of Enchantment: The Meaning and Importance of Fairy Tales* London: Thames and Hudson
Binns, Ronald (1990) 'Castles, Books and Bridges: Mervyn Peake and Iain Banks' *Peake Studies* 2:1 pp. 5–12
Blincoe, Nicholas and Matt Thorne (eds) (2003) *All Hail the New Puritans* London: Fourth Estate
Botting, Fred (1996) *Gothic* London: Routledge (The New Critical Idiom)
Bristol, Michael (1996) *Big-time Shakespeare* London: Routledge
Bristow, Joseph and Trev Lynn Broughton (eds) (1997) *The Infernal Desires of Angela Carter: Fiction, Femininity, Feminism* Harlow: Addison Wesley Longman
Brooks, Peter (1984) *Reading for the Plot: Desire and Intervention in Narrative* Oxford: Clarendon Press
Butler, Judith (1990) *Gender Trouble: Feminism and the Subversion of Identity* London: Routledge
—— (1993) *Bodies that Matter: On the Discursive Limits of 'Sex'* London: Routledge
Butor, Michel (1957) *L'Emploi du Temps* Paris: Editions de Minuit
—— (1967) *Portrait de l'Artiste en Jeune Singe* Paris: Gallimard
—— (1970) 'Research on the Technique of the Novel' in Richard Howard (ed.) *Inventory: Essays by Michel Butor* London: Jonathan Cape (essay first published in French 1964)
Camus, Albert (1961) *The Outsider* Harmondsworth: Penguin (first published in French 1942)
Carroll, Lewis (1889) *Sylvie and Bruno* London: Macmillan
—— (2001) *Alice's Adventures in Wonderland* London: Bloomsbury (first published 1865)
Clayborough, Arthur (1965) *The Grotesque in English Literature* London: Oxford University Press
Craig, Cairns (2002) *Complicity: A Reader's Guide* London: Continuum

Dacos, Nicole (1969) *La Découverte de la Domus Aurea et la Formation des Grotesques à la Renaissance* London: Warburg Institute
Davis, Lennard J. (1983) *Factual Fictions: the Origins of the English Novel* New York: Columbia University Press
—— (1987) *Resisting Novels: Ideology and Fiction* London: Methuen
Day, Aidan (1998) *Angela Carter: The Rational Glass* Manchester: Manchester University Press
De Groot, Jerome (2010) *The Historical Novel* Abingdon: Routledge (New Critical Idiom)
De Quincey, Thomas (1907) *Confessions of an English Opium-Eater* London: J.M. Dent (first published 1821)
Deleuze, Gilles and Félix Guattari (1986) *Kafka: Toward a Minor Literature* Dana Polan (trans.) Minneapolis: University of Minnesota Press (first published in French 1975)
—— (1988) *A Thousand Plateaus: Capitalism and Schizophrenia* Brian Mussumi (trans.) London: Athlone (first published in French 1980)
Derrida, Jacques (1978) 'Force and Signification' in Alan Bass (trans.) *Writing and Difference* London: Routledge and Kegan Paul (first published in French 1967, essay first published in French 1963)
—— (1982) 'Signature, Event, Context' in Alan Bass (trans.) *Margins of Philosophy* Chicago: University of Chicago Press (first published in French 1972)
—— (1994) *Specters of Marx: The State of the Debt, the Work of Mourning and the New International* Peggy Kamuf (trans.) London: Routledge (first published in French 1993)
Dick, Philip K. (1967) *Counter-Clock World* New York: Berkley
Dickens, Charles (1965) *Martin Chuzzlewit* London: New English Library (first published 1844)
Diedrick, James (1988) 'The Sublimation of Carnival in Ruskin's Theory of the Grotesque' *Victorian Newsletter* 74 (Fall) pp. 11–16
—— (1995) *Understanding Martin Amis* Columbia: University of South Carolina Press
Docherty, Thomas (1991) 'Postmodern Characterisation: The Ethics of Alterity' in Edmund J. Smyth (ed.) *Postmodernism and Contemporary Fiction* London: Batsford
Doody, Margaret Anne (1997) *The True Story of the Novel* London: HarperCollins (first published in the USA by Rutgers University Press 1996)
Douglas, Mary (1966) *Purity and Danger: An Analysis of the Concepts of Pollution and Taboo* London: Routledge and Kegan Paul

Du Maurier, George (2003) *Trilby* Peterborough, Ontario: Broadview Press (first published 1894)

Duggan, Robert (2006) '"Circles of Stage Fire": Angela Carter, Charles Dickens and Heteroglossia in the English Comic Novel' in Rebecca Munford (ed.) *Re-Visiting Angela Carter: Texts, Contexts, Intertexts* Basingstoke: Palgrave

—— (2007) 'Iain M. Banks, Postmodernism and the Gulf War' *Extrapolation* 48:3 (Winter). pp. 558–78

—— (2009) 'Big-time Shakespeare and the Joker in the Pack: The Intrusive Author in Martin Amis's *Money*' *JNT: Journal of Narrative Theory* 39:1 (Winter) pp. 86–108

—— (forthcoming) '"Our Close but Prohibited Union": Class and National Identity in Iain Banks's *The Steep Approach to Garbadale*' in Emma Miller and Miles Leeson (eds) *Writing Incest in the Post-War Years* Basingstoke: Palgrave

Duncker, Patricia (1984) 'Re-imagining the Fairy Tales: Angela Carter's Bloody Chambers' *Literature and History* 10 (Spring) pp. 3–14

Duperray, Max (1982) 'Insolite Modernité: *The Cement Garden* d'Ian McEwan, Chef-d'Oeuvre d'une Nouvelle Littérature de l'Angoisse' *Études Anglaises* 35:4 (October–December) pp. 420–9

Dwyer Hogg, Clare (2003) 'Adventures in Postmodernism' *The Independent* 21 June 2003 Magazine p. 22

Eco, Umberto (1987) 'The Comic and the Rule' in W. Weaver (trans.) *Travels in Hyperreality* London: Picador (essay first published in Italian 1980)

Edmond, Rod (1990) '"Kiss My Arse!" Epeli Hau'ofa and the Politics of Laughter' *Journal of Commonwealth Literature* 25:1 pp. 142–55

Edwards, Paul (1995) 'Time, Romanticism, Modernism and Moderation in Ian McEwan's *The Child in Time*' *English* 44:178 pp. 41–55

Egan, Jennifer (2010) *A Visit From the Goon Squad* New York: Random House

Eliot, George (1980) *Adam Bede* Harmondsworth: Penguin (first published 1859)

—— (1994) *Middlemarch* Harmondsworth: Penguin (first published 1871–2)

Fiedler, Leslie (1978) *Freaks: Myths and Images of the Secret Self* New York: Simon & Schuster

—— (1997) *Love and Death in the American Novel* Champaign, IL: Dalkey Archive Press (first published 1966)

Fielding, Henry (1987) *Joseph Andrews with Shamela and Other Writings*

New York and London: Norton Critical Edition (*Joseph Andrews* first published 1742, *Shamela* first published 1741)

Finney, Brian (1995) 'Narrative and Narrated Homicides in Martin Amis's *Other People* and *London Fields*' *Critique: Studies in Contemporary Fiction* 37:1 (Fall) pp. 3–15

Flannery, Dennis (2005) 'The Powers of Apostrophe and the Boundaries of Mourning: Henry James, Alan Hollinghurst, and Toby Litt' *Henry James Review* 26 pp. 293–305

Forster, E.M. (1976) *Aspects of the Novel* Harmondsworth: Pelican Books by Penguin (first published 1927)

Foucault, Michel (1991) *Discipline and Punish: the Birth of the Prison* A. Sheridan (trans.) Harmondsworth: Penguin (first published in French 1975)

Frehilly, Gerry (2001) Review of *deadkidsongs* in *New Statesman* 26 February 2001 p. 55

Freud, Sigmund (1960) *Jokes and their Relation to the Unconscious* (*Works* vol. VIII) London: Hogarth Press (first published in German 1905)

—— (1985) 'Creative Writers and Day-Dreaming' *Penguin Freud Library* 14 Harmondsworth: Penguin (essay first published in German 1908)

Frye, Northrop (1957) *Anatomy of Criticism: Four Essays* Princeton: Princeton University Press

Gale, Patrick (1997) Review of *Great Apes* in *The Independent* 26 April 1997 Books p. 6

Gamble, Sarah (ed.) (2001) *The Fiction of Angela Carter: A Reader's Guide to Essential Criticism* Basingstoke: Palgrave

Gasiorek, Andrzej (1995) *Post-War British Fiction: Realism and After* London: Edward Arnold

Gibson, Andrew (1996) *Towards a Postmodern Theory of Narrative* Edinburgh: Edinburgh University Press

Giger, H.R. (1996) *HR Giger ARh+* Cologne: Taschen

Goodwin, James (2009) *Modern American Grotesque: Literature and Photography* Columbus: Ohio State University Press

Golding, William (1958) *Lord of the Flies* London: Faber (first published 1954)

Gombrich, E.H. (1966) 'Norm and Form: The Stylistic Categories of Art History and their Origins in Renaissance Ideals' in *Norm and Form: Studies in the Art of the Renaissance* 3rd ed. London: Phaidon

Gray, Alasdair (1987) *Lanark: A Life in Four Books* London: Paladin (first published 1981)

—— (1992) *Poor Things* London: Bloomsbury

Greaney, Michael (2006) *Contemporary Fiction and the Uses of Theory* London: Palgrave
Grunenberg, Christopher (1997) *Gothic: Transmutations of Horror in Late-Twentieth-Century Art* Boston: Massachusetts Institute of Contemporary Art and London: MIT Press
Guerlac, Suzanne (1985) 'Delights of Sublime and Grotesque' *Diacritics* 15:3 (Fall) pp. 47–53
Harbord, Janet (1996) 'Performing Parts: Gender and Sexuality in Recent Fiction and Theory' *Women: A Cultural Review* 7:1 pp. 39–47
Hardy, Barbara (1970) *The Moral Art of Dickens* London: Athlone
Harpham, Geoffrey Galt (1982) *On the Grotesque: Strategies of Contradiction in Art and Literature* Princeton: Princeton University Press
Hayes, M. Hunter (2007) *Understanding Will Self* Columbia: University of South Carolina Press
Hazlitt, William (1934) *Complete Works* P.P. Howe (ed.) London: Dent and Sons
—— (1970) *Selected Writings* Ronald Blythe (ed.) Harmondsworth: Penguin
Head, Dominic (2002) *The Cambridge Introduction to Modern British Fiction, 1950–2000* Cambridge: Cambridge University Press
—— (2007) *Ian McEwan* Manchester: Manchester University Press
Hesse, Hermann (1972) *The Glass Bead Game* Richard and Clara Winston (trans.) Harmondsworth: Penguin (first published in German 1943)
Hill, Nancy (1981) *A Reformer's Art: Dickens' Picturesque and Grotesque Imagery* Athens, OH: Ohio University Press
Hogg, James (2002) *The Private Memoirs and Confessions of a Justified Sinner* Edinburgh: Edinburgh University Press (first published 1824)
Hollington, Michael (1980) 'Dickens's Conception of the Grotesque' *The Dickensian* 76 (Summer) pp. 91–9
—— (1984) *Dickens and the Grotesque* London: Croom Helm
Horace (1965) 'On the Art of Poetry' in *Classical Literary Criticism* Harmondsworth: Penguin
Hugo, Victor (1968) *Cromwell* Paris: Garnier-Flammarion (first published 1827)
Hunt, Anna (2006) '"The Margins of the Imaginative Life": The Abject and the Grotesque in Angela Carter and Jonathan Swift' in Rebecca Munford (ed.) *Re-Visiting Angela Carter: Texts, Contexts, Intertexts* Basingstoke: Palgrave
Hutcheon, Linda (1984) *Narcissistic Narrative: the Metafictional Paradox* London: Methuen (first published 1980)

—— (1985) *A Theory of Parody: The Teachings of Twentieth-Century Art Forms* London: Methuen
—— (1988) *A Poetics of Postmodernism: History, Theory, Fiction* London: Routledge
James, Henry (1961) 'The Limitations of Dickens' in George Ford and Lauriat Lane (eds) *The Dickens Critics* New York: Cornell University Press (essay first published 1865)
—— (2003) *The Turn of the Screw, The Aspern Papers and Two Stories* New York: Barnes and Noble Classics (*The Turn of the Screw* first published 1898)
Jameson, Fredric (1981) *The Political Unconscious: Narrative as a Socially Symbolic Act* Ithaca, NY: Cornell University Press
—— (1991) *Postmodernism or the Cultural Logic of Late Capitalism* London: Verso
Johnson, Heather (2000) 'Textualising the Double-gendered Body: Forms of the Grotesque in *The Passion of New Eve*' in Angela Easton (ed.) *Angela Carter* Basingstoke: Macmillan
Johnson, Samuel (1837) *Works* Vol. 1 New York: George Dearborn
Kafka, Franz (1998) *The Castle* Mark Harman (trans.) New York: Schocken Books (first published in German 1926)
—— (1999) *The Complete Short Stories* London: Vintage
Kayser, Wolfgang (1963) *The Grotesque in Art and Literature* Bloomington: Indiana University Press (first published in German 1957)
Knight, G. Wilson (1949) '*King Lear* and the Comedy of the Grotesque' in *The Wheel of Fire and Other Essays: Interpretations of Shakespearean Tragedy* 4th ed. London: Methuen (first published 1930)
Kristeva, Julia (1982) *Powers of Horror: An Essay on Abjection* Leon Roudiez (trans.) New York: Columbia University Press (first published in French 1980)
Kuryluk, Ewa (1987) *Salome and Judas in the Cave of Sex: The Grotesque: Origins, Iconography, Techniques* Evanston, IL: Northwestern University Press
Lacan, Jacques (1979) *The Four Fundamental Concepts of Psycho-Analysis* Alan Sheridan (trans.) Harmondsworth: Penguin (first published in French 1973)
Lamb, Charles (1980) 'On the Genius and Character of Hogarth' in Roy Park (ed.) *Lamb as Critic* London: Routledge and Kegan Paul (essay first published 1811)
Lawlor, C. (1993) 'The Classical and the Grotesque in the Work of Alexander Pope and Jonathan Swift' unpublished PhD thesis: Warwick

Lévi-Strauss, Claude (1966) *The Savage Mind* London: Weidenfeld and Nicolson (first published in French 1962)
Lewis, Wyndam (1934) *Men Without Art* London: Cassell
Lifton, Robert Jay (1986) *The Nazi Doctors: Medical Killing and the Psychology of Genocide* New York: Basic Books
Lloyd Smith, Allan (1996) 'Postmodernism/Gothicism' in Victor Sage and Allan Lloyd Smith (eds) *Modern Gothic: A Reader* Manchester: Manchester University Press
Lodge, David (1985) '*Middlemarch* and the Idea of the Classic Realist Text' in Arnold Kettle (ed.) *The Nineteenth Century Novel: Critical Essays and Documents* London: Open University Press and Heinemann Educational
—— (1988) 'The Novel Now: Theories and Practices' *Novel* 21:2/3 (Winter/Spring) pp. 125–38
—— (1992) *The Art of Fiction* Harmondsworth: Penguin (first published 1991–2)
Lynch, Deidre (1994) 'Overloaded Portraits: The Excesses of Character and Countenance' in Veronica Kelly and Dorothea Von Mucke (eds) *Body and Text in the Eighteenth Century* Stanford: Stanford University Press
—— (1998) *The Economy of Character: Novels, Market Culture and the Business of Inner Meaning* Chicago: University of Chicago Press
Lyotard, Jean-François (1984) 'Answering the Question: What is Postmodernism?' Régis Durand (trans.) in *The Postmodern Condition: A Report on Knowledge* Manchester: Manchester University Press (essay first published in French 1982, *The Postmodern Condition* first published in French 1979)
McCabe, Patrick (1992) *The Butcher Boy* London: Picador
—— (2006) *Winterwood* London: Bloomsbury
McDonagh, Martin (2001) *The Lieutenant of Inishmore* London: Methuen
McElroy, Bernard (1989) *Fiction of the Modern Grotesque* London: Macmillan
McGrath, Patrick (1989) *The Grotesque* London: Viking
—— (1991) *Spider* London: Viking
McGrath, Patrick and Bradford Morrow (eds) (1992) *The New Gothic: A Collection of Contemporary Gothic Fiction* London: Picador
McHale, Brian (1989) *Postmodernist Fiction* London: Routledge (first published 1987)
—— (1992) *Constructing Postmodernism* Abingdon: Routledge
McMillan, Dorothy (1995) 'Constructed out of Bewilderment: Stories

of Scotland' in Ian Bell (ed.) *Peripheral Visions: Images of Nationhood in Contemporary British Fiction* Cardiff: University of Wales Press

Malcolm, David (2002) *Understanding Ian McEwan* Columbia: University of South Carolina Press

Mann, Thomas (1955) *Death in Venice* H.T. Lowe-Porter (trans.) Harmondsworth: Penguin (first published in German 1912)

Marshall, Richard (2003a) 'The New Bawdy' 3am Magazine www.3ammagazine.com/litarchives/2003/oct/interview_toby_litt.html (accessed 25 March 2011)

—— (2003b) 'All Hail Matt Thorne' 3am Magazine www.3ammagazine.com/litarchives/2003/nov/interview_matt_thorne.html (accessed 25 March 2011)

Mars-Jones, Adam (1990) *Venus Envy* London: Chatto and Windus (Chatto and Windus Counterblasts no. 14)

—— (1998) 'Have a Heart' *The Independent* 6 September 1998 Review p. 16 (review of McEwan's *Amsterdam*)

Menke, Richard (1998) 'Narrative Reversals and the Thermodynamics of History in Martin Amis's *Time's Arrow*' *MFS Modern Fiction Studies* 44:4 (Winter) pp. 959–80

Miles, Margaret (1997) 'Carnal Abominations: The Female Body as Grotesque' in James Luther Adams and Wilson Yates (eds) *The Grotesque in Art and Literature: Theological Reflections* Grand Rapids, MI: Eerdmans

Mulvey-Roberts, Marie (ed.) (1998) *The Handbook to Gothic Literature* Basingstoke: Macmillan

Nairn, Thom (1993) 'Iain Banks and the Fiction Factory' in Gavin Wallace and Randall Stevenson (eds) *The Scottish Novel since the Seventies* Edinburgh: Edinburgh University Press

Nash, Christopher (1987) *World Postmodern Fiction: A Guide* London: Longman

Newman, Robert (1997) '(Re)Imaging the Grotesque: Francis Bacon's Crucifixion Triptychs' in Dudley Andrew (ed.) *The Image in Dispute: Art and Cinema in the Age of Photography* Austin: University of Texas Press

O'Brien, Flann (1967) *The Third Policeman* London: McGibbon and Kee

O'Connor, Joseph (1994) *The Secret World of the Irish Male* Dublin: New Island

O'Day, Marc (1994) '"Mutability is Having a Field Day": The Sixties Aura of Angela Carter's Bristol Trilogy' in Lorna Sage (ed.) *Flesh and the Mirror: Essays on the Art of Angela Carter* London: Virago

Palmer, Paulina (1987) 'From "Coded Mannequin" to Bird Woman:

Angela Carter's Magic Flight' in Sue Roe (ed.) *Women Reading Women Writing* Brighton: Harvester

Paulson, Ronald (1971) *Hogarth: His Life, Art and Times* New Haven, CT: Yale University Press

Peach, Linden (1998) *Angela Carter* Basingstoke: Macmillan

Peacock, Thomas Love (1927) *Melincourt:, or Sir Oran Haut-Ton* London: Macmillan (first published 1818)

Peake, Mervyn (1992) *The Gormenghast Trilogy* London: Mandarin (first published in three volumes 1946–59)

Pearson, Jacqueline (1999) '"These Tags of Literature": Some Uses of Allusion in the Early Novels of Angela Carter' *Critique: Studies in Contemporary Fiction* 40:3 (Spring) pp. 248–56

Poe, Edgar Allan (1986) 'The Masque of the Red Death' in *The Fall of the House of Usher and Other Writings* Harmondsworth: Penguin (first published 1967, story first published 1842)

Punter, David (1996) *The Literature of Terror* 2nd ed. vol. 2, London: Longman

Pykett, Lyn (1998) 'A New Way with Words? Jeanette Winterson's Post-Modernism' in Helena Grice and Tim Woods (eds) *'I'm Telling you Stories': Jeanette Winterson and the Politics of Reading* Amsterdam: Rodopi

Rabelais, François (1955) *Gargantua and Pantagruel* J.M. Cohen (trans.) Harmondsworth: Penguin (first published in French 1532–47)

Raine, Craig (1979) *A Martian Sends a Postcard Home* Oxford: Oxford University Press

Rhys, Jean (1966) *Wide Sargasso Sea* London: Deutsch

Ricks, Christopher (1982) 'Playing with Terror' *London Review of Books* 4:1 (21 January–3 February) pp. 13–14

Robbe-Grillet, Alain (1963) *Pour un Nouveau Roman* Paris: Editions de Minuit

Ruskin, John (1906) *Modern Painters* vol. III London: George Allen and Sons (first published 1856)

—— (1907) *Unto this Last and Other Essays* London: J.M. Dent and Sons (first published 1862)

—— (1908) *The Stones of Venice* vol. I London: George Allen and Sons (first published 1851–3)

—— (1911) *The Stones of Venice* vol. II London: George Allen and Sons (first published 1851–3)

—— (1912) *The Stones of Venice* vol. III London: George Allen and Sons (first published 1851–3)

—— (1928) *Ruskin as Literary Critic* A.H. Ball (ed.) Cambridge: Cambridge University Press
Russo, Mary (1995) *The Female Grotesque: Risk, Excess, Modernity* London: Routledge (first published in the USA 1994 by Routledge New York)
Ryan, Kiernan (1994) *Ian McEwan* Plymouth: Northcote House
—— (1999) 'Sex, Violence and Complicity: Martin Amis and Ian McEwan' in Rod Mengham (ed.) *An Introduction to Contemporary Fiction* Cambridge: Polity
Sage, Victor (1996) 'The Politics of Petrifaction: Culture, Religion, History in the Fiction of Iain Banks and John Banville' in Victor Sage and Allan Lloyd Smith (eds) *Modern Gothic: A Reader* Manchester: Manchester University Press
Sartre, Jean-Paul (1982) *Huis Clos* suivi de *Les Mouches* Paris: Gallimard Folio (first published 1947)
Schoene-Harwood, Berthold (2000) *Writing Men: Literary Masculinities from Frankenstein to the New Man* Edinburgh: Edinburgh University Press
Scott, Mary (1996) 'Adventures in Capitalism.' *New Statesman* 30 August 1996 p. 48
Scott, Walter (1835) *Prose Works* Edinburgh: Robert Cadell
Seaboyer, Judith (1999) 'Sadism demands a Story: Ian McEwan's *The Comfort of Strangers*' *MFS Modern Fiction Studies* 45:4 (Winter) pp. 957–86
Seaton, Matt (1996) 'Degree Show' *The Independent on Sunday* 23 June 1996 p. 39
Shelley, Mary (1992) *Frankenstein or The Modern Prometheus* Harmondsworth: Penguin Modern Classics (first published 1818)
Singley, Paulette (1997) 'Devouring Architecture: Ruskin's Insatiable Grotesque' *Assemblage* 32 pp. 108–25
Slay, Jack Jr. (1996) *Ian McEwan* New York: Twayne Publishers
Spencer, M.C. (1969) 'The Unfinished Cathedral: Michel Butor's *L'Emploi du Temps*' *Essays in French Literature* 6 (November) pp. 81–101
Spilka, Mark (1969) *Dickens and Kafka: A Mutual Interpretation* Gloucester, MA: Peter Smith
Stallabrass, Julian (1999) *High Art Lite* London: Verso
Stallybrass, Peter (1986) 'Patriarchal Territories: The Body Enclosed' in M. Ferguson et al. (eds) *Rewriting the Renaissance: The Discourse of Sexual Difference in Early Modern Europe* Chicago: University of Chicago Press

—— and Allon White (1986) *The Politics and Poetics of Transgression* London: Methuen

Stechow, Wolfgang (1997) 'Hieronymus Bosch: the Grotesque and We' in James Luther Adams and Wilson Yates (eds) *The Grotesque in Art and Literature: Theological Reflections* Grand Rapids, MI: Eerdmans

Sterne, Lawrence (1997) *The Life and Opinions of Tristram Shandy* Harmondsworth: Penguin (first published 1760)

Stevenson, Randall (1991) 'Postmodernism and Contemporary Fiction in Britain' in Edmund J. Smyth (ed.) *Postmodernism and Contemporary Fiction* London: Batsford

Swift, Jonathan (1973) 'A Modest Proposal' and *Gulliver's Travels* in *The Writings of Jonathan Swift* New York and London: Norton Critical Edition ('A Modest Proposal' first published 1729, *Gulliver's Travels* first published 1726)

—— (1992) *The Selected Poems* A. Norman Jeffares (ed.) London: Kyle Cathie

Tanner, Tony (1992) *Venice Desired* Oxford: Basil Blackwell

Taylor, Mark (1990) 'Nuclear Architecture ...' *Assemblage* 11 (April) pp. 8–21

Tew, Philip (2004) *The Contemporary British Novel* London: Continuum

Thomson, Philip (1972) *The Grotesque* London: Methuen (The Critical Idiom)

Tredell, Nicholas (ed.) (2000) *The Fiction of Martin Amis: A Reader's Guide to Essential Criticism* Cambridge: Icon

Uruburu, Paula M. (1986) *The Gruesome Doorway: An Analysis of the American Grotesque* New York: Peter Lang

Vattimo, Gianni (1988) *The End of Modernity* J.R. Snyder (trans.) London: Polity (first published in Italian 1985)

Vice, Sue (2000) *Holocaust Fiction* London: Routledge

Vitruvius Pollio (1999) *Ten Books on Architecture* Ingrid D. Rowland (trans.) Thomas Noble Howe (commentary and notes) Cambridge: Cambridge University Press

Vonnegut, Kurt (1972) *Slaughterhouse-Five or The Children's Crusade* London: Panther Books (first published 1969)

—— (1973) *Breakfast of Champions or Goodbye Blue Monday* London: Jonathan Cape

—— (1991) *Slapstick or Lonesome No More* London: Vintage (first published 1976)

—— (1997) *Mother Night* London: Vintage (first published 1961)

Wallace, David Foster (2000) *Brief Interviews with Hideous Men* London: Abacus (first published 1999)

Wallace, Gavin (1993) 'Voices in Empty Houses: The Novel of Damaged Identity' in Gavin Wallace and Randall Stevenson (eds) *The Scottish Novel since the Seventies* Edinburgh: Edinburgh University Press

Welsh, Irvine (1993) *Trainspotting* London: Secker and Warburg

—— (1998) *Filth* London: Vintage

Wheatcroft, Geoffrey (2000) 'Horrors Beyond Tragedy' *Times Literary Supplement* 5071 9 June pp. 9–10

Wilson, Leigh (2006) 'Possessing Toby Litt's Ghost Story' in Philip Tew and Rod Mengham (eds) *British Fiction Today* London: Continuum

Winterson, Jeanette (1989) *Sexing the Cherry* London: Bloomsbury

Wood, James (2002) 'V.S. Pritchett and English Comedy' in Zachary Leader (ed.) *On Modern British Fiction* Oxford: Oxford University Press

Yates, Wilson (1997) 'An Introduction to the Grotesque: Theoretical and Theological Considerations' in James Luther Adams and Wilson Yates (eds) *The Grotesque in Art and Literature: Theological Reflections* Grand Rapids, MI: Eerdmans

Yuan, Yuan (1996) 'The Lacanian Subject and Grotesque Desires: Between Oedipal Violation and Narcissistic Closure' *American Journal of Psychoanalysis* 56:1 pp. 35–47

Zipes, Jack (1979) *Breaking the Magic Spell: Radical Theories of Folk and Fairy Tales* Lexington: University Press of Kentucky

Index

Literary works can be found under authors' names

Addams, Charles 167, 181n.7
Allen, Woody 206–7
America 50n.1, 76–7, 82, 88, 111–12, 116n.9, 213, 250–1
Amis, Martin
  Dead Babies 85–6, 155n.1
  Experience 101, 116n.4–5
  Heavy Water and Other Stories 88, 219
  The Information 93, 95, 101, 104, 106, 110, 112, 116n.4
  London Fields 92–101, 108
  Money 86–100, 102–3, 107–9, 116n.2, 188, 196, 208
  Night Train 108
  Other People 91–2, 108
  The Rachel Papers 83–5, 106, 234
  Time's Arrow 86, 101–3, 110–15
  Yellow Dog 101, 107, 108
ape 140–3, 191, 199–203, 205–6

Bakhtin, Mikhail 19, 21–8, 44–6, 51n.7, 51n.9, 58–9, 61, 72–4, 86, 110, 148–9, 234, 249
Banks, Iain
  The Bridge 159–72, 180n.4, 181n.8, 190
  Complicity 156, 160–1, 173, 178, 181n.11
  The Crow Road 156, 161, 166–7, 173
  Espedair Street 152, 156, 173
  A Song of Stone 160, 165–6, 173
  Walking on Glass 157–8, 165
  The Wasp Factory 150–61, 167, 169–70, 173, 176, 178, 180n.1–2, 181n.7, 186–7, 228
Banks, Iain M.
  The Player of Games 161
barocco 49, 121
Barthes, Roland 82, 90–1, 152–4, 156–8, 172, 176–8, 213
Bataille, Georges 21–2, 51n.8
Benjamin, Walter 116n.6, 176–7
Burroughs, William 118–19, 182, 197–8
Butler, Judith 61, 125, 170, 185
Butor, Michel 158–9, 166, 181n.6

Caledonian antisyzygy 167–9
caricature 31–9, 52n.11–12, 83, 195
carnival 19–28, 44–6, 51n.9, 59, 70, 72–5, 77, 79–81
Carroll, Lewis 112–13, 199
Carter, Angela
  The Bloody Chamber 61–7, 69–71
  Heroes and Villains 64
  The Magic Toyshop 55, 60, 64, 79

Carter, Angela (*continued*)
   Nights at the Circus 44–5, 55, 66–75, 78–82
   The Passion of New Eve 53, 55–6, 76
   The Sadeian Woman 66
   Wise Children 73, 75–82
childhood 41, 85, 100–2, 116n.5, 117–18, 123–5, 127, 132–40, 143–6, 169, 189–91, 193, 199–200, 214n.3, 222–33, 240–5, 247n.1–2
clowns 71–2
comedy 20–3, 27, 33, 49, 52n.11, 72, 74–5, 96, 109, 114–15, 117, 135, 206–7, 217–18, 222–4

Davis, Lennard 39–40
Day, Aidan 59, 61, 73–4
decadence 50, 122, 126
Derrida, Jacques 171–80, 243
Dickens, Charles 3, 30–3, 39, 74, 83–4, 217, 221–2, 249
Diedrick, James 85, 91, 106, 114, 115n.1
dreams 15–18, 62, 77–8, 129–30, 144–5, 162, 164, 220, 246
drugs 18, 188–200, 207, 210–13, 218–19
Duggan, Robert 74, 98, 180n.3
Duncker, Patricia 65–6

evolution 140–3, 149, 229–30
excess 18, 20, 22, 33–6, 38–43, 57, 68–9, 85–8, 108, 121–2, 131, 151, 175–7, 180, 210–11, 246
fantasy 14–15, 17–19, 25, 41–6, 73, 82n.1, 124, 147–8, 168–71, 173, 182–3, 199–202, 206–7, 212, 221–2, 243–6

female grotesque 25–7, 68–70, 121, 137, 234
Fiedler, Leslie 54–5, 75
Fielding, Henry 33–8, 74, 80, 107
film 55, 71, 76–7, 93, 111–12, 170, 195, 202, 234–6, 240
force 171–80
Forster, E.M. 42–3
Foucault, Michel 216, 220–1, 238, 240
freaks 43, 45, 53, 69, 75
Freud, Sigmund 35, 52n.11, 62, 94, 143–5, 149, 202

gender 25–7, 56, 64–73, 79, 125, 127, 137–40, 153, 167, 170–1, 185–6, 228
Golding, William 124, 133, 170, 226, 229
gothic 39, 44–50, 54, 75, 169–71, 176, 225, 239
Goya, Francisco de 1, 6
Gray, Alasdair 45, 167–9, 181n.10, 250
griffins 17, 38–9
grottesche 14–20

Harpham, Geoffrey Galt 12–14, 17, 20, 28, 49, 51n.5, 110, 130, 173
hauntology 243–4
Hayes, M. Hunter 214n.2, 215n.8, 216
Head, Dominic 57–60, 146, 148
Hogarth, William 33–68, 52n.12
Holocaust 110–15, 116n.7–9
Hugo, Victor 13, 51n.2, 171

immaturity 50, 113, 123–4, 143, 146, 151
incest 79, 107, 123–5, 146, 158, 180n.3, 249

intertextuality 54, 59–61, 73, 76, 82, 85, 107, 126, 169–70, 216, 220, 245
intoxication 18–19, 174, 180, 210–13
inversion 9, 20–30, 72, 80, 110–15, 144, 223, 248–9
Ireland 27, 85, 169, 250

James, Henry 30, 39, 126, 239, 244–5

Kafka, Franz 26, 84, 122, 140, 164–6, 173–4, 176–7, 184–5, 202
Kayser, Wolfgang 6, 24–5, 51n.9
Kristeva, Julia 119, 123–4, 138

Lewis, Wyndham 208–9
Litt, Toby
　Adventures in Capitalism 216–22
　Corpsing 221–2
　deadkidsongs 222–33, 237, 244
　Exhibitionism 233–8
　Finding Myself 239–44
　Ghost Story 240–6
　Hospital 246
Little Artists 6
Lynch, Deidre 34–6, 89–90

McEwan, Ian
　Amsterdam 137, 143, 146–7
　Atonement 128, 147–8
　The Cement Garden 117–18, 122–5, 131–4, 138, 219, 226
　The Child in Time 131–40, 142–7, 193
　The Comfort of Strangers 126–31, 134–5, 141–2
　The Daydreamer 144–5
　Enduring Love 124, 128, 146

First Love, Last Rites 132–3, 136, 146, 219
In Between the Sheets 140–1
The Innocent 119–22, 131
Saturday 9, 147
McHale, Brian 45–6, 78
Malcolm, David 127
Mann, Thomas 24, 126, 128–31, 135
Menippean 24–5, 45, 53n.10, 59, 85, 115n.1, 185
metafiction 98, 107
metamorphosis 9, 56, 64, 69, 144–5, 164–5, 185, 196, 199, 218, 246, 248
modernism 24, 51n.9, 71, 78, 188, 208, 239, 244, 246, 253

national identity 27, 167–9, 186, 228, 230
New Puritans 235–7
nouveau roman 166–7, 172–3

parody 4, 20, 24, 44–5, 52n.13, 54, 79, 100, 108, 133, 203, 241
Peach, Linden 59, 64, 73, 80–1
pornography 62–3, 66, 86, 92–7, 101, 105, 235, 249
postmodernism 4, 44–7, 59–60, 74–5, 78, 109–10, 174, 206, 216–17, 220, 252
proportion 20, 38–41, 89–90, 108, 200, 203
Punter, David 169, 189–90

Rabelais, François 19–20, 22–6, 46, 68, 86, 185, 191–2, 201
realism 5, 7–8, 19, 24, 30–43, 47, 56–60, 90–1, 103–9, 122, 154–5, 168, 173, 176–80, 207–9, 221, 226, 237, 244, 251–3

regression 111, 131–43, 146
Renaissance 15–19, 46, 50n.1, 129
Rückert, Fredrich 222–3, 225
Rushdie, Salman 58–60, 82n.1, 235
Ruskin, John 15–19, 30–3, 35, 38–9, 41–2, 51n.4, 62, 126–9, 151, 161
Russo, Mary 25–7, 43, 61
Ryan, Kiernan 100, 118–20, 136–8, 143, 146

Sage, Victor 165, 169–70, 176–7
scale 6, 22–6, 68–9, 99, 104, 155, 160, 184–5, 191–5, 198–201, 206, 214n.5
Schoene-Harwood, Berthold 135, 138–9, 143, 167
science fiction 46, 111, 150, 159, 161–2, 172–3, 216
Scotland 9, 150, 160, 162, 166–9, 176, 181n.9–10
Scott, Walter 17–19, 41–2, 210–12
Self, Will
  The Book of Dave 212
  The Butt 185, 212–13
  Cock & Bull 185–6
  Great Apes 140, 195, 199–203, 205–6
  Grey Area 191, 193–5, 200, 204
  My Idea of Fun 184, 186–91, 195–8, 204–6, 208–9, 214n.2
  The Quantity Theory of Insanity 182–5, 200, 205, 207
  Sore Sites 198, 214n.7
  The Sweet Smell of Success 195–6

Tough, Tough Toys for Tough, Tough Boys 192–3, 196–8, 205, 214n.3, 214n.6
sex 53–4, 57, 62–7, 79, 85, 87, 89, 92–7, 100, 111, 119, 123–5, 130–3, 140–1, 146–7, 153, 157–8, 185–7, 190, 195–6, 200, 204–5, 211, 214n.6, 220–1, 233–6, 239, 249
Shakespeare, William 50n.1, 61, 73–4, 76–7, 107, 208
Shelley, Mary 42, 88, 169–70, 181n.10
Shelley, Percy Bysshe 232
sickness 15, 17–19, 118–19, 151
Stallybrass, Peter and Allon White 28–30, 43, 87, 101, 108
Swift, Jonathan 9, 22–6, 35, 45, 68, 73–4, 80, 84–5, 120–1, 191–2, 199–202, 207–8, 234

Thatcher, Margaret 139–40, 229
theatre 28–9, 77–81, 131
transgression 27–30, 43, 47, 72, 87, 102, 110, 179, 236–7

Venice 15–19, 51n.4, 126–31, 135, 151
violence 63, 72, 116n.9, 119–20, 127, 130, 150, 180, 186–7, 204–5, 211, 222, 224–33
visual art 6, 14–17, 33–9, 41, 90, 111, 164, 168, 202
Vonnegut, Kurt 112–13

Wilson, Leigh 241–3
Wordsworth, William 41, 144–5, 211, 225